AI-Powered Language Teaching

Christine Savvidou

AI-Powered Language Teaching

Transforming the Future of TESOL

palgrave
macmillan

Christine Savvidou
Department of Languages and Literature
University of Nicosia
Nicosia, Cyprus

ISBN 978-3-032-14501-7 ISBN 978-3-032-14502-4 (eBook)
https://doi.org/10.1007/978-3-032-14502-4

Cover credit: J Studios

This Palgrave Macmillan imprint is published by the registered company Springer Nature Switzerland AG
The registered company address is: Gewerbestrasse 11, 6330 Cham, Switzerland

For my parents—with love and gratitude.

Preface

I first heard about GPTs (Generative Pre-trained Transformers) shortly after the public launch of OpenAI's ChatGPT at the end of November 2022, and like many TESOL (Teaching English to Speakers of Other Languages) educators, I was uncertain about what this new technology might mean for my work. I began experimenting with the free version of ChatGPT 3.5 early on, asking it to respond to prompts, analyse texts, and generate examples for language learning. It quickly became clear that this was significantly different from any other digital tool I had used in TESOL. Its fluency, adaptability, and speed were unlike the familiar online learning platforms or language apps that had gradually become part of my professional toolkit over the last decade.

This realisation led to an early research question: could experienced TESOL teachers tell the difference between student writing and AI-generated text? In February 2023, together with two colleagues, I set up a small study asking experienced teachers to blind review essays: some were fully written by a GPT tool, some were partially generated with AI assistance, and others entirely authentic, written by students. The results of the study were striking. Human detection was no better than chance, and even AI detection tools, widely promoted at the time as a solution to the "problem," performed only slightly better, with an accuracy rate of about 60% (Alexander et al., 2023).

These findings created an immediate sense of uncertainty and urgency. If neither teachers nor technology could reliably detect AI-generated writing, what would this mean for teaching, assessment, and feedback? How would we preserve the processes of drafting, peer review, and critical reflection that are central to language learning?

Initially, these questions were not being widely discussed in my professional networks. Colleagues were hesitant to raise the issue, and students, too, said little about GenAI, at least in formal contexts. Yet when we began looking more closely, a different picture emerged. Research showed that many students had first learned about GenAI not in the classroom, but through social media platforms like TikTok. In some cases, they were better informed about the technology than their teachers. The gap between student practice and teacher awareness was widening rapidly.

It was out of this mixture of curiosity and urgency that the idea for this book emerged. What began as an attempt to understand the detectability of AI-generated student writing quickly developed into a deeper exploration of pedagogy, ethics, and professional identity in TESOL. It became apparent that this was not simply a matter of adding another pedagogical resource to the existing repertoire, in the way we had once integrated online learning platforms like Moodle into our teaching. GenAI was not just a delivery system or a digital library; it was a co-writer, a conversational partner, and, for some students, a constant study companion.

This raised deeper, almost existential questions for TESOL: What does it mean to learn a language when a machine can produce fluent, contextually appropriate, and grammatically correct text on demand? How should we assess student work in ways that remain authentic and fair? How do we preserve the processes of critical thinking, negotiation of meaning, and personal expression that are central to language learning? And perhaps most fundamentally, what is the role of the teacher when the boundaries between human and machine production are blurred?

These are not questions that can be answered by simply banning the use of GenAI in the classroom or outsourcing the problem to detection tools. They require a rethinking of our pedagogical frameworks, our assessment practices, and our professional identities. They also require us to engage with the ethical and ideological dimensions of GenAI, such as bias in training data, the reinforcement of standard language ideologies, the privacy and surveillance implications of cloud-based AI tools, and the persistent inequities in access to technology.

This book does not claim to have all the answers. Instead, it aims to map the terrain, drawing on empirical research, theoretical reflection, and the lived experiences of TESOL practitioners around the world. It is grounded in the belief that while GenAI represents a profound challenge, it also offers opportunities for innovation—but only if educators are prepared to engage with it critically, creatively, and ethically. Against this backdrop, conversations with my colleagues and students have been invaluable in shaping the ideas that follow.

The chapters that follow examine the historical, empirical, and pedagogical contexts for GenAI in TESOL, moving from the evolution of technology in second language education, through current classroom practices, to the ethical and professional challenges ahead. They explore teacher identity, critical AI literacy, and the need for policy frameworks that align with TESOL's social mission. This book is for student teachers, educators, researchers, and policymakers in the hope that it will challenge them to approach these ideas with critical curiosity, openness to the possibilities, as well as the challenges, that GenAI tools offer.

The questions raised here are urgent, and they are intended to provoke the reader to question their role, identity, and sense of agency as they interact with this technology. While much about teaching and learning with GenAI remains uncertain, the future of TESOL need not be approached with pessimism. It is my hope that by upholding the field's core principles, we can work with GenAI to expand access, empower learners, and advance our profession in ways that enrich and transform second language education.

Nicosia, Cyprus Dr. Christine Savvidou

References

Alexander, K., Savvidou, C., & Alexander, C. (2023). Who wrote this essay? Detecting AI-generated writing in second language education in higher education. *Teaching English with Technology*, 23(2), 25–43. https://doi.org/10.56297/buka4060/xhld5365

Acknowledgements I would like to express my sincere gratitude to the University of Nicosia for supporting this project and granting me the time and space to complete it. My colleagues, whose early collaboration inspired me to take this direction, have been an invaluable source of support and insight. I am equally indebted to the many students over the years, whose curiosity, questions, and openness continue to motivate me to explore the evolving role of TESOL.

This book has been enriched by the many educators around the world, who contributed to the study, generously sharing their time, perspectives, concerns, and hopes for the future of GenAI in our field. Their honesty and engagement have been central to this work.

I would like to express my sincere gratitude to all those who supported the development of this book. At Palgrave Macmillan, I would like to thank my editor, Cathy Scott, for her guidance and encouragement throughout the process. I am also deeply grateful to Karthikeyan Kalahasthi and Claudia Petter for their assistance and support in bringing this project to completion. I extend my sincere thanks to the reviewers whose thoughtful feedback strengthened this work. I am especially grateful to the initial reviewer, whose guidance encouraged the development of the empirical study at the heart of this book, and to the reviewer of the full manuscript, whose insightful comments helped refine and enhance the final version.

Finally, I am thankful to my family for their unwavering support and encouragement throughout this project.

I also acknowledge the use of GenAI tools, such as ChatGPT, which supported some drafting and language refinement during the preparation of this manuscript; all interpretations and conclusions remain entirely my own.

Competing Interests The author has no competing interests to declare that are relevant to the content of this manuscript.

Ethics Approval This book draws on data from an empirical study that was conducted in full accordance with the *British Educational Research*

Association (BERA) Ethical Guidelines for Educational Research (5th ed., 2024). All participants were fully informed about the purpose of the study, gave their voluntary consent to take part, and were assured that their anonymity and confidentiality would be maintained throughout.

Contents

About the Author

Dr. Christine Savvidou is an Associate Professor at the University of Nicosia and holds a doctorate in Teacher Education from the University of Nottingham, UK. She coordinates the PhD. TESOL programme at the University of Nicosia, where she teaches undergraduate and postgraduate courses and supervises PhD. research. Her research examines Teaching English to Speakers of Other Languages, second language teacher education, professional development, and professional knowledge and identity in second language teaching, with a particular focus on the intersection of technology and pedagogy. In recent years, she has explored the pedagogical implications of emerging technologies, including generative artificial intelligence, for language teaching and teacher education. A member of several professional associations, she is an active researcher and frequent presenter at international conferences. Her work has appeared in leading international refereed journals, including *Intercultural Education*, *Technology, Pedagogy and Education*,

Journal of Teacher Development, *Teachers and Teaching: Theory and Practice*, and *Teaching English with Technology*, among others. She is also co-organiser of the annual Advances in Second and Foreign Language Acquisition (ASeFOLa) Conference hosted at the University of Nicosia, Cyprus.

Abbreviations

AI	Artificial Intelligence
AIED	Artificial Intelligence in Education
BERT	Bidirectional Encoder Representations from Transformers
CALL	Computer-Assisted Language Learning
EFL	English as a Foreign Language
ESL	English as a Second Language
GDPR	General Data Protection Regulation
GenAI	Generative Artificial Intelligence
GPT	Generative Pre-trained Transformer
ITE	Initial Teacher Education
ITS	Intelligent Tutoring Systems
LLM(s)	Large Language Model(s)
MALL	Mobile-Assisted Language Learning
NLP	Natural Language Processing
OECD	Organisation for Economic Co-operation and Development
RLHF	Reinforcement Learning from Human Feedback
SLA	Second Language Acquisition
TAM	Technology Acceptance Model
TBLT	Task-Based Language Teaching
TESOL	Teaching English to Speakers of Other Languages

TPACK	Technological Pedagogical Content Knowledge
UNESCO	United Nations Educational, Scientific and Cultural Organization
ZPD	Zone of Proximal Development

List of Figures

List of Tables

1

Setting the Scene

1.1 Introduction

Few innovations have provoked as much debate in education as generative artificial intelligence (GenAI). For Teaching English to Speakers of Other Languages (TESOL) educators, it is not simply a new tool but a disruptive force that challenges long established practices of second language teaching, learning and assessment. Against this backdrop, and as GenAI becomes increasingly accessible, TESOL educators are beginning to explore its potential to transform their work. Many are using it to support lesson planning, materials development, and assessment, while others are experimenting with new ways to engage learners. When asked how they were using GenAI in their practice, educators described a wide range of uses:

> Quotation 1: "I use ChatGPT to generate texts for reading and to create vocabulary games. I also use it for writing, especially in correcting writing tasks for my students." (T.14, Algeria)
> Quotation 2: "It can be useful as a personal assistant. It can help answer questions related to teaching practices or suggest new techniques. It also helps to create teaching materials and exams." (T.12, Cyprus)

C. Savvidou, *AI-Powered Language Teaching*,
https://doi.org/10.1007/978-3-032-14502-4_1

> Quotation 3: "I had students generate pictures based on texts and they went through multiple iterations to get something that matched the text better. I hoped it would be a useful learning activity, engaging them with the text by thinking about how to visually represent it." (T.1, United States)

Beyond materials creation, some teachers are integrating AI into assessment processes:

> Quotation 4: "At our school, we use a platform called iTest for final exams, and AI assists teachers in grading translations and compositions. The AI gives an initial grade, and teachers review it to ensure it's reasonable." (T.4, China)

Others are exploring its potential to streamline feedback:

> Quotation 5: "I also tried using it during the exam period last year to help with marking writing essays, particularly summative essays." (T.3, China)

These examples illustrate how, since the launch of ChatGPT at the end of 2022, TESOL educators around the world have begun integrating GenAI into their practice in creative and context-specific ways. However, alongside this outward enthusiasm, questions are emerging about accuracy, bias, ethics, and the broader pedagogical implications of its adoption.

This chapter sets the scene for examining the role of GenAI in TESOL. It introduces the concept of GenAI, situates it within the historical trajectory of technology integration in language education, and outlines the theoretical frameworks guiding this book. Drawing on both recent literature and empirical data, including survey responses from 78 participants and interviews with 14 educators across diverse global contexts, this chapter provides a foundation for understanding how GenAI is adopted, perceived, and contested in TESOL settings.

The following section situates GenAI within the broader history of technology integration in TESOL, tracing the evolution from early language labs to the current era of AI-enhanced pedagogy.

1.2 TESOL and Technology Integration—An Overview

Over the past several decades, TESOL has undergone significant transformation, shaped by evolving pedagogical theories, global shifts in language use, and rapid technological development. Methodological approaches have progressed from teacher-centred, grammar-translation methods to communicative, learner-centred models (Nunan, 2022; Richards & Rodgers, 2001), with each stage influenced by available tools and resources.

The integration of technology into TESOL has followed a distinct trajectory. Early Computer-Assisted Language Learning (CALL) systems, grounded in behaviourist theory, emphasised repetitive drills focused on grammar and vocabulary. These later evolved into communicative CALL, aligning with shifts towards interaction-focused pedagogy and real-world language use (Chapelle, 2003).

Indeed, the rise of digital technology in the early twenty-first century has revolutionised TESOL in unprecedented ways with the introduction of multimedia resources, such as videos, podcasts, and interactive learning software. Not only do they provide teachers with a diverse array of tools to engage students, but they also allow for multimodal learning, catering to different learning styles and offering ways for students to engage in their own learning processes. Additionally, online learning management systems such as Moodle and Blackboard have facilitated asynchronous study, creating new possibilities for language education beyond the traditional classroom setting.

More recently, Kern (2024) has described the advent of AI technologies into TESOL as an 'inflection point' that invites language teachers to 'rethink how we organise our teaching in light of technology's affordances and be clear about what technology cannot do.' (p. 516). While previous technological advancements focused on providing access to content, AI has introduced the potential for personalised learning experiences and adaptive feedback that respond to individual student needs (Kabudi et al., 2021). Tools like automated writing evaluation systems (Barrot, 2023), speech recognition software (Johnson & Cardoso, 2024), and virtual tutors (Fandiño & Velandia, 2020) are already being used to assess and guide learners in real-time, creating tailor-made language-learning experiences that were not possible before.

The emergence of GenAI represents the latest phase in this progression. Using large data sets and machine learning models like Deep Neural Networks (DNNs) and Large Language Models (LLMs), GenAI is trained to respond to prompts to create new content such as text, quizzes, or feedback, and introduces new possibilities for personalised and automated language learning. Unlike traditional AI tools, which primarily process information, GenAI can produce unique outputs that are adapted to the specific needs of individual learners. This development not only enhances the efficiency of language teaching but also raises new questions about the role of educators in an AI-driven environment (Luckin et al., 2022). However, while this technology has the capacity to produce human-like content efficiently, it is still in its infancy in replicating human intelligence and is still prone to generating inaccurate information, often referred to as "hallucinations," or biased output. As a result, some commentators note that there is little reason for educators to be concerned about being replaced. As Thorne (2024) observes, "the most problematic term in GenAI is 'intelligence." As of this writing, there is no evidence linking GenAI to intelligence, thinking, or consciousness as these attributes relate to humans." (p. 369).

In the context of TESOL, the integration of GenAI represents a significant opportunity to bridge gaps in language instruction, particularly in under-resourced contexts where access to experienced language instructors may be limited (Holstein & Doroudi, 2022). However, it also presents challenges, including concerns about over-reliance on technology, the potential loss of human interaction in language learning, and the ethical implications of AI-generated content (Galaczi, 2023). Thus, while this technology is rapidly evolving, it still requires human intervention for reliable outcomes. This is a view echoed by Chapelle (2024), who takes an optimistic but cautious view of GenAI, urging educators to critically assess the role of technology in TESOL and the role of the educator in second language teaching.

As the following chapters will explore in greater depth, GenAI has the potential to reshape both the practice and pedagogy of TESOL, raising critical questions about how educators can make use of its benefits while mitigating its challenges.

1.3 What is GenAI?

"Generative AI systems can not only be used for artistic purposes to create new text mimicking writers or new images mimicking illustrators, but they can and will assist humans as intelligent question-answering systems." (Feuerriegel et al., 2024, p. 111).

GenAI refers to a subgroup of artificial intelligence systems that create new content, such as text, images, music, or code that is based on patterns found in the data they have been trained on. Unlike discriminative models, which are used for classification or prediction purposes (e.g. spam filters or human versus bot detection), GenAI is designed to produce new data that mirrors training data without replicating it exactly.

There are several characteristics that distinguish GenAI from other subsets of artificial intelligence. First, it has the ability to create novel content in the form of text, images, and code, with OpenAI's GPT and DALL-E being the most well-known examples. Second, these models, known as Large Language Models (LLMs), are trained on vast datasets, allowing them to process and understand language patterns and generate coherent responses (Barreto et al., 2023). This training involves processing vast amounts of text to predict the next word in a sentence, which allows the model to regenerate language that mimics human use. While LLMs have the ability to recognise word meanings, sentence structures, context and tone, they do not "understand" language the way humans do; rather, they generate language based on patterns and probabilities (Floridi, 2023). A third characteristic is the ability of GenAI to learn from human feedback, known as Reinforcement Learning from Human Feedback (RLHF). This training enables the LLMs to refine their outputs to align with the specific goals and instructions of users. Fourth, apart from the adaptability to create content across different fields such as education, finance, law, healthcare, technology, LLMs models are also capable of generating specialised content for areas like law, scientific research. A final characteristic of GenAI is creativity, as demonstrated by its adoption within the creative industries for content creation and personalised design (Amato et al., 2019).

In sum, GenAI stands out for its ability to create novel content, its reliance on pattern recognition rather than genuine comprehension, its capacity to learn and develop through human feedback, its adaptability across various fields, and its capacity for creativity. Despite this versatility, meaningful and accurate results still require critical human oversight. These distinctive characteristics have important implications for language teaching and learning, making it essential to consider the specific significance of GenAI within the TESOL context.

1.4 The Significance of GenAI for TESOL

Within TESOL, GenAI has transformative potential to create personalised learning plans, resources and quizzes that target specific learning objectives. Tafazoli (2024) argues that GenAI has the potential to deliver a wide range of up-to-date learning materials tailored to individual learners, to counter ideological bias, and to enhance cross-cultural communication. This personalisation not only democratises language teaching but also encourages engagement and aligns instruction with learners' needs.

Another significant feature of GenAI is its ability to provide real-time automated written corrective feedback that allows students to refine their skills independently (Godwin-Jones, 2022). While the automation of specific teaching processes may raise concerns about replacing human teachers, automated assessment is a feature of GenAI that supports teachers by generating and grading quizzes and by providing real-time feedback, without the labour- and time-intensive tasks usually required. Moreover, from a learner perspective, Kohnke (2024) observes that automated written evaluative systems "reduce anxiety because they are impersonal, [and] many learners prefer them to teacher feedback" (p. 2).

Alongside the potential to automate tasks like lesson planning and grading, GenAI can help reduce teachers' administrative workload, freeing time for greater student interaction and higher-quality instruction. Indeed, Moorhouse and colleagues (2024) demonstrate how pre-service teachers were able to use GenAI tools to save time improving lesson plans and creating context-based teaching materials, enabling them to devote more attention to student engagement.

With such potential, these developments highlight the urgency of critically examining how GenAI is being adopted, adapted, and contested in TESOL, which forms the basis for the rationale underpinning this book.

1.5 Rationale

Since the launch of ChatGPT on November 30, 2022, GenAI technology has become the fastest-growing consumer product in history with 1 million users within five days and over 100 million active users in under two months (Mahajan, 2023). Using the model of digitised technologies proposed by Diamandis and Kotler (2012), and later applied to educational contexts by Alier et al. (2024), the evolution of GenAI can be understood as following a trajectory that includes exponential growth (rapid adoption), disruption (transforming existing practices), demonetisation (reducing costs of previously expensive processes), and democratisation (widening access to advanced tools). As such, the impact of GenAI on education in general—and second language education in particular—is profound.

Before the most recent wave of AI developments, Diamandis and Kotler, in their 2012 book "Abundance: The Future is Better Than You Think," discussed the transformative potential of AI in education as a source of abundance, envisioning personalised AI tutors available anytime and anywhere. Based on ideas from Neil Jacobstein, Chair of the Artificial Intelligence and Robotics Track at Singularity University, they proposed a future in which education would be embedded in every aspect of life. This vision is especially significant when considering the millions of children worldwide whose access to education is limited. Knowing that free and personalised education is technically possible should be reason enough to motivate educators and policymakers to make this vision a reality. However, achieving it requires more than professional expertise to implement technological advancements; it calls for ongoing research, critical discourse, and deliberate action to address both the challenges and the opportunities of AI-driven education.

Although GenAI is rapidly expanding across education, research in TESOL is only beginning to emerge, reflecting the urgency of understanding its implications. However, as this research increases, its focus remains uneven, often concentrating on functional or technical applications rather than the broader pedagogical, ethical, and contextual dimensions. This creates an ongoing need for scholarship that situates GenAI within the larger historical, theoretical, and professional landscape of TESOL, while also considering its impact on teacher identity, learner engagement, and equitable access to education.

Therefore, it is hoped that this book will contribute to the scholarship on GenAI in TESOL by examining how these tools are currently being used in classrooms and by offering evidence-based insights into their pedagogical, ethical, and professional implications. The aim is to bridge the gap between research and practice, provide actionable recommendations for educators, and make a timely contribution to the academic discourse on AI-enhanced language education.

Moving on, the next section outlines the theoretical framework that guides this analysis, providing a structured lens for examining the issues raised here.

1.6 Theoretical Framework

The theoretical framework used in this book draws on established perspectives in TESOL and education to analyse the integration of GenAI into language teaching. Informed by Borg's (2003) framework of teacher cognitions, which emphasises how educators' beliefs are shaped by their learning experiences and practice, this approach considers how such cognitions influence the ways teachers engage with new technologies. The framework is structured around four key perspectives: Social Constructivism, Ethical Use of Technology, Critical Theory, and the Technology Acceptance Model (TAM), which together provide a multidimensional lens for examining GenAI in TESOL. In later chapters, this is extended through the inclusion of Posthuman Pedagogy, adding further insight into how teaching and learning with GenAI emerge from the interconnected relationships between teachers, learners, technologies, and educational environments.

1.6.1 SECT: A Conceptual Frame

The SECT framework (see Fig. 1.1), comprising **S**ocial Constructivism, **E**thical Use of Technology, **C**ritical Theory, and the **T**echnology Acceptance Model, provides a coherent structure for analysing how GenAI is adopted and integrated in TESOL contexts. These perspectives are complementary and together they address the pedagogical, ethical, critical, and adoption-related dimensions of GenAI in language education.

Social Constructivism highlights the role of collaboration, interaction, and scaffolded learning, positioning GenAI as a tool that can support learner-centred pedagogy when applied thoughtfully. The Ethical Use of

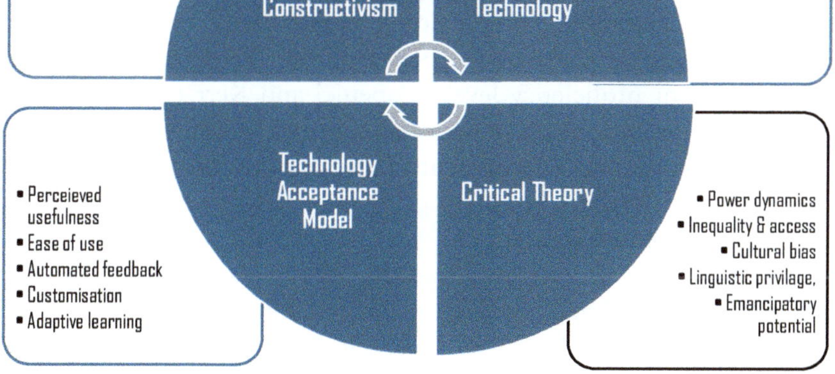

Fig. 1.1 SECT: A conceptual framework for viewing GenAI in TESOL

Technology addresses issues such as data privacy, bias, academic integrity, and the risks of "cognitive offloading" (Dawson, 2020), ensuring that GenAI is integrated in ways that protect learners and promote fairness. Critical Theory examines how GenAI is embedded within broader social and institutional power structures, exploring both the risks of reinforcing inequality and the potential for democratising access to language learning. The Technology Acceptance Model offers a framework for understanding how and why educators choose to adopt GenAI, with particular attention to perceived usefulness, ease of use, and teacher agency.

Together, these four perspectives underpin the book's practical and theoretical analyses, offering a balanced approach to understanding the promises and challenges of GenAI in language education. In later chapters, the framework is extended through the inclusion of posthuman pedagogy (Calderwood, 2025), to address the complex interplay between teachers, learners, technologies, and the educational environments in which they operate.

1.6.2 Social Constructivism and GenAI

Social constructivist pedagogy views learning as a socially mediated process in which knowledge is co-constructed through interaction and collaboration (Palinscar, 1998; Vygotsky, 1978). Within TESOL, GenAI can serve as a scaffold by providing personalised feedback (Barrot, 2023) and adaptive assessments (Naseer et al., 2024) that responds to learners' current proficiency levels. Popenici and Kerr (2017) note that AI has the capacity to act as a personalised tutor, guiding and managing students' learning and engagement. This supports the social constructivist view that learners build on prior knowledge through interaction with AI-generated resources.

For example, tools such as ChatGPT can generate targeted content that matches individual learning needs, enabling gradual progression with adaptive support (Pack & Maloney, 2023). Such scaffolding not only supports individual learning but can also facilitate collaborative activities, with AI-generated materials serving as the basis for group discussions, problem-solving tasks, and shared learning. Considered within the broader framework, social constructivism emphasises the importance of designing GenAI-enhanced activities that foster interaction, critical thinking, and learner autonomy.

1.6.3 The Ethical Use of GenAI

The ethical use of GenAI in TESOL encompasses issues such as data privacy, bias, academic integrity, and plagiarism. Large language models are trained on vast datasets, raising concerns about how personally identifiable information is stored and protected, with direct implications for student records in educational contexts (Duffourc et al., 2024). They may also unintentionally reinforce societal biases related to language, culture, gender, and ethnicity, potentially leading to inequitable learning experiences. Research has identified two main types of discriminatory output: explicitly demeaning and/or abusive content, and subtler prejudiced representations of protected groups (Hacker et al., 2025). While the latter may not be overtly discriminatory, its cumulative effect can reinforce societal inequalities over time.

Other ethical challenges arise from plagiarism and academic integrity. The ease of producing original-seeming AI-generated content creates risks that students may present such work as their own, undermining authentic learning. "Cognitive offloading" (Dawson, 2020; Perkins et al., 2024) further reduces the demand on students to develop and demonstrate their own skills in tasks such as writing or problem-solving, potentially weakening active engagement and critical thinking if not carefully managed. Viewed within the framework, the ethical-use perspective ensures that the integration of GenAI into TESOL balances innovation with responsibility, safeguarding both learners and the integrity of the educational process.

1.6.4 Critical Theory and GenAI

The framework for this book also draws on ideas from critical theory (Fuchs, 2021), which examines issues of power, inequality, emancipation, and the broader social implications of GenAI for TESOL. Through this lens, the analysis considers how GenAI operates within existing power structures and how it may perpetuate or reinforce social inequalities.

In the context of Artificial Intelligence in Education (AIED), digital literacy is an essential competency for educators. Defined as "the practices of communicating, relating, thinking and 'being' associated with digital media" (Jones & Hafner, 2021, p. 13), digital literacy also entails recognising that "literacies are never neutral: they are contextualized, situated, and circumscribed by different ideologies, inequalities, and relationships of power" (Darvin & Hafner, 2022, p. 867). This perspective raises critical questions about who designs GenAI systems, what cultural values are embedded within them, and how such values might perpetuate inequality or limit access for marginalised communities. Strengthening digital literacy in these ways enables educators to integrate GenAI into TESOL practices in ways that enhance learning while mitigating potential risks.

One of these risks concerns bias. Ferrara (2023) identifies multiple sources of bias in large language models, highlighting how such biases can shape and constrain educational applications. These range from multiple sources of bias embedded in training data, algorithms, labelling of training data by human annotators, product design decisions that prioritise specific demographics, among others. These biases, including linguistic, demographic, cultural, confirmation-based, and political, have significant implications for language learners from non-Western contexts, raising concerns about cultural hegemony and the perpetuation of inequalities in language education. This is illustrated by Alvero et al. (2024), who examined "Who does generative AI write like?" by comparing over 150,000 admissions essays submitted to a US private university with 25,000 ChatGPT-generated essays based on the same prompts. Their findings showed that, despite greater variability in human-written essays, AI-generated texts most closely resembled those written by male students from higher socio-economic backgrounds.

From a critical theory perspective, GenAI also brings into focus inequitable access to resources and the widening digital divide between those who benefit from AI tools and those who do not (Božić, 2023; Kitsara, 2022; Santiago-Ruiz, 2023). At the same time, this perspective recognises the emancipatory potential of AI technologies to expand educational opportunities and democratise access to learning for marginalised communities. In second language education, such potential can be realised by developing resources that support and empower learners from under-represented backgrounds. As Buddemeyer et al. (2022) observe, "Language is an act of identity, but AI has no identity other than that which its creators assign it. Technology creators who do not fully consider how identity information is encoded in AI dialogue risk creating representational harms that negatively impact users' interactions with the technology" (p. 366). If AI systems fail to reflect the diverse identities of second language learners, they risk perpetuating biases and misrepresenting learners' lived experiences.

Viewed within the SECT framework, critical theory provides a means to interrogate both the structural inequities and the transformative possibilities that GenAI presents for TESOL.

1.6.5 Technology Acceptance Model (TAM) and GenAI

The Technology Acceptance Model (TAM) (Davis, 1989, 1993) provides a framework for understanding the factors that influence an individual's decision to adopt and use new technologies. It emphasises two core constructs: perceived usefulness (PU), the degree to which a user believes a technology will enhance their performance, and perceived ease of use (PEoU), the extent to which the technology is seen as free from effort. Both directly shape user attitudes, intentions, and eventual uptake.

Applied to TESOL, TAM suggests that educators are more likely to integrate GenAI tools when they believe these tools can improve teaching and learning outcomes, such as by providing tailored feedback, generating lesson materials, or supporting learner autonomy. Conversely, if the tools are perceived as difficult to use, unreliable, or ethically problematic, adoption is less likely.

Building on TAM, the Unified Theory of Acceptance and Use of Technology (UTAUT) (Venkatesh et al., 2003) offers a broader framework that incorporates additional variables of technology adoption—performance expectancy, effort expectancy, social influence, and facilitating conditions. UTAUT extends TAM by recognising the social and institutional factors that shape technology acceptance, such as peer attitudes, organisational culture, and access to training and resources. In the context of GenAI adoption in TESOL, this model highlights how teachers' willingness to integrate AI tools depends not only on perceived usefulness and ease of use but also on institutional support and professional development.

Considered alongside the other perspectives in the framework, TAM and UTAUT together contribute to a broader understanding of how teacher agency, institutional contexts, and the capabilities of the technology itself interact to shape GenAI integration in TESOL. This framework is further enriched by posthuman pedagogy, discussed in later chapters on ethics and teacher education, which extends the analysis by examining how teaching and learning emerge from the interconnected relationships between human actors, AI tools, and the broader educational environment.

This framework not only provides a basis for analysing the pedagogical, ethical, and adoption-related dimensions of GenAI, but also informs the empirical investigation undertaken for this book, described in the following section.

1.7 An Empirical Approach

To complement the theoretical discussion, this book integrates findings from an original empirical study designed to explore how TESOL educators around the world are engaging with GenAI in their professional practice. Using a mixed-methods research design, the study gathered both quantitative and qualitative data to capture a wide range of experiences, perceptions, and contexts.

A purposive sampling strategy was used to recruit TESOL professionals with varying levels of experience with AI tools. An online survey was distributed via professional networks and TESOL community platforms. In total, 78 participants completed the survey, and 14 of these later took part in semi-structured interviews. Participation was voluntary, and the study followed the British Educational Research Association (BERA) Ethical Guidelines for Educational Research (5th ed., 2024), ensuring informed consent, anonymity, and confidentiality.

The procedure comprised two stages. First, an online questionnaire—administered via Google Forms—collected data on participants' demographic profiles, familiarity with GenAI, reported uses, perceived benefits, and concerns. The instrument included both Likert-scale items and open-ended questions allowing for elaboration on teaching practices and institutional contexts.

Second, follow-up semi-structured interviews were conducted with 14 participants who had indicated a willingness to share more about their experiences using GenAI. Interviews were conducted online. The interview protocol explored pedagogical applications of GenAI, ethical and institutional considerations, and perceived challenges and opportunities. Interviewees represented diverse professional backgrounds in TESOL working in higher education, language institutes, and schools across the United States, China, Japan, South Africa, Qatar, Cyprus, Greece, and Algeria. Interviews were audio-recorded and transcribed with participants' consent.

Quantitative data were analysed using descriptive statistics to identify patterns in GenAI adoption and perceptions, while qualitative data from open-ended responses and interviews were thematically analysed to highlight recurrent themes and contextual variations.

Participants, as a whole, represented a broad demographic and professional spectrum. They ranged in age from early-career educators to highly experienced practitioners, with the largest group (44.7%) aged 35–44 years. Most respondents identified as female (72.4%), followed by male (25%), with small proportions identifying as non-binary or preferring not to say. Educational backgrounds were strong, with 92.2% holding a master's degree or higher, and many also possessing professional TESOL certifications (e.g., CELTA, DELTA).

Participants worked in a variety of TESOL-related roles, including classroom teachers (73.1%), teacher trainers (20.5%), curriculum developers (11.5%), and school administrators (5.1%), often with overlapping responsibilities. Teaching contexts ranged from primary to adult education, with university-level teaching being the most common (61.5%). Geographically, the sample was weighted towards Europe (65.4%) and countries in West Asia and the Arabian Peninsula, including Qatar, Jordan, the Gulf States, the UAE, and Saudi Arabia (24.4%), with others from East and Southeast Asia, North America, Africa, and Australasia.

Familiarity with GenAI varied: 52.6% described themselves as "somewhat familiar," having experimented with tools in their teaching; 21.8% as "very familiar," using GenAI regularly; 16.7% as "slightly familiar" and 9% as "not familiar." This variation allowed for a wide range of perspectives, from early adopters to cautious observers.

While the sample is not fully representative of the global TESOL community, it offers valuable insight into an emerging area of practice at a critical point in its development. The study's findings are woven throughout the book, providing a grounded, practitioner-informed perspective that sits alongside the theoretical and policy discussions.

1.8 Scope of the Book

The book is specifically tailored to GenAI's applications and implications within the TESOL field, providing a targeted exploration of its educational potential and challenges. It addresses both the practical and theoretical dimensions of GenAI in TESOL, encompassing key areas such as personalised learning, automated feedback, ethical considerations (including data privacy, bias, and academic integrity), and the implications for teacher education. It also explores the future of AI-driven education and how best to prepare for it.

Empirical data collected from the literature is presented and discussed through the lens of the theoretical framework that guides the book. Alongside this, findings from original research conducted for this work are integrated throughout. These findings provide insights into TESOL educators' perceptions, uses, and challenges related to GenAI in diverse teaching contexts.

The scope does not extend to detailed examinations of other AI tools or broader applications outside TESOL. For example, AI applications such as learning analytics, virtual reality (VR), or augmented reality (AR) for immersive language learning are beyond the focus of this work, as are non-language-subject applications or the technical development of GenAI itself.

The discussion throughout the book is guided by the theoretical framework introduced in this chapter and is later expanded through the addition of posthuman pedagogy. This layered approach ensures that the analysis of GenAI integration in TESOL remains both conceptually grounded and responsive to the evolving relationships between teachers, learners, technologies, and educational contexts.

1.9 Overview

This book explores the transformative role of GenAI in TESOL, blending theoretical insights with empirical data to provide a comprehensive view of its impact on language education. This first chapter introduces the concept of GenAI in TESOL, outlines its significance, and establishes the SECT framework (Social Constructivism, Ethical Use of Technology, Critical Theory, Technology Acceptance Model) as the central analytical lens.

Chapter 2 examines the historical evolution of TESOL and the technologies that have shaped its practice, from early CALL systems to TELL and now GenAI. It connects these technological shifts to foundational SLA theories, demonstrating how each phase of technological integration has laid the groundwork for the emergence of GenAI. Drawing on empirical data and teacher reflections, Chapter 2 also highlights diverse approaches to technology adoption in TESOL, addressing both opportunities and barriers.

Chapter 3 shifts the focus to the present, offering a detailed analysis of GenAI's current applications in TESOL, including tools such as large language models (LLMs), virtual tutors, and translation software. It critically examines how these tools are being integrated into TESOL practices and their implications for pedagogy.

Chapter 4 provides practical strategies for enhancing language skills through GenAI, supported by examples and case studies on its use in teaching writing, speaking, reading, listening, and intercultural communication skills.

Chapter 5 addresses ethical and ideological tensions associated with GenAI in TESOL, such as bias, privacy concerns, over-reliance on GenAI tools, and issues of equity and access. It also explores the implications for teacher autonomy and the ways in which GenAI may embed unspoken values about language and pedagogy.

Chapter 6 focuses on language teacher education, examining strategies to prepare TESOL educators for integrating GenAI into their pedagogy. It outlines professional development approaches such as workshops, collaborative learning communities, and tailored training courses, and emphasises the importance of building critical AI literacy that blends technical competence with ethical and pedagogical reflection.

Chapter 7 concludes the book by synthesising the key insights, theoretical contributions, and practical recommendations from across the chapters. It reflects on how GenAI is reshaping TESOL practice, pedagogy, and professional identity, and calls for an approach that maintains the relational, critical, and ethical ethos of language teaching.

The analysis across these chapters is guided by the theoretical framework introduced in Chapter 1, which is later extended through the incorporation of posthuman pedagogy. This combined approach offers both a conceptual and practical basis for examining GenAI integration in TESOL.

1.10 Conclusion

This chapter introduced the concept of GenAI and its implications for the field of TESOL. It outlined the theoretical framework that is rooted in Social Constructivism, Ethical Use of Technology, Critical Theory, and the Technology Acceptance Model (TAM), and noted that in later chapters this framework is extended through the inclusion of Posthuman Pedagogy. Together, these perspectives provide a structured lens for critically examining the impact of GenAI, particularly in relation to pedagogy, ethics, professional practice, and the evolving relationships between teachers, learners, technologies, and educational environments.

The chapter also described the empirical basis for the book, drawing on survey responses from 78 TESOL educators and follow-up interviews with 14 participants from diverse geographical and educational contexts. These educator voices will appear throughout the book, complementing the theoretical and policy perspectives with practice-based insights.

As we close this first chapter, it is useful to return to the voices of educators who are navigating the opportunities and challenges of GenAI in their teaching. Many are using GenAI with caution but are beginning to see GenAI as a valuable addition to their professional toolkit:

> Quotation 6: "In the beginning, when I first heard about ChatGPT and similar tools, I didn't use them at all because they were unknown to me. But once I started using them, I found them useful, and my view has been positive since. Initially, I was more hesitant, but now I see the benefits." (T.7, South Africa)
>
> Quotation 7: "I think it will be very helpful for both language learning and teaching. Yes, it will revolutionise the process. It's a very important part of technology. I mean now we are talking about AI just like 20 years ago we were talking about PowerPoint and slides." (T.2, China)

While some remain wary of over-reliance, they still recognise its potential:

> Quotation 8: "I'm definitely concerned about over-reliance. Some universities now say, 'If you can't say it, how are you writing it?' I apply that to my teaching too." (T.10, Cyprus)
>
> Quotation 9: "I truly believe that AI can never ever replace a teacher. There is always some kind of connections that need to be established between a teacher and a student, and this is something that AI cannot provide. This is for sure. But the benefit would be the kind of, let's say, activities AI can provide. Like, it helps with saving time." (T.8, Qatar)

Others focus on demystifying GenAI for their students:

> Quotation 10: "One of my goals is to demystify it for them since much of what they hear about AI is negative. I'm old enough to remember the

backlash against Wikipedia when it first came out, but now it's widely accepted. I think AI will follow a similar path." (T.1., US)
Quotation 11: "I think there's no way to avoid these new technologies, much like when the calculator was first introduced. We should focus on the positive aspects and handle any potential drawbacks carefully. We shouldn't reject it outright." (T.14, Algeria)

These reflections reveal a profession in transition that is moving from uncertainty towards cautious optimism, with educators actively seeking ways to integrate GenAI responsibly and meaningfully into their practice. They highlight the need for both critical engagement and pedagogical creativity, ensuring that the use of GenAI strengthens rather than diminishes the relational and ethical foundations of TESOL.

Moving on, Chapter 2 builds on this foundation by providing a historical overview of technology integration in TESOL, tracing the evolution from early CALL systems to the current GenAI landscape, and situating today's developments within the broader trajectory of language teaching and learning.

References

Alier, M., Peñalvo, F. J. G., & Camba, J. D. (2024). Generative artificial intelligence in education: From deceptive to disruptive. *International Journal of Interactive Multimedia and Artificial Intelligence, 8*(5), 5–14. https://doi.org/10.9781/ijimai.2024.02.011

Alvero, A. J., Lee, J., Regla-Vargas, A., Kizilcec, R. F., Joachims, T., & Antonio, A. L. (2024). Large language models, social demography, and hegemony: Comparing authorship in human and synthetic text. *Journal of Big Data, 11*(1), 138. https://doi.org/10.1186/s40537-024-00986-7

Amato, G., Behrmann, M., Bimbot, F., Caramiaux, B., Falchi, F., Garcia, A., ... & Vincent, E. (2019). AI in the media and creative industries. arXiv preprint arXiv:1905.04175

Barreto, F., Moharkar, L., Shirodkar, M., Sarode, V., Gonsalves, S., & Johns, A. (2023, February). Generative artificial intelligence: Opportunities and challenges of large language models. In *International Conference on Intelligent Computing and Networking* (pp. 545–553). Springer Nature Singapore. https://doi.org/10.1007/978-981-99-3177-4_41

Barrot, J. S. (2023). Using automated written corrective feedback in the writing classrooms: Effects on L2 writing accuracy. *Computer Assisted Language Learning, 36*(4), 584–607. https://doi.org/10.1080/09588221.2021.1936071

Borg, S. (2003). Teacher cognition in language teaching: A review of research on what language teachers think, know, believe, and do. *Language Teaching, 36*(2), 81–109. https://doi.org/10.1017/s0261444803001903

British Educational Research Association. (2024). *Ethical guidelines for educational research* (5th ed.). https://www.bera.ac.uk/publication/ethical-guidelines-for-educational-research-2024

Božić, V. (2023). Artifical intelligence as the reason and the solution of digital divide. *Language Education and Technology, 3*(2).

Buddemeyer, A., Nwogu, J., Solyst, J., Walker, E., Nkrumah, T., Ogan, A., ... & Stewart, A. (2022, September). Unwritten magic: Participatory design of AI dialogue to empower marginalized voices. In *Proceedings of the 2022 ACM conference on information technology for social good* (pp. 366–372). https://doi.org/10.1145/3524458.3547119

Calderwood, S. J. (2025). An exploration of human and platform intra-actions in a digital teaching and learning environment. *Learning, Media and Technology, 50*(2), 263–275. https://doi.org/10.1080/17439884.2023.2285820

Galaczi, E. (2023). *English language education in the era of generative AI: Our perspective.* Cambridge English.

Chapelle, C. A. (2003). *English language learning and technology: Lectures on applied linguistics in the age of information and communication technology.* John Benjamins. https://doi.org/10.1075/lllt.7

Chapelle, C. A. (2024). Open generative AI changes a lot, but not everything. *Modern Language Journal (John Wiley & Sons, Inc.), 108*(2). https://doi.org/10.1111/modl.12927

Darvin, R., & Hafner, C. A. (2022). Digital literacies in TESOL: Mapping out the terrain. *TESOL Quarterly, 56*(3), 865–882. https://doi.org/10.1002/tesq.3161

Davis, F. D. (1989). Perceived usefulness, perceived ease of use, and user acceptance of information technology. *MIS Quarterly*, 319–340. https://doi.org/10.2307/249008

Davis, F. D. (1993). User acceptance of information technology: System characteristics, user perceptions and behavioral impacts. *International Journal of Man-Machine Studies, 38*(3), 475–487. https://doi.org/10.1006/imms.1993.1022

Dawson, P. (2020). Cognitive offloading and assessment. In M. Bearman, P. Dawson, R. Ajjawi, J. Tai, & D. Boud (Eds.), *Re-imagining University Assessment in a Digital World* (pp. 37–48). Springer International Publishing. https://doi.org/10.1007/978-3-030-41956-1_4

Diamandis, P. H., & Kotler, S. (2012). Abundance: The future is better than you think. *Simon and Schuster*. https://doi.org/10.1177/1946756713478580

Duffourc, M., Gerke, S., & Kollnig, K. (2024). Privacy of personal data in the generative AI data lifecycle. *New York University Journal of Intellectual Property & Entertainment Law, 13*(2), 219–268. https://doi.org/10.2139/ssrn.4899219

Fandiño, F. G. E., & Velandia, A. J. S. (2020). How an online tutor motivates E-learning English. *Heliyon, 6*(8). https://doi.org/10.1016/j.heliyon.2020.e04630

Ferrara, E. (2023). Should ChatGPT be biased? Challenges and Risks of Bias in Large Language Models. *arXiv*. https://doi.org/10.2139/ssrn.4627814

Feuerriegel, S., Hartmann, J., Janiesch, C., & Zschech, P. (2024). Generative AI. *Business & Information Systems Engineering, 66*(1), 111–126. https://doi.org/10.1007/s12599-023-00834-7

Floridi, L. (2023). AI as agency without intelligence: On ChatGPT, large language models, and other generative models. *Philosophy & Technology, 36*(1), 15. https://doi.org/10.1007/s13347-023-00621-y

Fuchs, C. (2021). What is critical theory? In *Foundations of critical theory* (pp. 17–51). Routledge. https://doi.org/10.4324/9781003199182-2

Godwin-Jones, R. (2022). Partnering with AI: Intelligent writing assistance and instructed language learning. *Language Learning & Technology, 26*(2), 5–24. https://doi.org/10.10125/73474

Hacker, P., Zuiderveen Borgesius, F., Mittelstadt, B. D., & Wachter, S. (2025). Generative discrimination: What happens when generative AI exhibits bias, and what can be done about it. In P. Hacker, A. Engel, S. Hammer, & B. Mittelstadt (Eds.), *The Oxford handbook of the foundations and regulation of generative AI.* (1st ed.). Oxford University Press. https://doi.org/10.1093/oxfordhb/9780198940272.013.0016

Holstein, K., & Doroudi, S. (2022). Equity and artificial intelligence in education. In *The ethics of artificial intelligence in education* (pp. 151–173). Routledge. https://doi.org/10.4324/9780429329067-9

Johnson, C., & Cardoso, W. (2024). Hey Google, let's write: Examining L2 learners' acceptance of automatic speech recognition as a writing tool. *CALICO Journal, 41*(2). https://doi.org/10.1558/cj.22431

Jones, R. H., & Hafner, C. A. (2021). Understanding digital literacies: A practical introduction. *Routledge*. https://doi.org/10.4324/9781003177647

Kabudi, T., Pappas, I., & Olsen, D. H. (2021). AI-enabled adaptive learning systems: A systematic mapping of the literature. *Computers and Education: Artificial Intelligence, 2*, Article 100017. https://doi.org/10.1016/j.caeai.2021.100017

Kern, R. (2024). Twenty-first century technologies and language education: Charting a path forward. *Modern Language Journal (John Wiley & Sons, Inc.), 108*(2). https://doi.org/10.1111/modl.12924

Kitsara, I. (2022). Artificial intelligence and the digital divide: From an innovation perspective. In *Platforms and artificial intelligence: The next generation of competences* (pp. 245–265). Springer International Publishing. https://doi.org/10.1007/978-3-030-90192-9_12

Kohnke, L. (2024). Exploring EAP students' perceptions of GenAI and traditional grammar-checking tools for language learning. *Computers and Education: Artificial Intelligence, 7*, Article 100279. https://doi.org/10.1016/j.caeai.2024.100279

Luckin, R., Cukurova, M., Kent, C., & Du Boulay, B. (2022). Empowering educators to be AI-ready. *Computers and Education: Artificial Intelligence, 3*, Article 100076. https://doi.org/10.1016/j.caeai.2022.100076

Mahajan, V. (2023). 100+ incredible ChatGPT statistics & facts in 2024.

Moorhouse, B. L., Wan, Y., Wu, C., Kohnke, L., Ho, T. Y., & Kwong, T. (2024). Developing language teachers' professional generative AI competence: An intervention study in an initial language teacher education course. *System, 125*, Article 103399. https://doi.org/10.1016/j.system.2024.103399

Naseer, F., Khalid, M. U., Ayub, N., Rasool, A., Abbas, T., & Afzal, M. W. (2024). Automated assessment and feedback in higher education using generative AI. In R. C. Sharma & A. Bozkurt (Eds.), *Transforming education with generative AI: Prompt engineering and synthetic content creation* (pp. 433–461). IGI Global. https://doi.org/10.4018/979-8-3693-1351-0.ch021

Nunan, D. (2022). The changing landscape of English language teaching and learning. In E. Hinkel (Ed.), *Handbook of practical second language teaching and learning* (pp. 3–23). Routledge. https://doi.org/10.4324/9781003106609

Pack, A., & Maloney, J. (2023). Potential affordances of generative AI in language education: Demonstrations and an evaluative framework. *Teaching English with Technology, 23*(2), 4–24. https://doi.org/10.56297/BUKA4060/VRRO1747

Palinscar, A. S. (1998). Social constructivist perspectives on teaching and learning. *Annual Review of Psychology, 49*(1), 345–375. https://doi.org/10.1146/annurev.psych.49.1.345

Perkins, M., Roe, J., Postma, D., McGaughran, J., & Hickerson, D. (2024). Detection of GPT-4 generated text in higher education: Combining academic judgement and software to identify generative AI tool misuse. *Journal of Academic Ethics, 22*(1), 89–113.https://doi.org/10.48550/arXiv.2305.18081

Popenici, S. A., & Kerr, S. (2017). Exploring the impact of artificial intelligence on teaching and learning in higher education. *Research and Practice in Technology Enhanced Learning, 12*(1), Article 22. https://doi.org/10.1186/s41039-017-0062-8

Richards, J. C., & Rodgers, T. S. (2001). Major language trends in twentieth-century language teaching. In *Approaches and methods in language teaching* (pp. 1–2). Cambridge University Press. https://doi.org/10.1017/cbo9780511667305.002

Santiago-Ruiz, E. (2023). Writing with ChatGPT in a context of educational inequality and digital divide. *International Journal of Education and Development Using Information and Communication Technology, 19*(3), 28–38.

Tafazoli, D. (2024). Exploring the potential of generative AI in democratizing English language education. *Computers and Education: Artificial Intelligence, 7*, Article 100275. https://doi.org/10.1016/j.caeai.2024.100275

Thorne, S. L. (2024). Generative artificial intelligence, co-evolution, and language education. *Modern Language Journal, 108*(2), 567–572. https://doi.org/10.1111/modl.12986

Venkatesh, V., Morris, M. G., Davis, G. B., & Davis, F. D. (2003). User acceptance of information technology: Toward a unified view1. *MIS Quarterly, 27*(3), 425–478. https://doi.org/10.2307/30036540

Vygotsky, L. S. (1978). *Mind in society: The development of higher psychological processes*. Harvard University Press.

2

From CALL to AIED—The Role of Technology in TESOL

2.1 Teachers Reflecting on Technology in TESOL

Over the past five decades, technology has transformed the landscape of TESOL, advancing from simple tools like audio recordings and language labs to sophisticated digital platforms, multimedia resources, and, more recently, GenAI-driven applications. This chapter traces the evolution of technology integration in TESOL, emphasising the pivotal role of educators and theoretical frameworks in this transformation. By examining key milestones, including the shift from Computer-Assisted Language Learning (CALL) to Technology-Enhanced Language Learning (TELL), and the emergence of Artificial Intelligence in Education (AIED), it provides a historical and theoretical foundation for understanding how GenAI is reshaping TESOL today. Furthermore, it draws on empirical data collected from TESOL educators, highlighting their reflections on the challenges and opportunities of adopting GenAI in practice. Finally, it addresses the ethical and pedagogical implications of AI in TESOL, offering insights into its transformative potential and the considerations for its responsible integration.

C. Savvidou, *AI-Powered Language Teaching*,
https://doi.org/10.1007/978-3-032-14502-4_2

To gain a deeper understanding of how this technological evolution has impacted teaching practices, insights from TESOL educators were gathered through interviews. Their reflections highlight both the challenges and opportunities presented by integrating new technologies into the classroom. From initial scepticism to embracing GenAI, several teachers noted how innovations in AI mirror earlier technological shifts, such as the introduction of PowerPoint, emphasising that eventually all tools become embedded in routine classroom practice:

> Quotation 1: "Philosophy is a big word, but it [GenAI] has certainly changed my teaching. …COVID forced us to rethink how we teach, which was stressful but ultimately healthy. Now, AI is just another change to navigate, and we have some tools from that earlier experience to help us manage it." (T.1, United States)
> Quotation 2: "I think it [AI] will be very helpful for both language learning and teaching. Yes, it will revolutionise the process. It's a very important part of technology. I mean, now we are talking about AI just like 20 years ago we were talking about PowerPoint and slides. It will become more and more popular, I believe." (T.2, China)
> Quotation 3: "I'm old enough to remember the backlash against Wikipedia when it first came out, but now it's widely accepted. I think AI will follow a similar path." (T.13, Greece)

Teachers' sense of continuity with earlier technological shifts highlights their belief that GenAI will eventually be normalised as a standard classroom tool, much like Wikipedia and PowerPoint.

Despite this growing acceptance, several educators also voiced concerns that GenAI could reshape the teachers' professional role by altering the student–teacher relationship, encouraging over-reliance or enabling misuse:

> Quotation 4: "I don't believe AI will replace teachers... it helps with saving time, like generating pictures or resources quickly, but it won't ever replace the teacher–student connection." (T.8, Qatar)

Quotation 5: "AI has both advantages and disadvantages. It makes it easier to collect data and prepare classes, but there are challenges like plagiarism... I worry that students may become lazier and more dependent on AI." (T.4, China)
Quotation 6: "AI introduces a new way of learning and thinking critically, and it's not going away. We need to adapt, but I worry about students relying too much on it, like when they ask AI to summarise an article instead of reading it themselves." (T.9, Cyprus)

These reflections reveal how teachers are negotiating the evolving role of GenAI in language education, weighing its potential to improve teaching and learning against the risks of reduced learner autonomy, academic integrity concerns, and the erosion of critical thinking skills. These insights set the stage for the discussion that follows in this chapter.

2.2 A Brief History of Technology in TESOL

The history of modern TESOL has been a history of technology adoption. The initial stages of technology adoption in language teaching saw the use of basic tools like audio recordings, film strips, projectors and infrastructure in the form of language labs. The development of early Computer-Assisted Language Learning (CALL) systems provided grammar drills and vocabulary exercises, marking the beginning of computer-based learning (Garrett, 2009; Warschauer & Healey, 1998). Most of this early technology was aimed at improving speaking and listening skills and bringing authentic language use into the classroom.

In his overview of the development of technology in TESOL, Bax (2003) outlined three phases from the later twentieth century to the beginning of the twenty-first century.

The first phase included a 'restricted' version of CALL in the 1970s and 1980s, characterised by the use of mainframe computers and teaching approaches primarily focused on grammar drills and repetitive practice exercises. During this phase, the approach was aligned with traditional language learning methods such as grammar-translation and audio-lingual practices, and the use of technology, such as overhead projectors, scantrons, and early computers, was seen as a tutor, providing direct, controlled instruction primarily designed to reinforce language rules and vocabulary. Systems such as PLATO (University of Illinois) and TICCIT (Brigham Young University) exemplified this period with their drill-and-practice activities, automated testing, and limited learner control (Davies et al., 2013; Levy, 1997; Morton, 1976).

The second phase of development in the 1980s to 1990s saw a transition to more 'open' CALL with communicative language teaching, which emphasised interactive and flexible language learning. As personal computers, films, television programmes, and CD-ROMs became more widespread, TESOL educators promoted skills development through simulations, games, and multimedia, often with the aid of whiteboards and language labs equipped with headphones. Authoring tools such as CALIS (Kossuth, 1987) enabled teachers to design custom activities, while early text-based simulations such as 'Granville: The Prize Holiday Package' (Cambridge University Press, 1986) incorporated authentic materials, such as maps, prices, and menus, to support decision-making tasks and contextual language use (Torlot, 1993). Despite these increased capabilities, technology remained supplementary rather than being fully integrated into the curriculum.

The third phase, beginning at the onset of the twenty-first century, aimed at an integrated version of CALL and the normalisation of technology within language education. During this period, interactive whiteboards, laptops, and internet access became common in classrooms, supporting communicative and integrative approaches. Concordancing software such as Micro-OCP (Hockey & Martin, 1988) paved the way for Data-Driven Learning (DDL), which encouraged learners to explore authentic language corpora and identify patterns inductively (Dodd, 2014). This shift aimed for technology to be embedded within everyday teaching practice, supporting various learning approaches, including content-based, task-based, and project-based learning. The rise of mobile devices such as iPads and smartphones extended this integration further, allowing for personalised, on-the-go learning experiences.

These three phases highlight the evolution of technology integration in TESOL over the past fifty years. This progression, from restricted, controlled use to more interactive and adaptive systems, not only sets the

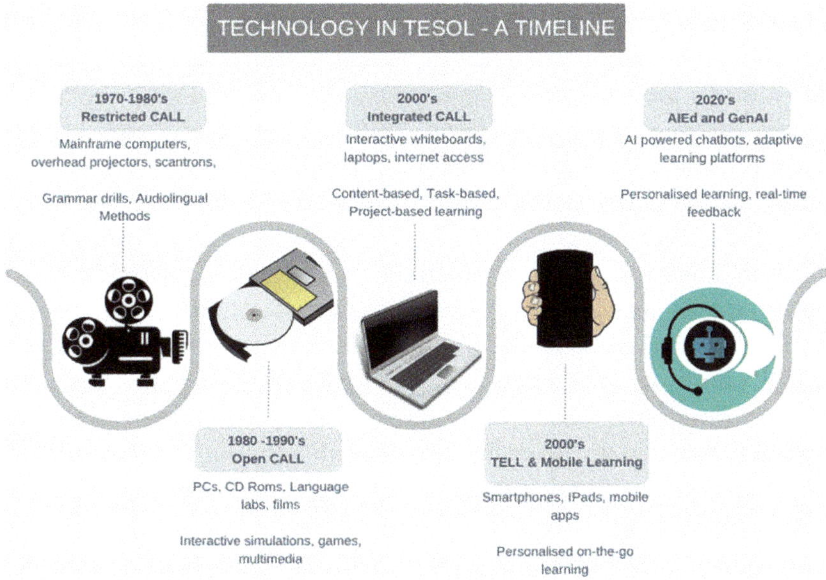

Fig. 2.1 Development of technology in TESOL: An overview

stage for the introduction of GenAI into the modern educational landscape but also provides a valuable context for understanding its adoption. Figure 2.1 summarises the development, providing an overview of how technology integration in TESOL has evolved over the last five decades.

2.3 Trends in Technology Adoption in TESOL

Building on this historical trajectory, research on technology adoption in TESOL has shown that successful integration depends not only on technological availability but also on educators' pedagogical beliefs, institutional contexts, and training. Studies of CALL and subsequent digital innovations emphasise that teachers adopt technology when it aligns with communicative and learner-centred approaches (Bax, 2003; Chapelle, 2001; Garrett, 2009; Warschauer & Healey, 1998). At the same time, constraints such as limited infrastructure, insufficient professional development, and resistance to change have often hindered implementation (Davies et al., 2013; Tondeur et al., 2017). As digital learning environments expanded, research also highlighted the shift towards greater teacher agency and the role of digital literacies in shaping practice (Darvin & Hafner, 2022). More recent work on AI in education underscores similar adoption patterns while introducing new ethical and pedagogical concerns (Chapelle, 2024; Holmes et al., 2019; Kern, 2024; Pedro et al., 2019). This body of research provides a foundation for understanding current trends in GenAI adoption in TESOL and situates the present study within this broader context.

To build on these insights, the survey conducted for this book asked TESOL educators to describe their experience with integrating new technologies (not only GenAI) into their teaching over the years. Their responses revealed three main patterns of adoption: frequent use of new technologies, occasional use depending on relevance, and cautious or limited adoption. Because participants could select more than one option, the percentages reported here indicate the proportion who chose each category, rather than mutually exclusive groups.

A majority of educators (64.1%) identified themselves as frequent users of technology in their teaching. They demonstrated adaptability by integrating platforms such as Moodle, Google Classroom, and multimedia tools to support assessment, grading, collaboration, and interactive lessons through videos, podcasts, and digital games. These experiences with digital platforms have prepared this group to adopt newer technologies such as GenAI, which builds on these foundations, as one survey participant noted:

> Quotation 7: "Past experiences with technology integration have significantly influenced my readiness to use generative AI tools in the classroom by building familiarity with digital tools and increasing adaptability. Platforms like Moodle and Google Classroom introduced me to managing online content and interacting with students in virtual spaces. Tools like Duolingo and multimedia resources have shown me the benefits of interactive, personalized learning experiences. My experience with online assessments has made me comfortable with automated feedback, preparing me to embrace AI-powered evaluation and teaching tools. These experiences have fostered a mindset of flexibility and innovation,

making the transition to generative AI smoother and more intuitive." (Survey Participant)

Approximately 33.3% of educators described their approach as occasional, adopting technologies only when they perceived clear benefits. This group valued practicality and preferred to balance innovation with proven effectiveness. They expressed concerns about the relevance of certain tools, ensuring that new technologies aligned with their specific teaching objectives. They were also conscious of the learning curve required in mastering new tools, particularly those requiring substantial setup or customisation. As one survey participant reflected:

> Quotation 8: "In the past I have been cautious integrating new technologies, mostly due to a lack of technical experience with those tools. AI seems easier to integrate, and the students are more receptive to its use." (Survey Participant)

Finally, a small percentage (5.1%) of educators reported rarely or never integrating new technologies into their classrooms, citing concerns about tools failing during critical teaching moments and limited exposure to, or training in, using digital tools effectively. As one participant explained:

> Quotation 9: "Haven't really seen any influence. I think I am not a fast adopter of new innovations, so that might explain why I don't jump right away at adopting new technology in my professional or personal life." (Survey Participant)

These three patterns illustrate how prior experiences with technology influence educators' openness to GenAI, suggesting that familiarity with digital platforms can facilitate smoother adoption, while limited exposure or cautious approaches may slow integration.

2.4 The Rise of Digital Tools and Multimedia

Educators' prior experiences with technology are closely connected to the rise of digital tools and multimedia. These innovations marked a turning point in TESOL, enabling more interactive, engaging, and flexible approaches to language teaching and learning. From basic applications such as Microsoft Word for creating class materials, to ELT websites, internet-based projects, blogs, wikis, and podcasts, the range of multimedia resources has been significant in facilitating interactive learning (Dudeney & Hockly, 2007). More recently, the adoption of digital learning platforms such as Moodle, Google Classroom, and Blackboard Learn has supported online collaboration, resource sharing, and personalised learning. These platforms have transformed traditional teaching methods by enabling more interactive and student-centred learning environments.

Similarly, the shift from face-to-face to online assessment practices has also addressed several key issues, including time management, content complexity, student responsibility, and informal assessment opportunities. Online assessments and examination techniques can automate grading and feedback, improving efficiency and test security. However, the increasing automation of assessment raises important pedagogical questions: to what extent do these systems capture the full complexity of language proficiency, and how might they shape what is valued in language learning? As Beebe et al. (2010) note, there remains a need for pedagogical frameworks that address not only the delivery of content in online contexts but also the mediation of learning through teacher presence, feedback, and interaction.

Over the last two decades, the rapid growth and integration of technology in education have been widely supported by academics, institutions, and governments, contributing to the broader digitalisation of education. While the overall stance on implementation has been positive, scholars have also urged caution. For example, Selwyn (2016), in "Is Technology Good for Education?", emphasises the importance of understanding technology integration within its wider social, economic, and cultural contexts, rather than viewing it as an isolated component. In TESOL, this means recognising that the benefits of digital learning, such as improved access and efficiency, are unevenly distributed, often reflecting existing inequalities in internet connectivity, institutional infrastructure, and teacher training. Furthermore, the very platforms that enable collaborative, student-centred learning also collect and store large amounts of learner data, raising concerns over privacy, surveillance, and the commercialisation of educational information.

Taken together, these issues highlight a persistent tension: technology offers genuine pedagogical opportunities, yet its integration must be critically mediated to ensure that innovation does not come at the expense of equity, learner agency, or the nuanced goals of language education. These concerns are highly relevant to the adoption of GenAI, which reflects many of the promises and challenges associated with earlier waves of digital innovation in TESOL.

Turning to the survey data, when asked which technological innovations had best prepared them for GenAI, many participants identified specific technological innovations as foundational in preparing them for the integration of GenAI tools in TESOL. Digital learning platforms such as Moodle and Google Classroom were cited by 65.4% of respondents as the most significant, credited with familiarising educators with online resource management, digital assessments, and collaborative functions. Multimedia resources, including podcasts, videos, and interactive content, were recognised by 52.6% of participants for their role in engaging students through varied content formats that appeal to different learning styles. Language learning applications such as Duolingo and Rosetta Stone were mentioned by 48.7% of respondents, reflecting their contribution to integrating technology in ways that enhance language acquisition through gamification and personalised practice. Online assessment tools, including TOEFL iBT and IELTS online, were selected by 26.9% of participants, valued for their capacity to provide automated grading and real-time feedback—capabilities that directly anticipate more advanced AI-driven applications.

The findings suggest that educators' prior exposure to various digital tools has played a crucial role in preparing them for the integration of GenAI in TESOL. Through regular use of digital learning platforms like Moodle and Google Classroom, educators have developed key skills in managing digital content, organising online activities, and facilitating student engagement through virtual interfaces. This aligns with the Technology Acceptance Model (TAM), which emphasises that positive experiences with technology can shape users' attitudes towards adopting new tools (Marangunić & Granić, 2015). Within this model, two factors are central to technology adoption: perceived usefulness (the degree to which the person believes that the technology will enhance their job performance) and perceived ease of use (the degree to which the person believes that using the technology will be free of effort) are central to technology adoption.

Furthermore, the findings suggest that educators who have previously integrated videos, podcasts, and interactive activities into their lessons may have a stronger understanding of how to apply and adapt content to sustain student engagement. This experience can be directly transferred to the use of GenAI, which can generate and adapt materials, such as customised exercises or visual aids, thereby extending the trend towards multimodal learning.

> Quotation 10: "Sometimes even if I need some pictures, instead of looking or surfing the internet—maybe spending an hour or two just to find something relevant—I could just give a prompt to the AI, and then it generates the picture that suits the context that I want to have in that picture." (T.8, Qatar)
> Quotation 11: "Yes, I've started to use it in other ways. One example is using its art capabilities to generate images. I had students generate pictures based on texts, and they went through multiple iterations to get something that matched the text better." (T.1, United States)

In these instances, AI image generators were perceived as both time-saving and user-friendly, enabling teachers to create materials and design learning activities that were communicative, creative, and tailored to specific lesson contexts.

Additionally, language learning applications such as Duolingo have familiarised educators with the potential of automated, adaptive learning systems. These apps provide personalised feedback and track student progress, features that are now being enhanced and expanded through GenAI technologies. With more than 300 million people having used the gamified mobile-assisted language learning (MALL) application

Duolingo (Shortt et al., 2023), many educators are already accustomed to how technology can support personalised learning. This familiarity increases the likelihood that they will recognise the benefits of AI for customising lesson content to meet individual student needs. Such perceptions align with the principles of the Technology Acceptance Model (TAM), which emphasises that perceived usefulness and ease of integration strongly influence educators' readiness to adopt new technologies (Marangunić & Granić, 2015).

Lastly, when asked about past technological innovations which had prepared them for GenAI, educators cited the benefits of online assessment tools, such as TOEFL iBT and IELTS online, for providing automated grading and feedback, making the transition to AI-driven assessments a natural progression.

> Quotation 12: "I definitely use ChatGPT, especially for tests and quizzes." (T.10, Cyprus)
>
> Quotation 13: "We use ChatGPT to design test papers. We also use it in our daily teaching practice to search for professional terms or terminology. Some teachers even use ChatGPT or similar software to correct students' writing assignments. We also use platforms like Moodle to collect data on their homework submissions, participation, and performance in discussions. It even grades quizzes and tests, making it easier for teachers to access the grades at the end of the semester." (T.4, China)

These tools can provide real-time, personalised feedback on writing or speaking tasks, building on the automated systems teachers are already comfortable using. This adaptability reflects the growing awareness of digital literacies among TESOL educators—particularly since the COVID-19 pandemic—not only to identify which digital literacies matter in the language classroom, but also to reflect on their own digital practices and recognise how personal preferences shape professional choices (Darvin & Hafner, 2022). In essence, the use of earlier digital tools has laid a strong foundation by helping educators develop technical skills, build confidence in using technology, and recognise the pedagogical benefits of digital resources. These experiences have made the transition to GenAI smoother for many educators, as they are building on existing familiarity with educational technologies rather than starting from scratch.

By understanding the historical progression from traditional teaching aids to complex digital platforms, educators and researchers can appreciate how each phase of technological development has prepared the field for this next wave of innovation. Even more importantly, is the idea that language and technology are critical agents of societal change. Drawing on Rogers' Diffusion of Innovations model (2003), the adoption of new ideas or technologies describes how new ideas or technologies spread gradually across society, influenced by different groups along an adoption curve. This adoption unfolds through a series of categories, such as 'innovators,' early adopters,' early majority,' 'late majority,' and 'laggards,' with each contributing differently to the diffusion process. Within TESOL, early adopters play a critical role in guiding and influencing their peers through their openness to technology. Their integration of tools like language and technology in the classroom builds foundational skills in learners, supporting individual growth and societal development. In the context of GenAI, these early adopters are, once again, shaping how this emerging technology is understood, implemented, and normalised, while later adopters engage with the technology when clearer pedagogical frameworks and institutional supports are established within TESOL.

2.5 Second Language Acquisition Theories in the GenAI Era

This section reviews key Second Language Acquisition (SLA) theories, which provide insights into how language learning occurs and guide the design of technology-enhanced instruction in TESOL. It also considers how these theories can inform educators' decisions when selecting and applying technologies, including emerging tools such as GenAI.

Building on this foundation, Krashen's (1992)Input Hypothesis emphasises the importance of comprehensible input—language slightly above the learner's current proficiency level ($i + 1$) in language learning. GenAI tools, such as ChatGPT, QuillBot, and ReadTheory can facilitate this by generating graded reading materials or simplified texts tailored to learners' abilities. For instance, a teacher might use ChatGPT to rewrite authentic news articles at different proficiency levels or employ Google's Read Along for adaptive listening practice. These applications allow learners to access materials appropriate to their level while maintaining engagement. However, this raises questions about the accuracy and appropriateness of AI-generated simplifications. Without teacher mediation, learners may be exposed to oversimplifications or subtle distortions that affect comprehension and cultural literacy.

While Krashen highlights input, Swain's (2005) Output Hypothesis shifts attention to the importance of the student actively producing language as a way of consolidating learning. GenAI supports this through AI chatbots such as ChatGPT, Duolingo Max, or Microsoft Copilot, which simulate conversational practice and provide real-time, contextual feedback on grammar and vocabulary. Similarly, writing assistants such as Grammarly and Write & Improve (Cambridge) help learners draft and revise texts with instant, targeted feedback. Yet, the use of such tools raises concerns about "cognitive offloading" (Dawson, 2020; Perkins et al., 2024), where learners may become overly dependent on automated corrections rather than developing self-monitoring skills essential for independent language production.

Extending this focus, Long's (1980) Interaction Hypothesis stresses the value of meaningful interaction, where negotiation of meaning supports both input and output. GenAI tools increasingly replicate these interactional dynamics through AI tutors such as ChatGPT's role-play modes, ELSA Speak, or TalkPal AI, which allow learners to ask follow-up questions, receive pronunciation feedback, and engage in simulated dialogue. Collaborative tools like Google Gemini can also support group projects by generating ideas or feedback for team-writing tasks. However, unlike human interlocutors, GenAI may not always provide genuinely adaptive or socially appropriate feedback, potentially limiting the richness of interactional negotiation. Moreover, without careful instructional design, learners may passively receive AI-generated suggestions without engaging in deeper communicative problem-solving.

Beyond SLA-specific theories, social constructivism provides a broader educational lens, highlighting how knowledge is co-constructed through social interaction and collaboration in authentic contexts. GenAI can support this through collaborative writing platforms, such as Google Docs or Jasper AI, enabling learners to co-create and revise shared texts, or through immersive simulations in ChatGPT's custom role-play environments where learners interact with AI-generated characters. However, while the idea of technology as a mediating tool is well established, emerging research suggests that significant challenges remain in facilitating truly productive communication in AI-supported language learning within real classroom contexts (Yang & Kyun, 2022). In particular, AI-mediated exchanges may lack the spontaneity and unpredictability of peer-to-peer interaction.

Finally, critical theory adds a reflective dimension, urging educators to consider issues of power, equity, and ideology in the adoption of new technologies such as GenAI (see Chapter 5 for further discussion). Disparities in access due to socio-economic factors may lead to inequitable educational experiences. For instance, students from under-resourced backgrounds may lack access to the latest language-learning software, high-speed internet, or even reliable devices, which could marginalise them in increasingly digital TESOL environments. While a Social Constructivist perspective supports the use of technology to enrich language. Critical Theory urges TESOL practitioners to address the inequities that the digital divide brings, ensuring that technological advancements in language education benefit all learners regardless of their socio-economic status.

Taken together, these theories highlight the ways in which language learning can be supported through input, output, interaction, and critical reflection, offering a foundation for understanding how technology shapes TESOL practice.

2.6 From CALL to TELL and Beyond

Building on the earlier discussion of CALL and its historical development (see 2.2), this section examines the pedagogical evolution from CALL to TELL and, more recently, to GenAI Understanding this trajectory reveals how each phase's innovations and limitations have shaped the adoption of GenAI in TESOL. While CALL introduced the first digital affordances for language learning, TELL expanded the focus to interactivity and personalisation, creating the pedagogical conditions for GenAI's emergence as a significant turning point in language education.

2.6.1 Technology-Enhanced Language Learning (TELL)

Building on CALL's legacy, which progressed from restricted to integrated stages (Bax, 2003), language education in the 1990s and 2000s shifted towards TELL. This represented a conceptual move from the computer as a tutor to viewing technology as an interactive, networked learning environment supporting communication, collaboration, and autonomy. TELL integrated multimedia, internet connectivity, and collaborative platforms such as Moodle and Blackboard, enabling both synchronous and asynchronous interaction. Role-play simulations, web-based projects, and adaptive learning systems like Rosetta Stone illustrated the move towards learner-centred, personalised pathways (Shute & Zapata-Rivera, 2007; Tseng et al., 2008).

Mobile-assisted language learning (MALL) further extended flexibility and access, while immersive environments such as 'Second Life' demonstrated the potential for simulated real-world language use (Deutschmann & Panichi, 2009; Stevens, 2006). TELL also expanded teachers' Technological Pedagogical Content Knowledge (TPACK), a framework emphasising the intersection of content, pedagogy, and technology necessary for effective teaching with digital tools (Mishra & Koehler, 2006).

However, the effectiveness of TELL was shaped by contextual factors, such as uneven digital infrastructure, varying teacher digital literacy, and the persistence of traditional assessment practices. Although it broadened pedagogical possibilities, it still relied heavily on pre-programmed content and could not fully reproduce the spontaneity of human interaction. These limitations created space for the next stage in technology integration with GenAI.

2.6.2 Transitioning to GenAI

The transition to GenAI builds on TELL's adaptability and interactivity while overcoming some of its constraints by generating content in real-time, simulating human-like conversation, and adapting dynamically to learner input. Tools such as ChatGPT and Grammarly can provide instant, context-specific feedback; generate texts, prompts, or visuals tailored to learner needs, and support multimodal learning across text, speech, and image formats.

Chapelle (2024), like Kern (2024), frames this as an "inflection point" in language teaching, requiring educators to re-evaluate their methods to integrate GenAI's unique capabilities while addressing its ethical and pedagogical implications.

GenAI's responsiveness aligns closely with key SLA principles: comprehensible input (Krashen's Input Hypothesis, 1992) through adaptive text and multimodal resources; opportunities for output (Swain's Output Hypothesis, 2005) via AI-driven conversation and writing practice; negotiation of meaning (Long's Interaction Hypothesis, 1980) in adaptive chatbot interactions; and collaborative knowledge-building (social constructivism) supported through AI-mediated group projects and role-play simulations. At the same time, GenAI introduces new challenges not seen in CALL or TELL, including the need to critically evaluate AI outputs, guard against bias and unfair representation, and prevent over-reliance on automated feedback.

In sum, the journey from CALL to TELL to GenAI reflects a steady shift from behaviourist, drill-based instruction to interactive, adaptive, and increasingly personalised learning environments. Each phase has expanded the teacher's toolkit while also raising new pedagogical and ethical questions. GenAI's emergence offers unprecedented opportunities to align technology use with SLA theory, but it also demands that TESOL educators critically mediate its integration to ensure that technological possibilities support, rather than replace, the human dimensions of language learning.

2.7 The Transformative Potential of GenAI

The development of Natural Language Processing (NLP) has laid the groundwork for today's GenAI tools, which are significantly influencing language learning. Early NLP systems began with basic tasks such as identifying sentence structure but advanced with the adoption of statistical methods, enabling computers to recognise language patterns with greater accuracy (Jurafsky & Martin, 2023; Young et al., 2018). The introduction of neural networks and deep learning further enhanced NLP's capacity to process complex sentences and identify relationships within text (Young et al., 2018).

A major breakthrough came with transformer models, such as BERT (Bidirectional Encoder Representations from Transformers) and GPT (Generative Pre-trained Transformer), which enable more accurate and context-aware sentence processing. For example, BERT and other transformer-based models form the basis of many question–answering systems, helping students retrieve information from texts and underpinning grammar-checking and writing assistance applications (Devlin et al., 2019; Vaswani et al., 2017).

Whereas BERT-based models are widely used in classification tasks—supporting functions such as question-answering, error detection, and adaptive feedback—GPT models, by contrast, excel in text generation. As Brown et al. (2020) demonstrate, GPT-3 can generate coherent responses from prompts; when applied to TESOL, this capacity supports chatbots that simulate authentic conversation, creative writing activities, and personalised exercises such as vocabulary drills. Together, these models illustrate how the functionalities of LLMs can be adapted to foster meaningful and interactive language learning.

For language educators, these developments mean that GenAI can facilitate highly personalised and interactive learning experiences through dynamic content generation, real-time feedback, and adaptive learning pathways (Maity & Deroy, 2024). However, the same features that make GenAI powerful also present pedagogical challenges. AI-generated output is not always accurate, and without teacher mediation, learners risk exposure to linguistic inaccuracies or culturally inappropriate content.

Building on these advancements, it is essential to consider how educators themselves perceive the role of GenAI in the classroom, particularly in comparison to previous technologies. Survey findings indicate that TESOL educators generally view GenAI as a significant advancement in educational technology (see Fig. 2.2). Among the 78 respondents, 55.1% reported that they consider GenAI more transformative than earlier tools such as digital learning platforms and multimedia resources. In contrast, 20.5% expressed uncertainty about its overall impact, and 19.2% perceived it as equally transformative when compared to prior innovations. A smaller proportion, 5.2%, viewed GenAI as less transformative. Overall, these findings suggest that while most educators recognise GenAI's potential to reshape language teaching, a substantial minority remain cautious about its implications or view its influence as comparable to that of past technological developments.

However, other research reveals that this generally positive attitude is not shared by all educators in different regions or sectors of education. A UK study of more than one thousand educators (YouGov, 2023) found varied perspectives on the transformative potential of AI over the next five years (see Fig. 2.3). While 27% of respondents believed that AI would enable more time for meaningful student interaction, 38% disagreed. Similarly, 23% expected AI to have a positive impact on classroom practices, whereas 35% did not share this view. A significant proportion of teachers expressed neutrality or uncertainty about AI's capacity to save teaching time and improve classroom methods.

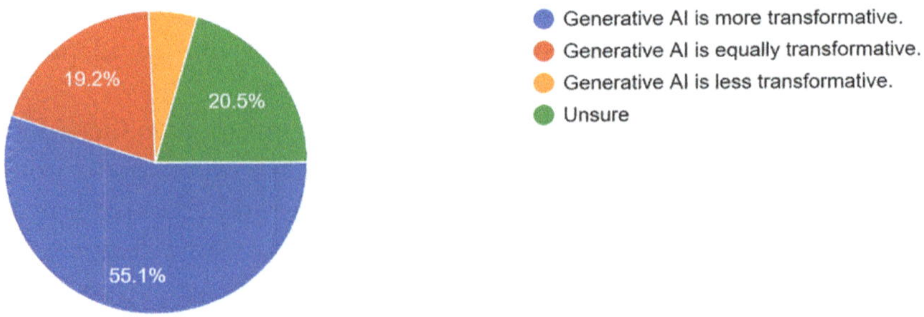

Fig. 2.2 How educators compare GenAI to previous technology in TESOL (e.g., digital learning platforms, multimedia tools)

These findings indicate that, even within contexts where AI adoption is progressing, scepticism and hesitation remain, highlighting the importance of addressing educators' concerns alongside promoting its pedagogical benefits.

These insights provide a useful foundation for examining the factors that influence educators' acceptance of AI, as outlined in the Technology Acceptance Model (TAM) (Davis, 1989). For educators who view GenAI as highly transformative, its 'perceived usefulness,' such as the ability to

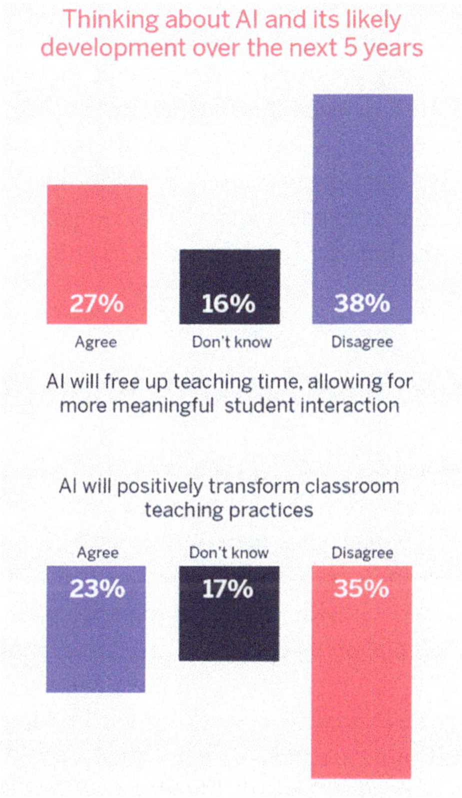

Fig. 2.3 UK teachers' attitudes on the transformative potential of AI in classroom teaching. *Source* YouGov (2023). The rise of AI in education: Exploring the impact of artificial intelligence on UK schools. Bett UK. https://uk.bettshow.com/the-rise-of-ai-in-education

create personalised, interactive learning experiences, may be a decisive factor in their enthusiasm. In contrast, educators with limited experience may have reservations about its 'perceived ease of use' compared to existing tools.

For instance, a recent study on Iranian EFL teachers' acceptance of ChatGPT found that their willingness to adopt the tool was primarily influenced by core TAM variables including Perceived Usefulness (PU), Perceived Ease of Use (PEoU), Attitude Toward Using Technology (ATU), and Behavioral Intention to Use (BIU) (Dehghani & Mashhadi, 2024). Teachers who viewed ChatGPT as beneficial and user-friendly were more likely to consider integrating it into their teaching. However, the influence of colleagues or broader societal expectations, known as Subjective Norm (SN), did not significantly affect acceptance, suggesting that teachers' openness to ChatGPT was shaped more by their own judgements than by external pressures. This finding reinforces the idea that while perceived effectiveness and ease of integration are key motivators, social influences may be less impactful in teachers' decisions to use GenAI.

2.8 GenAI vs. Traditional Technology Tools

To explore how educators' past experiences with technology have shaped their readiness to adopt GenAI, survey participants were asked an open-ended question: "How have past experiences with technology integration influenced your readiness to use generative AI tools in your classroom?" Their responses reveal a wide range of perspectives from enthusiasm and adaptability to caution, scepticism, and concerns over institutional readiness.

Many educators described how working with earlier digital platforms increased their willingness to experiment with GenAI. Prior success in integrating technology into lessons appeared to build both confidence and a mindset open to innovation.

> Quotation 14: "My experience using tools like Microsoft Teams made me feel more confident to use AI efficiently." (Survey Participant)

> Quotation 15: "Experimentation with one tool makes it easier to accept experimentation with another." (Survey Participant)

These responses suggest that familiarity with digital teaching environments fosters a sense of preparedness, making the transition to GenAI feel like a natural next step rather than a disruptive shift. Such findings align with broader research on technology adoption in TESOL. Warschauer (2002) and Bax (2003) both highlight how teachers' prior experiences with CALL and emerging digital tools shape their developing practices and openness to innovation. Chapelle (2001) similarly notes that teachers' existing beliefs and experiences with digital platforms influence how they evaluate and integrate new technologies.

Some teachers pointed to concrete examples, such as apps, multimedia resources, or gamified activities, that demonstrated the value of personalised and interactive learning, which they now see mirrored and extended in GenAI.

> Quotation 16: "Tools like Duolingo and multimedia resources have shown me the benefits of interactive, personalised learning experiences." (Survey Participant)
> Quotation 17: "Having experience with gamification tools made it easier to adopt AI." (Survey Participant)

These comments highlight that when teachers have already used tools offering adaptivity and engagement, they are more receptive to AI systems that build on these same principles. This pattern is consistent with developments in CALL and mobile-assisted learning. For example, Shortt et al. (2021) show that gamified platforms such as Duolingo enhance motivation and engagement, while Dudeney and Hockly (2007) highlight how multimedia tools can support more interactive and learner-centred practices.

Not all educators felt ready to adopt GenAI, even with prior experience. Some expressed a slower pace of adoption or a preference for tried-and-tested methods, indicating that confidence in technology integration varies significantly.

> Quotation 18: "AI usage feels different from other technology integration, so I had to read articles and watch tutorials to feel more prepared." (Survey Participant)
> Quotation 19: "It's not easy for me to adapt to technology." (Survey Participant)

These perspectives reflect broader findings that teachers' confidence and AI-readiness are decisive predictors of adoption. Liu (2025) shows that educators who feel under-skilled or lack confidence are significantly less likely to integrate AI tools, even when they recognise potential benefits.

For some respondents, readiness was less about personal skills and more about the availability of institutional resources, infrastructure, and professional development opportunities.

> Quotation 20: "In the past, I worked at institutes with no digital learning platforms, so it was difficult to integrate technology without institutional backing." (Survey Participant)
> Quotation 21: "The challenge lies in whether the institution provides adequate resources and training to support new technologies like AI." (Survey Participant)

These reflections reinforce the idea that creating institutional readiness through infrastructure, policy, and professional development is a critical factor in determining whether GenAI can be meaningfully integrated into teaching practice. This perspective is echoed in wider research. Pedro et al. (2019) note that without adequate infrastructure, training, and governance, AI innovations are unlikely to be sustainably integrated. UNESCO (2023) similarly identifies digital access and policy clarity as major barriers, reinforcing that institutional readiness is as important as individual teacher competence.

In sum, while many educators view past technology integration as a stepping stone towards embracing GenAI, others remain hesitant due to personal confidence, perceived complexity, institutional constraints, or a lack of clear connection between earlier tools and current AI applications. This variation reflects patterns highlighted in the Technology Acceptance Model (TAM), discussed earlier, where PU and PeoU influence adoption, but other factors, such as institutional support and personal digital literacy, also play a decisive role in shaping readiness for GenAI integration.

2.9 Critical Perspectives on AI in TESOL

The evolution of technology in TESOL, from CALL to TELL to AIED, has brought significant opportunities for language learning alongside some critical challenges and ethical considerations. Drawing on critical theory, this section explores how issues of bias, inequity, and ethical responsibility shape the adoption of GenAI tools in education. Building on these concerns, the following section turns to the practical barriers that influence technology integration in TESOL.

2.9.1 Barriers to Technology Integration in TESOL

Historically, the integration of technology in TESOL has faced persistent barriers, many of which continue to affect the adoption of AIED tools. For instance, early CALL systems were limited by the high cost of mainframe computers and the restricted availability of software (Hubbard, 2021). As TESOL moved into the era of TELL, the rise of multimedia platforms and mobile learning tools began addressing accessibility, yet inequities remained, particularly in under-resourced regions (Tafazoli & Picard, 2023). Despite their transformative potential, AIED tools risk deepening these divides because of their reliance on technological infrastructure and high development costs (Pedro et al., 2019).

National-level investment can make a difference. For instance, in 2016, China's Ministry of Education mandated 8% of local government education budgets to be allocated to digitisation, marking a significant investment in educational technology. With 95% of schools connected to the internet, China has positioned itself for one of the largest digital education experiments globally. This extensive infrastructure ensures that schools are equipped to integrate advanced AI technologies (Pedro et al.,

2019). In contrast, many under-resourced countries struggle with inadequate infrastructure and limited budgets, hindering progress towards AI adoption in education.

The COVID-19 pandemic further exposed the scale of global educational inequalities. Although 91% of countries implemented online learning platforms, these tools reached only around a quarter of students worldwide. An estimated half a billion students, or 31% of learners worldwide, mainly from rural areas (70%) and poorer households (72%), were excluded from remote learning entirely (UNESCO, 2023). For these students, countries relied on low-tech solutions such as radio and television broadcasts, supported by paper-based materials and mobile phones to facilitate interaction. The challenges of digital inequality in education, presented by the COVID-19 pandemic, demonstrate that in many contexts the infrastructure required for technologies like AIED does not yet exist. As UNESCO (2023) notes, such disparities reveal that the infrastructure needed for effective AI integration simply does not exist in many parts of the world. This deepening digital divide—where schools in wealthier nations have full access to AI tools, while underfunded schools cannot meet even basic technological requirements—makes the recognition of internet access as a fundamental human right even more urgent (Mutoni, 2017).

A further barrier is the lack of teacher training. In CALL's early days, teachers were often left to explore software independently, leading to uneven implementation (Levy, 1997). Today, research suggests that despite the fact that most language teachers believe GenAI tools will significantly affect the language curriculum, instruction, and assessment methods, many lack confidence and competence to use them effectively. Without targeted professional development, the adaptive and interactive capabilities of AIED may remain underused (Moorhouse & Kohne, 2024).

Institutional resistance has also played a role in slowing technological adoption. From CALL to TELL, concerns about costs and efficacy have frequently hindered innovation (Chapelle, 2001; Hubbard, 2021). Moreover, in the context of AIED, resistance to change is not only a matter of institutional inertia but also reflects institutions' ethical responsibility to balance the risks of inaction against the potential benefits of innovation (Holmes et al., 2019). Critical Theory further highlights that, without institutional commitment to equity, the benefits of AI integration remain concentrated among those already privileged, thereby reinforcing educational inequalities.

2.9.2 Ethical Implications of Bias in AI Systems

One of the most significant challenges associated with GenAI is bias. LLMs are trained on vast datasets that often reflect and reproduce existing societal biases, resulting in discriminatory or culturally inappropriate content. For example, gender stereotypes can appear in AI-generated materials, such as associating "doctor" with male pronouns and "nurse" with female pronouns (Bender et al., 2021). In the TESOL classroom, such biases risk misrepresenting cultures, marginalising certain perspectives, and undermining inclusive learning environments. A further risk is 'algorithmic toxicity,' whereby models produce offensive or inappropriate content that can erode trust in the technology (Bender et al., 2021).

As LLMs draw on vast amounts of learner data, concerns about privacy become increasingly pressing. Tools like ChatGPT collect user input to refine their models, raising questions about compliance with regulations such as the General Data Protection Regulation (GDPR). In one notable case, ChatGPT was temporarily banned in Italy due to concerns over its handling of personal data (Shailendra et al., 2024). Such incidents highlight the importance of transparent data governance and robust safeguards to protect learners' personal information.

Another ethical issue is the potential over-reliance on AI tools, which could undermine teacher autonomy. While CALL and TELL emphasised the language teacher's role as a facilitator responsible for guiding students in using digital technologies, and fostering active engagement and collaboration (Smith, 2017; Son, 2018), the capabilities of GenAI risk shifting attention from teachers' expertise. Research by Frøsig and Romero (2024) suggests that while GenAI can assist in tasks like idea generation and co-creation, it may also reduce the perceived need for teachers' professional skills and judgement. Echoing this concern, a report by the U.S. Department of Education emphasises the importance of maintaining a balance between the use of AI tools and preserving educators' critical role in guiding and mentoring students (Cardona et al., 2023).

In sum, the progression from CALL to GenAI in TESOL highlights both the opportunities and challenges of integrating advanced technologies. Addressing barriers to access and training while navigating ethical concerns around bias, privacy, and teacher autonomy is critical to ensuring that GenAI tools enhance, rather than negatively disrupt, language education. These considerations are explored further in Chapter 5.

2.10 Conclusion

The integration of technology in TESOL, from early CALL systems to the emergence of GenAI, reflects a dynamic interplay between pedagogical innovation and technological advancement. Each phase—CALL, TELL, and now GenAI—has built upon its predecessor to enhance language learning through personalisation, collaboration, and accessibility. Through the lens of the SECT framework, this chapter has demonstrated how Social Constructivism, Ethical Use of Technology, Critical Theory, and the Technology Acceptance Model provide a structured way to understand the integration of AI in language teaching. The discussion has highlighted both opportunities and challenges, particularly in fostering personalised, dynamic learning environments while addressing ethical concerns such as bias, privacy, and teacher autonomy.

2.10.1 Final Reflections from TESOL Educators

The voices of TESOL educators illustrate how these theoretical perspectives and historical developments translate into classroom realities, revealing both the opportunities and challenges of integrating GenAI into language teaching. Some educators see it as a catalyst for inclusivity and engagement:

> Quotation 22: "Students react more and everyone participates. Some students are introverted and don't like speaking up, but with AI, everyone can type their answers. This encourages more participation from all students." (T.4, China)
> Quotation 23: "Maybe we could get rid of some boring tasks and focus on interacting and doing more authentic problem-solving tasks. AI could leave space for us to prioritise interaction that can't be done by machines." (T.13, Greece)

However, other educators are more cautious, warning that AI can hinder collaboration when overused or misapplied:

> Quotation 24: "AI makes it easier for students to participate in class discussions by quickly searching for terms or answers. But on the other hand, it can make students lazier and more dependent…they rely on AI rather than discussing ideas with their peers." (T.5, China)

Some educators note that GenAI can even reduce group engagement if not carefully managed:

> Quotation 25: "When I introduced the idea of creating personalised chatbots, they ended up going into their own little smartphone bubbles and stopped talking. I was hoping they'd share their screens and say, "Hey, check this out," but instead, it hindered group communication." (T.6, Japan)

Despite these concerns, several educators see clear potential for GenAI to enhance collaborative work, provided that both teachers and students receive adequate training in its use:

> Quotation 26: "Some students use it to save time and effort, but that can be a problem. It comes down to training—both teachers and students need proper training on how to use AI effectively and responsibly." (T.7, South Africa)
> Quotation 27: "If I were to integrate AI into group work, students could potentially use it to collaborate on research or summarise studies within a shared document." (T.3, China)

These reflections suggest that while GenAI can facilitate collaboration, inclusivity, and engagement, it can also reduce interaction and foster dependency if used without clear pedagogical strategies. Effective integration, therefore, requires teacher guidance, structured activities, and explicit training in responsible AI use.

In sum, this chapter has shown how TESOL educators' experiences with past technological transitions inform their readiness for GenAI adoption. The journey from CALL to AIED underscores the evolving role of the second language teacher as facilitator, mentor, and critical evaluator in increasingly automated environments. The perspectives and practices highlighted here set the stage for the next chapter, which examines the current state of GenAI in TESOL, focusing on practical strategies for implementation and the broader implications for language teaching in a rapidly changing educational landscape.

References

Bax, S. (2003). CALL—Past, present and future. *System, 31*(1), 13–28. https://doi.org/10.1016/S0346-251X(02)00071-4

Beebe, R., Vonderwell, S., & Boboc, M. (2010). Emerging patterns in transferring assessment practices from face-to-face to online environments. *Electronic Journal of e-Learning, 8*(1), 1–12. https://academic-publishing.org/index.php/ejel/article/view/1581

Bender, E. M., Gebru, T., McMillan-Major, A., & Shmitchell, S. (2021). On the dangers of stochastic parrots: Can language models be too big? In *Proceedings of the 2021 ACM Conference on Fairness, Accountability, and Transparency* (pp. 610–623). https://doi.org/10.1145/3442188.3445922

Brown, T. B., Mann, B., Ryder, N., Subbiah, M., Kaplan, J., Dhariwal, P., & Amodei, D. (2020). Language models are few-shot learners. *Advances in Neural Information Processing Systems, 33*, 1877–1901. https://doi.org/10.48550/arXiv.2005.14165

Cardona, M. A., Rodríguez, R. J., & Ishmael, K. (2023). Artificial intelligence and the future of teaching and learning. Office of Educational Technology. https://tech.ed.gov/files/2023/05/ai-future-of-teaching-and-learning-report.pdf

Chapelle, C. A. (2001). Computer applications in second language acquisition. *Cambridge University Press*. https://doi.org/10.1017/cbo9781139524681

Chapelle, C. A. (2024). Open generative AI changes a lot, but not everything. *Modern Language Journal (John Wiley & Sons, Inc.)*, *108*(2). https://doi.org/10.1111/modl.12927

Darvin, R., & Hafner, C. A. (2022). Digital literacies in TESOL: Mapping out the terrain. *TESOL Quarterly*, *56*(3), 865–882. https://doi.org/10.1002/tesq.3161

Davies, G., Otto, S. E. K., & Rüschoff, B. (2013). Historical perspectives on CALL. In M. Thomas, H. Reinders & M. Warschauer (Eds.), *Contemporary computer-assisted language learning* (pp. 19–38). Bloomsbury Academic. https://doi.org/10.11139/cj.30.3.449-451

Davis, F. D. (1989). Perceived usefulness, perceived ease of use, and user acceptance of information technology. *MIS Quarterly*, 319–340. https://doi.org/10.2307/249008

Dawson, P. (2020). Cognitive Offloading and Assessment. In M. Bearman, P. Dawson, R. Ajjawi, J. Tai, & D. Boud (Eds.), *Re-imagining University Assessment in a Digital World* (pp. 37–48). Springer International Publishing. https://doi.org/10.1007/978-3-030-41956-1_4

Dehghani, H., & Mashhadi, A. (2024). Exploring Iranian English as a foreign language teachers' acceptance of ChatGPT in English language teaching: Extending the technology acceptance model. *Education and Information Technologies*, 1–22. https://doi.org/10.1007/s10639-024-12660-9

Deutschmann, M., & Panichi, L. (2009). Talking into empty space? Signalling involvement in a virtual language classroom in Second Life. *Language Awareness*, *18*(3–4), 310–328. https://doi.org/10.1080/09658410903197306

Devlin, J., Chang, M. W., Lee, K., & Toutanova, K. (2019, June). BERT: Pre-training of deep bidirectional transformers for language understanding. In *Proceedings of the 2019 conference of the North American chapter of the association for computational linguistics: human language technologies, volume 1 (long and short papers)* (pp. 4171–4186).

Dodd, B. (2014, June). Exploiting a corpus of written German for advanced language learning. In *Teaching and language corpora* (pp. 131–145). Routledge. https://doi.org/10.4324/9781315842677-11

Dudeney, G., & Hockly, N. (2007). *How to teach English with technology*. Pearson Education Limited. https://doi.org/10.4000/apliut.1348

Frøsig, T. B., & Romero, M. (2024). Teacher agency in the age of generative AI: towards a framework of hybrid intelligence for learning design. *arXiv preprint* arXiv:2407.06655. https://doi.org/10.48550/arXiv.2407.06655

Garrett, N. (2009). Computer-assisted language learning trends and issues revisited: Integrating innovation. *The Modern Language Journal, 93*(s1), 719–740. https://doi.org/10.1111/j.1540-4781.2009.00969.x
Hockey, S. M., & Martin, J. (1988). *Oxford Concordance Program: Users' manual, version 2*. Oxford University Computing Service. https://doi.org/10.1093/llc/2.2.125
Holmes, W., Bialik, M., & Fadel, C. (2019). *Artificial intelligence in education promises and implications for teaching and learning*. Center for Curriculum Redesign. https://doi.org/10.58863/20.500.12424/4276068
Hubbard, P. (2021). An invitation to CALL: Foundations of computer-assisted language learning. *Asia-Pacific Association for Computer-Assisted Language Learning(APACALL)*. https://doi.org/10.5040/9781350020436.ch-010
Jurafsky, D., & Martin, J. H. (2023). *Speech and language processing* (3rd ed.). Pearson. https://doi.org/10.1162/coli.b09-001
Kern, R. (2024). Twenty-first century technologies and language education: Charting a path forward. *Modern Language Journal (John Wiley & Sons, Inc.), 108*(2). https://doi.org/10.1111/modl.12924
Kossuth, K. (1987). *CALIS (computer assisted language instruction system)*. Duke University.
Krashen, S. (1992). The input hypothesis: An update. In *Linguistics and language pedagogy: The state of the art* (pp. 409–431).
Levy, M. (1997). Computer-assisted language learning: Context and conceptualization. *Oxford University Press*. https://doi.org/10.1093/oso/9780198236320.001.0001
Liu, N. (2025). Exploring the factors influencing the adoption of artificial intelligence technology by university teachers: The mediating role of confidence and AI readiness. *BMC Psychology, 13*(1), 311. https://doi.org/10.1186/s40359-025-02620-4
Long, M. H. (1980). *Input, interaction, and second language acquisition*. University of California.
Maity, S., & Deroy, A. (2024). Generative AI and its impact on personalized intelligent tutoring systems. *arXiv*. https://doi.org/10.48550/arXiv.2410.10650
Marangunić, N., & Granić, A. (2015). Technology acceptance model: A literature review from 1986 to 2013. *Universal Access in the Information Society, 14*(1), 81–95. https://doi.org/10.1007/s10209-014-0348-1
Mishra, P., & Koehler, M. J. (2006). Technological pedagogical content knowledge: A framework for teacher knowledge. *Teachers College Record, 108*(6), 1017–1054. https://doi.org/10.1111/j.1467-9620.2006.00684.x

Moorhouse, B. L., & Kohnke, L. (2024). The effects of generative AI on initial language teacher education: The perceptions of teacher educators. *System, 122*, Article 103290. https://doi.org/10.1016/j.system.2024.103290

Morton, R. P. (1976). The variety of TICCIT systems—An overview. *ACM SIGCSE Bulletin, 8*(1), 144–148. https://doi.org/10.1145/952989.80346

Mutoni, D. (2017). *A revolutionary connectivity: Internet access as the ultimate human right and socioeconomic force*. New Degree Press.

Pedro, F., Subosa, M., Rivas, A., & Valverde, P. (2019). *Artificial intelligence in education: Challenges and opportunities for sustainable development.* UNESCO. https://unesdoc.unesco.org/ark:/48223/pf0000366994

Perkins, M., Roe, J., Postma, D., McGaughran, J., & Hickerson, D. (2024). Detection of GPT-4 generated text in higher education: Combining academic judgement and software to identify generative AI tool misuse. *Journal of Academic Ethics, 22*(1), 89–113.https://doi.org/10.48550/arXiv.2305.18081

Rogers, E. M. (2003). *The diffusion of innovations* (5th ed.). The Free Press.

Selwyn, N. (2016). *Is technology good for education?* John Wiley & Sons.

Shailendra, S., Kadel, R., & Sharma, A. (2024). Framework for adoption of generative artificial intelligence (GenAI) in education. *IEEE Transactions on Education, 67*(5), 777–785. https://doi.org/10.1109/TE.2024.3432101

Shortt, M., Tilak, S., Kuznetcova, I., Martens, B., & Akinkuolie, B. (2021). Gamification in mobile-assisted language learning: A systematic review of Duolingo literature from public release of 2012 to early 2020. *Computer Assisted Language Learning, 36*(3), 517–554. https://doi.org/10.1080/09588221.2021.1933540

Shute, V. J., & Zapata-Rivera, D. (2007). Adaptive technologies. *ETS Research Report Series, 2007*(1), i–34. https://doi.org/10.1002/j.2333-8504.2007.tb02047.x

Smith, K. (2017). The role of a learning facilitator. In D. J. Clandinin & J. Husu (Eds.), *Teachers as self-directed learners* (Self-Study of Teaching and Teacher Education Practices (Vol. 18, pp. 91–106). Springer. https://doi.org/10.1007/978-981-10-3587-6_6

Son, J. B. (2018). Teachers' roles in the CALL classroom. In *Teacher development in technology-enhanced language teaching* (pp. 19–32). Palgrave Macmillan. https://doi.org/10.1007/978-3-319-75711-7_2

Stevens, V. (2006). Second life in education and language learning. *TESL-EJ, 10*(3), 1–4.

Swain, M. (2005). The output hypothesis: Theory and research. *Handbook of research in second language teaching and learning.* Lawrence Erlbaum Associates. https://doi.org/10.4324/9781410612700-38

Tafazoli, D., & Picard, M. (2023). CALL teacher education and professional development: Contextual challenges in under-represented contexts. In D. Tafazoli & M. Picard (Eds.), *Handbook of CALL teacher education and professional development* (pp. 15–32). Springer. https://doi.org/10.1007/978-981-99-0514-0_2

Tondeur, J., Van Braak, J., Ertmer, P. A., & Ottenbreit-Leftwich, A. (2017). Understanding the relationship between teachers' pedagogical beliefs and technology use in education: A systematic review of qualitative evidence. *Educational Technology Research and Development, 65*(3), 555–575. https://doi.org/10.1007/s11423-016-9481-2

Torlot, B. J. (1993). *Willkommen in München: A HyperCard database for use in teaching German* [Educational resource]. Loughborough University. https://doi.org/10.26174/thesis.lboro.14304029.v1

Tseng, J. C., Chu, H. C., Hwang, G. J., & Tsai, C. C. (2008). Development of an adaptive learning system with two sources of personalization information. *Computers & Education, 51*(2), 776–786. https://doi.org/10.1016/j.compedu.2007.08.002

UNESCO. (2023). *Global education monitoring report 2023: Technology in education—A tool on whose terms?* Target 4.A: Education facilities and learning environments. United Nations Educational, Scientific and Cultural Organization (UNESCO). https://gem-report-2023.unesco.org/

Vaswani, A., Shazeer, N., Parmar, N., Uszkoreit, J., Jones, L., Gomez, A. N., Kaiser, Ł., & Polosukhin, I. (2017). Attention is all you need. In *Advances in Neural Information Processing Systems* (Vol. 30, pp. 5998–6008). Curran Associates, Inc. https://papers.nips.cc/paper/2017/hash/3f5ee243547dee91fbd053c1c4a845aa-Abstract.html

Warschauer, M. (2002). A developmental perspective on technology in language education. *TESOL Quarterly, 36*(3), 453–475. https://doi.org/10.2307/3588421

Warschauer, M., & Healey, D. (1998). Computers and language learning: An overview. *Language Teaching, 31*(2), 57–71. https://doi.org/10.1017/s0261444800012970

Yang, H., & Kyun, S. (2022). The current research trend of artificial intelligence in language learning: A systematic empirical literature review from an activity theory perspective. *Australasian Journal of Educational Technology, 38*(5), 180–210. https://doi.org/10.14742/ajet.7492

YouGov. (2023). *The rise of AI in education: Exploring the impact of artificial intelligence on UK schools*. Bett UK. https://uk.bettshow.com/the-rise-of-ai-in-education

Young, T., Hazarika, D., Poria, S., & Cambria, E. (2018). Recent trends in deep learning based natural language processing. *IEEE Computational Intelligence Magazine, 13*(3), 55–75. https://doi.org/10.1109/mci.2018.2840738

3

The Current State of GenAI in TESOL

3.1 Overview

Building on the historical and theoretical perspectives introduced in the previous chapter, this chapter examines how TESOL educators are currently using GenAI in their practice. Drawing on data from the empirical study alongside emerging literature, it explores teachers' perceptions, experiences, and applications of GenAI in language teaching. These accounts shed light on broader trends in GenAI adoption in classrooms, highlighting both opportunities for innovation and the challenges that accompany this rapidly developing field. Beginning with some of the voices of TESOL educators in the study, many participants acknowledged its potential to enhance classroom engagement, foster creativity and update their instruction.

> Quotation 1: "Students are motivated because AI makes it easier for them to participate." (T.5, China)

> Quotation 2: "I had students generate pictures based on texts, and they went through multiple iterations to get something that matched the text better." (T.1, USA)

C. Savvidou, *AI-Powered Language Teaching*,
https://doi.org/10.1007/978-3-032-14502-4_3

These comments suggest that, when integrated thoughtfully, GenAI can enhance participation and create a more supportive learning environment for diverse learners. At the same time, educators voiced concerns about over-reliance on AI and the risks to academic integrity.

> Quotation 3: ": My main concern is whether students will use it for their benefit. I worry about critical thinking. It's fast and does the research, but I don't like the lazy aspect—like when students just ask AI to summarize an academic article instead of reading it themselves." (T.11, Cyprus)

> Quotation 4: "Overreliance is a possibility if we don't teach the learners how to use it, not to do things really quickly and really easily, just to use it to write an essay or something like that, but how to use it to get ideas." (T.13, Greece)

Such reflections emphasise the need for clear guidance on responsible AI use and the development of students' critical thinking skills.

A further theme related to the importance of teaching learners to evaluate GenAI outputs critically.

> Quotation 5: "Students may think they're improving, but in reality, it might not reflect their true language proficiency." (T.14, Algeria)

> Quotation 6: "AI tools help students generate ideas for essays, but unchecked use leads to plagiarism and challenges in summative assessments." (T.3, China)

These comments points to teachers concerns that students do not blindly trust AI-generated information but, instead, engage with it as a tool for learning.

Finally, teachers recognised the adaptive and personalised learning opportunities provided by GenAI.

> Quotation 7: "Students have become independent to a certain extent due to adaptive AI platforms, which customise tasks based on their level of understanding." (T.8, Qatar)

Overall, these perspectives highlight the two-fold nature of GenAI in TESOL. While teachers appreciate its potential to engage students, foster creativity, and support personalised learning, they also recognise the need for critical guidance to address ethical concerns, over-reliance, and the importance of maintaining academic rigour.

3.1.1 The Evolution of AI for Personalised Learning

Distinguished by its ability to generate human-like text, simulate life-like conversations, and create interactive, adaptive teaching materials, GenAI represents a significant advancement in educational technology. However, as outlined in Chapter 2, AI in education is not a new concept and has been applied in educational settings for more than 50 years. The concept of 'Intelligent Tutoring Systems' (ITS) evolved from earlier terms, such as 'Computer-Aided Instruction' (CAI), 'Intelligent Computer-Aided Instruction' (ICAI) (Self, 1988), and was also referred to as 'Adaptive Tutoring Systems' (ATS) (Streitz, 1988), and 'Knowledge Communication Systems' (KBTS) (Wenger, 1987). Building on Bloom's (1984) research that one-to-one tutoring is more effective than conventional group instruction improving students grades by an average of two standard deviation points, ITS aimed to recreate such personalised learning environments.

The first ITS, SCHOLAR, developed by Carbonell (1970), demonstrated this potential through a semantic network that generated lesson content, posed questions, and provided corrective feedback. At any point, SCHOLAR could accept questions or requests from the student, generating responses by making calculations and inferences programmed into the system. The dialogue was unanticipated, adapting dynamically to the learner's input (see Fig. 3.1).

This first ITS set the groundwork for developing models that could adapt to individual learners' needs and simulate interactive human tutoring interactions. Moreover, the benefits of ITS for education can be seen in personalised learning paths, automated feedback and assessment, engagement analytics, gamification, automation of repetitive tasks

SCHOLAR: WHAT IS THE LANGUAGE OF ARGENTINA?
Student: *PROBABLY SPANISH*
SCHOLAR: VERY GOOD. APPROXIMATELY WHAT IS THE AREA OF ARGENTINA?
Student: *TELL ME SOMETHING ABOUT PERU*
SCHOLAR: PERU IS A COUNTRY. IT IS LOCATED IN SOUTH AMERICA. THE CAPITAL OF PERU IS LIMA. NOW ANSWER THE QUESTION YOU DIDN'T ANSWER BEFORE.

Fig. 3.1 Excerpt of a scholar–student dialogue (Carbonell & Collins, 1974, p. 8)

(e.g. grading), and tools for accessibility, including text-to-speech functionalities for learners with specific learning needs (Pinkwart, 2016). This continuity from early ITS to current GenAI tools highlights a long-standing goal in language education: the creation of adaptive, learner-centred systems that respond dynamically to learner needs.

Unlike general AI tools, GenAI tools such as ChatGPT, Google Translate and Grammarly excel at creating personalised and adaptive content. One example is the use of AI-generated writing prompts, such as those offered by platforms like Reimagine AI, which can stimulate imaginative thinking, helping writers explore new perspectives and develop original content. Research on human-AI creativity in pre-writing tasks (Wan et al., 2024) found that these tools can act as collaborators by providing adaptable suggestions that writers can build upon. In this way, GenAI becomes a valuable resource for fostering innovative thinking and creative expression.

Additionally, accessibility to real-time language tutors such as ChatGPT, Duolingo Max, and iVR-based platforms like Immerse, can simulate authentic conversational practice providing learners with interactive, context-driven dialogues that replicate real-world communication. Research has shown that using chatbots for conversational practice can enhance speaking proficiency by providing opportunities for repeated practice and error correction with minimal foreign language anxiety (Zhang et al., 2023). Furthermore, immersive virtual reality environments have been found to significantly improve learners' communicative competence by simulating realistic social interactions (Lee et al., 2024). All in all, these capabilities make GenAI uniquely suited to the diverse needs of TESOL learners and go beyond what earlier ITS could offer.

Moreover, beyond the classroom, GenAI supports educators by generating lesson plans, automating assessments, and tailoring resources to learners' proficiency levels. Indeed, survey results indicate that the majority of TESOL educators in this study (71.8%) are already using GenAI tools in such ways. Analysis and discussion of the empirical findings of the survey and interviews are discussed further in greater depth throughout this chapter.

This chapter also employs a multi-theoretical framework to analyse the current state of GenAI in TESOL. Social constructivism emphasises its collaborative potential, while critical theory examines issues of equity and inclusivity. The Ethical Use of Technology framework highlights concerns around privacy, bias, and accountability. Finally, the Technology Acceptance Model (TAM) provides insights into educators' adoption of these tools, focusing on perceived usefulness and external barriers. Together these perspectives frame the analysis of empirical findings, exploring how TESOL educators are using GenAI tools, the benefits they report, and the ethical challenges they face.

By first mapping the range of GenAI tools currently in use, the next section provides the necessary context for understanding how these technologies are shaping teaching practices and learner engagement in TESOL.

3.2 Categories of GenAI Tools in TESOL

GenAI tools are transforming TESOL by providing innovative resources that support both educators and learners. These tools can be broadly categorised by function: writing support, interactive conversational agents, content generation, and real-time feedback systems. Survey data from this study reveal varied patterns of use: 65% of respondents reported employing automated language assessments, 56.7% used writing support tools, and 48.3% relied on AI-generated translation and summarisation tools. In addition, conversational tools like virtual language tutors (23.3%) and pronunciation tools with AI-generated feedback (20%) were also noted. These findings indicate a clear preference for tools that improve efficiency and personalisation in teaching, while tools focused on student interaction and skill-building are less widely adopted. The following section examines these categories in turn, drawing on empirical findings and considering how these tools align with TESOL pedagogical goals and theoretical perspectives.

3.2.1 Writing Support Tools

Writing support tools are among the most widely used GenAI resources in TESOL, with tools such as ChatGPT, Gemini, Grammarly, and DeepL commonly employed for activities such as creating writing prompts, enhancing grammar instruction, and generating translations. These tools can act as virtual tutors offering personalised learning experiences (Kim et al., 2025) and significantly reduce preparation time for educators. However, over-reliance on such tools may diminish learners' ability to develop independent writing skills. Critics argue that frequent use can lead to superficial learning, where students focus on correcting errors rather than understanding the underlying rules of language (Ozer, 2024).

Survey results indicate that 56.7% of educators use GenAI for writing support, making it one of the most common applications in TESOL. Teachers noted that AI-generated prompts, grammar suggestions, and translation tools can help meet diverse learner needs, particularly in mixed-proficiency classrooms, aligning with findings from the research literature (Innaci & Jona, 2024; Karpouzis et al., 2024; Wang & Dang, 2024). One educator shared their experience with AI-generated writing prompts:

> Quotation 8: "One example of how generative AI has enhanced my classroom instruction is through the use of AI-generated writing prompts. For a writing unit, I utilized an AI tool to create tailored prompts based on each student's proficiency level and interests." (Survey Participant)

Writing support tools such as Grammarly are valued for their ability to provide quick, automated feedback on grammar and style (Lazic et al., 2020). Despite these benefits, such tools have been criticised for prioritising surface-level corrections, such as grammar, spelling, and punctuation, while neglecting higher-order concerns such as coherence, argumentation, and organisation (Godwin-Jones, 2022).

GenAI writing tools also promote skill-building through examples and experimentation. For instance, one educator remarked:

> Quotation 9: "Students who had difficulty in understanding how to paraphrase managed to improve themselves since they had the chance to see plenty of examples before they start working on their own projects and then experiment by uploading their work online and see if they are correct or not. (Survey Participant)"

While such experimentation is valuable, it is also noted that these tools might promote over-reliance by students who might not make an effort to recall or use new language independently (Marzuki et al., 2023).

Beyond such technical support, some educators emphasise the role of GenAI in fostering creativity. Tools like ChatGPT can be used to encourage learners to experiment with language, explore writing styles, and engage in imaginative tasks (Begian-Lewis & Hart, 2024; Doshi & Hauser, 2023).

One educator shared how they integrate AI tools into creative writing lessons:

> Quotation 10: I have a vocabulary-based lesson where students learn new adjectives to describe landscapes or cityscapes. The activation involves students describing a landscape or cityscape they are very familiar with and then using an AI image creator to see how closely their description matches the generated picture. (Survey Participant)

While such tasks can stimulate creative thinking, several studies warn that AI-generated outputs may prioritise fluency over originality. Doshi and Hauser (2023) found that while GenAI can encourage creative experimentation, it may also reduce the diversity of novel content, producing formulaic results. Kreminski (2024) refers to this as the "dearth of the author" phenomenon, where AI-supported writing allows users to produce text with minimal creative decisions, leading to generic writing outputs. As Kreminski explains, "the naïvely AI-augmented author is not absent or dead, but their intent is stretched so thinly over their writing that they may feel barely present" (2024, 1).

In sum, GenAI writing support tools can enhance skill development, creativity, and personalisation in TESOL, but their integration requires careful scaffolding. Used without guidance, they risk encouraging over-reliance, limiting originality, and overlooking deeper aspects of writing competence.

3.2.2 Conversational Agents

Conversational agents (CAs) are among the most transformative GenAI tools in TESOL, offering new possibilities for speaking and listening practice. Many people are already familiar with general-purpose CAs such as Google, Alexa, Cortana and Siri, which simulate real-time conversations through natural language processing (NLP). In TESOL, tools such as ChatGPT and Duolingo Max act as virtual practice partners providing immediate feedback and personalised dialogue. According to survey data, 23.3% of TESOL educators report using virtual language tutors, while 20% utilised pronunciation tools with AI-generated feedback. Additionally, 37.2% of educators found CAs useful for teaching speaking and 34.6% for teaching listening. Research also indicates that such tools can reduce second language anxiety, creating safer spaces for learners to experiment with language (MacIntyre & Gregersen, 2012). As one of the interviewees notes:

> Quotation 11: It could also lower anxiety, especially in second language teaching, where students often feel nervous about speaking with real people. AI could be a good tool for that. (T.1, United States)

CAs can be categorised based on their functionality and interaction styles, ranging from rule-based systems to advanced generative models.

3.2.3 Rule-Based Conversational Agents

Early CAs relied on fixed scripts, making them effective for targeted vocabulary and grammar drills but limited in handling spontaneous input. For example, ELIZA, developed in the 1960s, demonstrated the potential and limits of this approach by using pattern-matching to a conversation with a Rogerian psychotherapist (Weizenbaum, 1966). For example, when a user stated, "I feel sad," ELIZA might respond, "Why do you feel sad?" or if the user mentioned their mother, it would reply, "Tell me more about your mother." These responses created the illusion of understanding by reflecting or rephrasing user input. However, ELIZA's capabilities were limited to superficial text manipulation; it had no comprehension of context, meaning, or human emotions. Its apparent depth depended entirely on user interpretation, revealing the limitations of early NLP in genuine conversational ability.

Another example, relating to TESOL, ISI ("Io Sono Io"), developed for Italian-speaking primary school children learning English, provided structured, goal-oriented speech-based tasks such as describing physical characteristics, (for example, hair colour or eye size) (Catania et al., 2021). While effective for specific outcomes, rule-based systems like ISI are limited by their narrow topic scope, inability to engage in unscripted conversations, and their susceptibility to misinterpretations due to accents or pronunciation errors.

3.2.4 Retrieval-Based Conversational Agents

Retrieval-based systems store large banks of predefined responses to simulate more natural dialogue. Tools like Duolingo, Rosetta Stone, Babbel, and Mondly provide contextualised feedback through role-play scenarios such as ordering food or asking for directions (Loewen et al., 2019). These platforms make use of predefined responses to help learners practice vocabulary, grammar, and conversational skills, often through role-playing activities like ordering food or asking for directions.

A.L.I.C.E. (Artificial Linguistic Internet Computer Entity) developed in the 1990's demonstrated large-scale scripted dialogue, while Jabberwacky incorporated self-learning capabilities, dynamically expanding its conversational repertoire from user interactions (Fryer & Carpenter, 2006). While A.L.I.C.E. used predefined patterns and scripts, Jabberwacky learned by storing every conversation with users in its database so that during every interaction it analysed inputs which it then paired with corresponding responses building a repository of conversational patterns. While ALICE was programmed with 45,000 conversational patterns, Jabberwacky 'learnt more than 8 million on its own' (Fryer & Carpenter, 2006, p.10). However, these systems struggle with maintaining context over extended conversations and, as they depend on learner inputs, they risk introducing errors or inappropriate responses.

3.2.5 Generative Conversational Agents

Generative conversational agents represent the most advanced category of conversational tools. Unlike their predecessors, these agents generate original, context-aware responses tailored to learners' proficiency levels and interests. Simplistically, these CAs work by transcribing speech to text, then using natural language understanding techniques to determine meaning, which prompts an AI-generated response which is then converted to speech (Xiao et al., 2024).

Advanced conversational agents (CAs) are not new in language learning and have significantly enhanced learning by providing interactive and personalised experiences. For instance, AI-driven chatbots are able to simulate real-world conversations, adapting to learners' proficiency levels and offering immediate feedback on grammar and vocabulary. For example, Vesselinov and Grego (2012) found Duolingo improved beginner Spanish proficiency by an average of 91.4 points over eight weeks, while Mondly increased Danish learners' productive vocabulary in four weeks (Jensen & Cadierno, 2024). However, Mondly's rapid introduction of new lexical items without sufficient repetition weakened long-term retention, emphasising the need for supplementary instructional strategies that emphasise repetition and targeted practice.

These platforms utilise natural language processing to create engaging dialogues, allowing learners to practice in a low-pressure environment without fear of criticism from peers or instructors (MacIntyre & Gregersen, 2012). Research has evaluated the effectiveness of chatbots as conversational partners in language learning, especially in relation to reducing language anxiety. In one study, Belda-Medina and Calvo-Ferrer (2022) examined the perceptions of 176 pre-service teachers from Spain and Poland who interacted with three chatbots—Replika, Kuki, and Wysa—over four weeks. Results showed that across the board, chatbots reduced language anxiety, increased confidence, and provided non-judgmental practice opportunities.

However, in another study of CAs such as Replika and other generative-based systems (Zhai et al., Zhai et al., 2024), issues of trust-worthiness arose due to fabricated citations, non-existent references, and false information, which misrepresented key ideas. Learners struggled to assess the reliability of GenAI outputs, and educators had to remain vigilant in monitoring their use to ensure the reliability and appropriateness of the content generated. Another drawback was highlighted in this study when it was also noted that, despite their potential for engagement, generative CAs can unintentionally hinder peer interaction when not carefully structured into collaborative tasks, which was a point noted by one of the teachers in the study:

> Quotation 12: "When I introduced the idea of creating personalized chatbots, they ended up going into their own little smartphone bubbles and stopped talking." (T.11, Japan)

While conversational agents can enhance fluency, confidence, and learner engagement, their integration in TESOL raises key issues. Generative models can introduce bias, inaccuracies, and inappropriate content, requiring educators to monitor use closely. Accessibility also remains uneven, with institutions in resource-limited contexts facing barriers to adoption (Varsik & Vosberg, 2024). Finally, CAs should supplement rather than replace human interaction, ensuring learners still engage in authentic, negotiated communication (Xiao et al., 2023).

In sum, CAs, whether rule-based, retrieval-based or generative, offer scalable and personalised language learning experiences. Their greatest strength lies in lowering anxiety, tailoring dialogue to learners' needs and supporting practice beyond the classroom. However, their limitations must be carefully managed with rigorous pedagogy and teacher oversight to support the development of learners' speaking and listening skills.

3.2.6 Content Generation

TESOL educators are increasingly integrating GenAI tools into their teaching, particularly for content generation. Survey data indicates that 67.9% of respondents report using GenAI to create teaching materials, while 50% employ it for lesson planning and curriculum design. These trends align with findings by Karpouzis et al. (2024), who show that AI-driven platforms can streamline material preparation and allow educators to customise resources for diverse learner needs. Such tools can generate high-quality reading passages and corresponding exercises tailored to specific proficiency levels, making lesson content more relevant and engaging. Evidence from a study of Chinese educators revealed that AI system-generated materials were not only deemed appropriate for learners but, in many cases, surpassed the quality of human-written content (Xiao et al., 2023). This capacity for rapid, targeted content production highlights the potential of GenAI to enhance instructional efficiency and adaptivity in TESOL.

Survey results also indicate that 44.9% of respondents use GenAI to create reading or listening materials, underscoring its potential to support language skill development through tailored content. A further 28.2% report using GenAI to provide differentiated learning experiences, designing tasks that address varied proficiency levels and learning styles within the same classroom. By enabling personalised materials, tasks, and assessments, these tools can facilitate differentiated instruction at scale. For example, ChatGPT has been shown to generate customised reading passages, exercises, and formative feedback, supporting learners across a range of abilities. In a study by Li, Zhang, and Cai (2024), ChatGPT was used to implement differentiated instruction for learners of Chinese as a second language with varied proficiency levels. The tool generated outputs such as tailored reading passages, comprehension questions, and writing prompts, which were evaluated for linguistic accuracy, relevance, and engagement. Findings indicated that ChatGPT-supported materials improved learner outcomes by addressing individual needs while enhancing learner engagement.

In this study, survey data revealed that TESOL educators employ a range of GenAI tools to support both classroom instruction and related tasks. Responses to the open-ended question, "Please describe how generative AI has influenced your approach to teaching, if at all," indicated that ChatGPT was the most frequently cited, valued for generating lesson ideas, quizzes, reading texts, study guides, and tailored activities. Other commonly mentioned tools included Claude, Grammarly, Quillbot, Canva, Quizizz, Kahoot, Twee, Notion AI, and Education Copilot, which educators used for rewriting and simplifying texts, refreshing older materials, creating accessible resources for students with disabilities, and supporting planning and assessment. The following comment from survey participants illustrate the variety of ways GenAI supports content generation, grouped by key functions.

For planning diverse classroom activities and materials, one participant recounted:

> Quotation 13: "I use AI to create grammar and vocabulary activities, role play scripts." (Survey Participant)

While another participant commented:

> Quotation 14: "It has only made my life easier in terms of material preparation." (Survey Participant)

As a tool for assisting lesson planning, Karpouzis et al. (2024) note that GenAI can save time and help educators personalise materials to meet diverse learning needs. For enhancing accessibility and multimodality, one participant noted:

> Quotation 14: "With generative AI, I can easily convert textual material to audio materials that suit my students better:" (Survey Participant)

This aligns with the discussion by Anis and Khan (2023), who note that multimodal AI resources can significantly improve inclusivity for learners with specific visual or auditory processing needs and/or preferences. Nevertheless, it is also argued that potential for greater accessibility on current models still requires further development (Godwin-Jones, 2024).

It was also reported how GenAI tools were used to streamline assessment, with one participant reporting:

Quotation 15: "By using Forms, I can generate a quiz in minutes." (Survey Participant).

As Marzuki et al. (Marzuki et al., 2023) observe, while automation can save educators significant preparation time, they also risk reducing opportunities for teachers to create assessments that evaluate critical thinking and problem-solving skills.

Finally, another key function for teachers in generating content included planning and differentiated instruction, as was noted by one educator:

> Quotation 16: "Through AI, it becomes more practical for teachers to organize the syllabus and produce multiple activities for diverse students with different needs." (Survey Participant)

This reflects Li et al. (Li et al., 2024) findings that GenAI can facilitate differentiated instruction by tailoring content to multiple proficiency levels. However, such differentiation relies heavily on the teacher's ability to evaluate AI outputs for pedagogical appropriateness and accuracy.

While it is argued that AI content generation should be part of the TESOL educator's toolkit (Koraishi, 2023), educators are also urged to consider its limitations. AI-generated content has been criticised for lacking nuance and cultural relevance. For instance, it has been argued that GenAI content has a tendency towards Western-centric perspectives, thereby alienating students in non-Western contexts (Nyaaba et al. Nyaaba et al., 2024). These cultural biases risk producing content that fails to reflect the lived experiences of students from non-Western countries, with generated materials that fail to reflect their cultural contexts and lived experiences effectively. Moreover, the MIT Sloan Teaching &

Learning Technologies group (n.d.) highlights the known tendency of GenAI tools to produce content that is skewed or misleading, emphasising the need for critical evaluation of AI outputs in educational settings. Specifically, GenAI technology tools have been shown to produce images and text that perpetuate gender, racial (Nicoletti & Bass, 2023), and political biases (Heikkilä, Heikkilä, 2023). These ethical challenges and limitations are discussed further in Chapter 5. As such, there is a need for educators to be prepared to critically evaluate and adapt AI-generated content to ensure accuracy, relevance, and alignment with pedagogical goals. Moreover, while such tools might be time-saving, there is also concern that GenAI can limit creativity and originality, leading to homogenised learning resources.

In sum, these examples illustrate how GenAI tools are becoming increasingly embedded in TESOL practice, supporting lesson planning, differentiated instruction, and the creation of varied, personalised resources for diverse learners. However, their effective use demands critical oversight to prevent over-reliance, superficial engagement, and the perpetuation of cultural or societal biases. While GenAI can improve teaching efficiency, enhance accessibility and foster creativity, its integration must remain both effective and ethical, ensuring outputs align with pedagogical goals and reflect inclusive, culturally responsive second language education.

3.2.7 Real-Time Feedback

AI-powered tools provide instant feedback on grammar, pronunciation, and vocabulary, helping learners self-correct. For instance, Automated Writing Evaluation (AWE) tools like Gemini and Grammarly offer real-time corrections during writing and speaking exercises. As previously mentioned, survey findings indicate that 65% of TESOL educators use automated language assessment tools, and 20% utilise pronunciation tools with AI-generated feedback. When asked in which areas of language teaching they found GenAI tools most beneficial, 61.5% of participants reported assessment and feedback in AI-generated quizzes and personalised tests. Many appreciated the immediate and actionable nature of

AI-generated feedback. These systems empower learners by promoting independent learning and immediate skill improvement.

When asked how GenAI tools have enhanced their classroom instruction, teachers noted that the immediacy of AI feedback not only supported skill development but also freed them to focus on other instructional priorities. For example, several educators described using AI tools in class to clarify concepts, extend activities, and tailor feedback to individual learner levels:

> Quotation 17: "AI can provide students live feedback while working on a certain task. This means that I can focus on other aspects in class and even monitor independent learning more effectively." (Survey Participant)

> Quotation 18: "AI tools provide immediate, tailored feedback. The AI can suggest more precise vocabulary or offer multiple ways to rephrase sentences for clarity. It also adapts feedback based on the student's language level, offering simpler explanations to beginners and more advanced tips to higher-level students." (Survey Participant)

In addition to improving the quality of instructional feedback, educators observed that GenAI tools reduced learner anxiety by enabling low-stakes, self-paced practice. For instance, some students who initially struggled with paraphrasing developed greater confidence by experimenting with AI-generated examples.

> Quotation 19: "Students who had difficulty in understanding how to paraphrase managed to improve themselves since they had the chance to see plenty of examples before they started working on their own projects and then experiment by uploading their work online and see if they are correct or not." (Survey Participant)

Such reflections highlight the potential of GenAI to foster engagement and autonomy, while allowing teachers to allocate more attention to higher-order instructional goals.

The benefits of AI-powered tools in providing real-time feedback are well supported by research. Jubier et al. (2024) highlight how Automated Writing Evaluation (AWE) tools like Grammarly enhance learner autonomy by enabling students to identify and correct errors independently, fostering self-regulation and reducing anxiety. In writing instruction, Li et al. (Li et al., 2023) emphasise GenAI's ability to deliver tailored grammar, vocabulary, and stylistic suggestions, allowing educators to differentiate instruction effectively. By aligning feedback with learners' proficiency levels, these systems allow students to progress at their own pace while sustaining motivation and engagement. Similarly, Qassrawi et al. (2024) demonstrate that AI-powered pronunciation tools, such as Google Assistant, significantly improve EFL learners' fluency, vocabulary, content, and spoken grammar. Students reported that these tools allowed them to practice independently and receive supportive, non-judgemental feedback in low-pressure settings, which is especially advantageous for learners with low confidence in their oral skills.

Despite their advantages, AWE tools are not without limitations. Ding and Zou (2024) note that platforms like Grammarly often prioritise surface-level corrections, such as grammar, spelling, and syntax, while neglecting deeper-level writing errors such as organisation and content and higher-order thinking skills such as critical analysis and creativity. As a result, learners may develop overly mechanical approaches to writing without fully understanding the nuances of effective communication.

Another significant challenge is the risk of over-reliance on AWE tools, as noted by Koltovskaia (2020). Excessive dependence on automated feedback can lead to passive learning, where students accept AI-generated corrections without critically analysing their mistakes. This can hinder deeper learning and limit the development of independent problem-solving skills.

Cultural relevance also remains an issue. Liu (2023) argues that AI tools trained on Western-centric data sets may fail to accommodate diverse linguistic norms, potentially offering culturally irrelevant or inaccurate feedback for non-native learners. While AI can provide instant corrections, human teachers are still essential for delivering nuanced feedback, emotional support, and addressing learners' broader educational needs. For example, in a study of pronunciation tools, Jeon, Lee, and Coronel-Molina (2024) examined the use of the AI chatbot "PengTalk" in a South Korean elementary school. Through student reflections and interviews, their findings indicated that while the chatbot improved speaking confidence and enabled self-paced practice, it also reinforced native-speaker norms, narrowing students' perceptions of English diversity.

In sum, GenAI tools are reshaping TESOL practice across four main functions: writing support, conversational practice, content generation, and real-time feedback. Writing tools like ChatGPT, Grammarly, and DeepL help create tailored prompts, enhance grammar instruction, and support creative assignments, though over-reliance can limit skill development. Conversational agents such as Duolingo Max provide low-pressure speaking and listening practice that reduces language anxiety but may reinforce native-speaker norms and present learners with inaccuracies. In content generation, tools like ChatGPT and Canva enable efficient production of personalised, accessible materials, yet risks of cultural bias and content irrelevance remain. Real-time feedback systems foster learner autonomy and reduce stress through instant, adaptive corrections, but tend to prioritise surface-level issues over deeper critical engagement. Together, these tools offer efficiency, personalisation, and engagement, but their integration demands critical oversight to ensure pedagogical value and equity.

3.3 GenAI for Teacher Support

As discussed in Chapter 2, the Technology Acceptance Model (TAM) (Davis, 1989) offers a useful lens for understanding TESOL educators' adoption of GenAI tools for teacher-focused tasks. Survey and interview findings suggest that perceived ease of use and usefulness strongly influence uptake. GenAI has rapidly become an invaluable resource for lesson planning, resource creation, and assessment design, allowing teachers to devote more time to pedagogy and student engagement. However, adoption is shaped not only by these perceived benefits but also by cultural relevance, privacy, over-reliance, and institutional support.

Many educators praised the efficiency and adaptability of tools like ChatGPT for lesson planning, assessment design, and activity creation.

Quotation 20: "It saves lots of time. Instead of looking for lots of resources, you just have it at the tip of your finger." (T.8, Qatar)

Other participants also emphasised the versatility of AI tools in supporting teaching tasks.

Quotation 22 "AI tools like ChatGPT help me prepare my classes. I don't rely entirely on them, but I see them as complementary tools, like a helper or a copilot." (T.7, South Africa)

Quotation 23: "Sometimes, you know, there are some activities that you might not think of. And then just like you're discussing with a peer or colleague about something, so you're having another perspective... AI is like a second voice." (T.7, Qatar)

Aligning with recent research, these insights illustrate the perceived usefulness and ease of use of GenAI tools in supporting teaching tasks, including lesson planning (Karpouzis et al., 2024) and resource creation, such as worksheets, texts, and assessment materials (Koraishi, 2023). By reducing preparation time and providing adaptable solutions, they enable educators to devote more attention to interactive, personalised student engagement.

However, as discussed in Chapter 2, TAM also reveals challenges that hinder adoption. Some educators expressed scepticism about the reliability and cultural relevance of AI-generated materials.

Quotation 24: "AI discriminates between countries. It provides more positive information about developed countries and more negative information about developing countries." (T.12, Cyprus)

Such biases raise concerns about the cultural appropriateness of AI-generated content and its implications for global education equity, as noted by another educator:

Quotation 25: "There may be political or ideological sensitivities around what is considered acceptable information, especially with Western AI tools like ChatGPT. What's acceptable in one country might not be in

> another, and there could be a clash between certain facts or belief." (T.3, China)

Such concerns align with evidence that GenAI systems can reproduce cultural and political biases. Jeon et al. (Jeon et al., 2024) found that AI tools reflect ideological and linguistic preferences, while Nicoletti and Bass (2023) showed that generative models often amplify Western-centric or racialised representations.

Concerns over privacy and data collection emerged as another barrier to adoption:

> Quotation 26: "AI tools collect user data to build profiles, and we don't know how that information will be used in the future." (T.12, Cyprus)

Concerns were also expressed around cultural responsiveness and contextual relevance.

> Quotation 27: "In Algeria, we often use a competency-based approach, but AI tools tend to reflect Western teaching methods, which don't align with our context." (T.14, Algeria)

These concerns point to the importance of data transparency and localisation in AI tool design. Uddagiri and Isunuri (2024) emphasise that inadequate data transparency and opaque AI governance structures undermine educators' trust, while UNESCO (2023) notes that limited localisation and contextualisation remain major barriers to equitable technology integration across diverse educational systems.

Furthermore, concerns about over-reliance on AI were seen as diminishing its perceived usefulness:

> Quotation 28: "You still need to know what you want to achieve before you can use it effectively… and the results depend on what we ask for. So, teachers need to improve their technical skills and update their professional knowledge in order to use AI effectively. It's more demanding than just referring to textbooks or reference books like before." (T.5, China)

> Quotation 29: "Teachers have become so over-reliant that sometimes they take the content as it is. And later on, when we sit together and discuss whatever they have used, then they come to realize, oh, no. That actually doesn't fit what I want to use it for." (T.8, Qatar)

These reflections reinforce the necessity of balancing AI-driven automation with human oversight to maintain instructional quality. Teachers must develop both technical competence and critical judgement to ensure AI outputs are adapted to pedagogical aims rather than accepted uncritically. Research shows that limited familiarity with AI tools can contribute to uncertainty and uncritical use (Kim & Kim, 2022), while broader evidence indicates that over-reliance on AI can reduce cognitive engagement (Zhai et al., Zhai et al., 2024).

Educators were also keen to stress that institutional policy and training are essential for effective GenAI integration.

> Quotation 30: "I'd like more uniformity and guidelines, but there's none at the moment. Since I only use AI for in-class experiments and nothing that affects final grades, I try to avoid any ethical grey areas." (T.3, China)

> Quotation 31: "My institution hasn't provided clear guidelines on how to integrate AI into our teaching, so I'm hesitant to use it extensively. They just tell you that it's important but show us how… guide us. This is lacking unfortunately." (T.8, Qatar)

These perspectives illustrate how the absence of clear institutional guidance can create uncertainty and limit adoption. Similar concerns are observed in other educational contexts. Al-Zahrani and Alasmari (2025) reported that institutional uncertainty and inconsistent national policies were major barriers in the MENA region. Likewise, Islam et al. (2024) found that inadequate institutional policies impeded teacher adoption of AI in Bangladeshi universities.

As outlined in the Technology Acceptance Model (see Chapter 2), such external variables moderate educators' willingness to integrate new tools, reinforcing the need for robust support systems, clear guidelines, and targeted training.

Another hindrance to adoption centred on educators' ethical concerns about students' over-reliance on AI, particularly its effect on critical thinking and originality.

> Quotation 32: "Students tend to use it without critical thinking. If they need to learn vocabulary or complete sentences, they rely on AI too much. That doesn't necessarily mean they're actually learning. So in that sense, it's not the best tool for students." (T.10, Cyprus)

> Quotation 33: " It's fast and does the research, but I don't like the lazy aspect, like when students just ask AI to summarize an academic article instead of reading it themselves." (T.11, Cyprus)

Such comments reflect the apprehension that AI, if used uncritically, could encourage superficial learning habits and undermine the development of independent academic skills. This concern aligns with research showing that uncritical use of GenAI can potentially undermine student learning through over-reliance and plagiarism (Ozer, 2024). Additionally, these concerns also extend to planning and assessment, where teachers have expressed concern that AI could reduce their role to assistants relying on AI-generated content (Kim & Kim, 2022).

> Quotation 34: "There's a risk that teachers might stop engaging critically with the materials they use, instead relying entirely on AI-generated outputs." (Survey Participant)

The adoption of GenAI tools in TESOL is shaped by both the perceived technological benefits, including efficiency, adaptability, and resource generation, and the perceived challenges, including bias, privacy, over-reliance, and lack of institutional support. TAM offers insight into the drivers and barriers of adoption, while ethical considerations stress the importance of cultural inclusivity, teacher autonomy, and critical engagement.

Moving forward, integration must be supported by clear guidelines (see Chapter 5) and professional development opportunities (see Chapter 6) to ensure these tools are used effectively and responsibly.

3.4 GenAI for Enhancing Learner Engagement

Engaging learners is central to effective TESOL practice, fostering active participation, sustaining motivation, and facilitating meaningful language acquisition. While GenAI tools offer new opportunities to enhance engagement, their integration into TESOL classrooms also raises important theoretical and practical considerations. Drawing on social constructivist and critical theory perspectives, this section examines the role of GenAI in promoting learner engagement, supported by qualitative data from TESOL educators.

Social constructivism emphasises the co-construction of knowledge and the importance of scaffolding in supporting language development through active participation and collaboration (Vygotsky, 1978). GenAI tools such as ChatGPT, Grammarly, and Duolingo Max align with this framework by enabling learners to interact with content and peers in dynamic ways. In this context, GenAI can act as the "more knowledgeable other" (MKO) (Vygotsky, 1978), offering scaffolding, personalised learning pathways, and opportunities for collaborative knowledge-building.

For example, many educators in this study often highlighted the role of GenAI in encouraging self-directed learning and independent skill development.

> Quotation 35: "I use ChatGPT to generate texts for reading and to create vocabulary games. It helps students engage independently while improving their skills." (T.14, Algeria)

> Quotation 36 "It tells students if they've missed a word, pronounced something wrong, or skipped something. They can do this independently at home, which motivates them." (T.10, Cyprus)

These reflections illustrate how GenAI tools can motivate learners to take ownership of their learning while providing immediate, personalised feedback that supports skill development beyond the classroom. Research supports this link between AI tools and autonomous learning. Belda-Medina and Calvo-Ferrer (2022) found that the integration of chatbots into language learning increased learners' willingness to communicate, while Loewen et al. (2019) showed that mobile AI platforms foster self-paced, autonomous learning.

Similarly, other educators noted the collaborative functions of GenAI tools. One educator highlighted the potential of one specific application with AI-powered transcription and summarisation.

> Quotation: 37: "If integrated well, it helps students collaborate on research or summarise shared documents." (T.3, China)

Such applications not only promote language development but also encourage critical thinking and teamwork, essential components of collaborative learning. Similarly, conversational agents like Duolingo Max provide learners with opportunities to practice speaking and listening skills in low-pressure environments, simulating real-world conversations. As one of the educators explained:

> Quotation: 38 "I think AI can be very useful in language teaching, especially because of its interactivity. You could have students submit their chat logs with AI or screenshots of their interactions, which could be less stressful for them than interacting with a teacher." (T.1, United States)

These insights reflect the dual role of GenAI as both a facilitator of interaction and a supportive tool for learners who may feel intimidated in traditional classroom settings. Similar benefits have been observed in other contexts where AI-mediated interaction provides a low-anxiety environment for speaking and listening practice. Zhang et al. (2023), for example, reported that chatbot-based activities improved learners' speaking proficiency while reducing communication-related anxiety.

Some educators identified ways in which AI tools could support participation, particularly for introverted learners:

> Quotation 39: "AI is interactive, so it can engage with each student individually, giving them a personalized learning experience. This is especially

helpful for students who are introverted or shy and don't want to interact with their teachers." (T.2, China)

> Quotation 40: "Students react more, and everyone participates. Some students are introverted and don't like speaking up, but with AI, everyone can type their answers. This encourages more participation from all students." (T.4, China)

These examples illustrate how AI tools can bridge gaps in traditional teaching methods, providing a platform where all learners feel comfortable participating. This aligns with research showing that conversational agents help learners feel comfortable and more willing to communicate; for example, Catania et al. (2021) observed that children engaged more readily with an AI agent that addressed them personally and used a familiar tone.

Despite the many positive examples of student engagement in TESOL, some educators were uncertain how such tools explicitly supported collaborative learning. One educator admitted:

> Quotation 41: "I don't know yet. That's why we need professional development. I'm not sure how it will help with collaboration or writing." (T.11, Cyprus)

This sentiment was echoed by another educator from the United States, who observed that AI tools might foster interaction with the technology itself rather than among peers:

> Quotation 42: "I think it has, but maybe not in terms of collaboration with each other—more like collaboration with the tool. It feels like a collaboration in some ways because AI is interactive and conversational, so students might see it as a form of interaction." (T.1, United States)

Similarly, another interviewee who had previously highlighted potential uses (Quotation 37) also continued to note its limitations:

> Quotation 43: "Students could potentially use it to collaborate on research or summarize studies within a shared document. But beyond

> that, I'm not sure how else AI could enhance student interaction." (T.3, China)

In some instances, educators found that AI tools could hinder group communication rather than enhance it. As discussed earlier in relation to conversational agents, one educator found that integrating personalised chatbots had unintended effects on collaboration:

> Quotation 44: "When I introduced the idea of creating personalized chatbots, they ended up going into their own little smartphone bubbles and stopped talking. I was hoping they'd share their screens and say, 'Hey, check this out,' but instead, it hindered group communication." (T.6, Japan)

This example, while illustrating the technical potential of conversational agents, also highlights the risk that students may engage more with the tool than with each other, ultimately reducing opportunities for meaningful peer interaction.

These perspectives demonstrate the mixed responses among TESOL educators regarding AI's role in collaborative learning. While AI offers valuable opportunities for personalisation and engagement, its potential to foster meaningful collaboration among students is still an area of uncertainty and, in some cases, concern. Research mirrors these concerns. For example, Wan et al. (2024) found that learners sometimes preferred collaborating with GenAI over peers because it responded predictably and aligned with their ideas, which can inadvertently reduce peer interaction. Such findings highlight the need for careful task design to ensure that AI supports, rather than replaces, human collaboration.

The integration of GenAI into social constructivist practices is not without challenges. Over-reliance on AI tools can lead to surface-level engagement, where learners focus on completing tasks efficiently rather than engaging deeply with the content. Without teacher guidance, learners may treat GenAI outputs as definitive answers, undermining critical thinking and the exploratory nature of collaborative learning. One educator warned:

> Quotation 45: "It's easy for students to rely too much on these tools, and the problem is they don't always use them critically. They need to be able to assess the information AI provides, as it can generate hallucinations or inaccurate content. Students often find it convenient and may blindly trust the information, thinking they're saving time and effort." (T.9, Cyprus)

Such overuse of AI can dilute the collaborative and creative processes central to constructivist pedagogy, reducing learning to a mechanical exercise of input and output.

Reflecting on their earlier experiences with AI-based classroom activities, one educator stressed the importance of maintaining student ownership of their work:

> Quotation 46: "Students got value from it, but I emphasized that AI can't replace their voice in writing. AI can assist in research, but students' voices are what matter in their work. That's the advice I'd give – use AI as an assistant but remind students that their voice is irreplaceable." (T.6, Japan)

These reflections reinforce the need for teacher-led guidance to ensure that GenAI use complements, rather than replaces, learners' authentic contributions and curriculum-specific requirements. The teacher further cautioned GenAI against uncritical use:

> Quotation 47: "Students might ask AI how to write an essay and get some basic guidelines, but those guidelines may not be suited to their curriculum. For example, they might get instructions based on a different educational system, or the AI might give them irrelevant or overly complex information. Without human guidance, they might become confused." (T.6, Japan)

This concern mirrors wider research showing that students require support to use AI critically and in ways that preserve their own ideas and identities. As Godwin-Jones (2024) argues, AI literacy must be both critical and agentive so that learners do not uncritically accept AI-generated suggestions.

Overall, these reflections illustrate the role of GenAI tools as a potential More Knowledgeable Other (MKO) in TESOL, especially in enhancing learner engagement. By providing personalised feedback, fostering autonomy, and encouraging interaction, these tools align with social constructivist principles of guided learning within the Zone of Proximal Development (ZPD). Educators observe that GenAI supports self-directed learning, motivates introverted students, and personalises interactions to meet diverse learner needs. However, challenges remain. Over-reliance on these tools risks undermining critical thinking, with students sometimes treating GenAI outputs as definitive answers without deeper engagement. Additionally, while AI fosters individual interaction, its ability to facilitate meaningful peer collaboration remains inconsistent. To ensure that GenAI serves as an effective MKO, educators must actively mediate their use, balancing technological support with teacher-led instruction to maintain critical enquiry, creativity, and meaningful collaboration.

3.5 Current Adoption Trends in TESOL

The integration of GenAI tools into TESOL is reshaping language education, though adoption patterns vary across contexts. Findings from the international survey conducted for this study revealed that 71.8% of TESOL educators are currently using GenAI tools in their teaching. While this figure invites comparison with broader studies, there is limited statistical data on GenAI use in TESOL, making it challenging to contextualise these findings fully. For example, a survey of 500 U.S. educators conducted in October 2023 found that 60% had integrated AI into their classrooms (Forbes Advisor, 2024, June 6). While such comparisons highlight the growing importance of AI across education, the uneven distribution of responses in this TESOL dataset means that regional or global adoption trends cannot be reliably inferred. This highlights the need for larger-scale, TESOL-specific research to provide a clearer picture of global integration.

However, insights from broader studies help contextualise these trends beyond the limitations of the TESOL dataset used for this study. For example, Al-Zahrani and Alasmari (2025) examined GenAI adoption across the Middle East and North Africa (MENA) region, surveying 508 participants from 259 institutions across 19 countries. Their findings highlight significant disparities between high-income countries, such as Saudi Arabia and the United Arab Emirates, which benefit from robust infrastructure, substantial investments, and national strategies like Saudi Vision 2030 and UAE Centennial 2071, and lower-middle-income countries such as Sudan, Mauritania, and Yemen, where adoption is hindered by economic constraints, inadequate infrastructure, and unclear policies. These findings emphasise the importance of addressing structural barriers to ensure equitable access to AI technologies across regions. This issue of equity in AI integration will be further explored in Chapter 5, particularly in relation to ethics and access.

GenAI tools are being used across all levels of TESOL education. Of those educators who said that they are currently using GenAI tools in their teaching (71.8%), findings indicate broad uptake across all sectors with the highest reported use in adult education (69.2%) and the lowest in primary education (56.3%). These findings provide a descriptive snapshot of current patterns, highlighting general trends across levels of education. However, they should not be taken as statistically significant, since many educators teach across multiple levels and the sample size is not statistically representative.

In comparison to other studies in education, Pettersson et al. (2024) observed that over half of university educators in Sweden had already integrated GenAI into their teaching. Secondary school educators in this dataset reported an even higher rate (75%), suggesting particularly strong uptake within this sector. Findings also demonstrated that educators in primary education demonstrated a somewhat lower adoption rate (60%), though this still indicates a significant level of integration.

In comparison, the use of GenAI in UK primary and secondary schools was shown to have increased rapidly, from 17% in April 2023 to 42% by November 2023 (Department for Education, 2024). Likewise, a US study found that only 18% of K–12 public school teachers reported using AI in 2024 (Diliberti et al., 2024), suggesting there may be a more cautious adoption at lower levels of education. These disparities emphasise that while GenAI is gaining traction across education, the speed and scale of uptake vary depending on national contexts, resources, and policies.

Survey findings also identified several key applications of GenAI tools that enhance teaching effectiveness and learner engagement. The most frequently cited use was the creation of teaching materials such as AI-generated worksheets, quizzes, and presentation (67.9%), followed by lesson planning and curriculum design (50%). Educators also reported using GenAI for generating reading or listening materials (44.9%), providing differentiated learning tasks (28.2%), grading and feedback (26.9%), and administrative tasks such as preparing forms or reports (32.1%). These results suggest that TESOL educators are primarily relying on GenAI for content generation and preparation, while tasks such as assessment and feedback remain less common. However, it is important to note that while these findings provide valuable insights into TESOL practice, there are currently no large-scale international studies that map how GenAI is being applied across education globally. Existing research remains fragmented, often limited to national or regional contexts, which highlights the need for broader comparative studies to establish global trends.

However, the broader research literature shows that GenAI tools are being adopted across a wide range of academic disciplines, with applications tailored to subject-specific needs. In mathematics education, GenAI supports large-class management by providing real-time feedback while offering tailored assistance to individual learners (Abd Algani & Shine, 2025; Bernardi et al., 2024; Wardat et al., 2023). In engineering, AI is increasingly applied in project-based learning, where it can assess design tasks and suggest improvements, particularly in structural and mechanical contexts (Khan et al., 2024; Nikolic et al., 2023; Zhang & Chang, 2024). In the performing arts, GenAI tools are used for lesson planning, pedagogy, and assessment (Clark-Fookes, 2025), while research in music education shows their impact on instruction and engagement. For example, the Artificial Intelligence Virtual Artist (AIVA) has been found to enhance student creativity and learner engagement (Yin & Guo, 2024), and AI chatbots have demonstrated modest improvements in learners' musical performance (8%) but substantial benefits in teaching (95%) (Li & Wang, 2023). Similarly, in law, GenAI is being adopted as a personalised tutor, helping students grasp complex legal concepts and receive tailored feedback (Murray, 2023).

Taken together, these applications demonstrate the expanding role of GenAI across diverse academic disciplines, reinforcing its potential to reshape pedagogy, assessment, and learner engagement. However, while fields such as mathematics or engineering often measure outcomes in terms of efficiency and accuracy, TESOL involves additional challenges linked to culture, communication, and creativity, which shape both the real and perceived barriers that educators associate with GenAI adoption in TESOL. These are examined in the following section.

3.6 Challenges and Barriers

Survey findings reveal that TESOL educators face a range of obstacles when integrating GenAI tools into their teaching. The most frequently reported challenge was a lack of training and professional support (67.9%), emphasising the importance of sustained professional development in this area. Cost and limited access to tools were also significant concerns (55.1%), alongside issues of privacy and security (35.9%). In addition, one-third of respondents (33.3%) pointed to the absence of tools appropriate for their specific teaching contexts. The least cited concern was resistance from students or institutions (20.5%), though this figure still represents a significant minority. Collectively, these findings emphasise the need for professional development opportunities, affordable and accessible AI tools, and clear institutional and policy frameworks to address both technical and ethical concerns in TESOL education.

The most frequently cited barrier to integrating GenAI tools in TESOL is the lack of training and professional support, reported by 67.9% of educators. This challenge is critical, as insufficient training reduces both the perceived ease of use and perceived usefulness of GenAI tools, which are the two key constructs that directly influence adoption, as outlined in the Technology Acceptance Model (Davis, 1989; see Chapter 2). Without appropriate training, educators may view GenAI as overly complex or irrelevant to their teaching, resulting in low uptake and limited impact. As one educator reflected:

> Quotation: 48: "I don't feel prepared enough as a teacher to use it. I don't think I have the right tools or knowledge yet. We definitely need professional development on AI. If I knew how to incorporate it properly, like using translingual methods or other ELT approaches, I'd definitely use it." (T.11)

These findings mirror international studies that consistently show that insufficient teacher training is a major barrier to AI adoption, with evidence from the U.S. (Diliberti et al., 2024), the U.K. (Department for Education, 2024), the EU (Cukurova et al., 2024), the MENA region (Al-Zahrani & Alasmari, 2025), and Bangladesh (Islam et al., 2024), among others.

Cukurova et al. (2024) further argue that teachers must be equipped to critically evaluate the social and educational implications of GenAI, identify potential biases, and guide students in navigating its ethical and personal impacts. Existing frameworks, such as the European Framework for the Digital Competence of Educators (DigCompEdu) (Redecker, 2017), already provide guidance for developing digital competence in teaching, including resource selection, assessment practices, and fostering learner autonomy and inclusivity. However, while such frameworks aim to integrate GenAI effectively into pedagogy, foster innovation, and address diverse learning needs, they remain advisory, unless they are adopted as mandatory professional standards within teacher certification and in-service training programmes (see Chapter 6 for further discussion).

Cost or access emerged as the second most significant barrier, cited by 55.1% of respondents. This challenge is particularly acute in resource-constrained settings, where educators may lack the infrastructure or funding to integrate GenAI tools effectively, perpetuating a digital divide. As noted in broader studies (e.g., Al-Zahrani & Alasmari, 2025), such disparities are evident across regions, with adoption shaped by differences in investment, infrastructure, and national policy. One interviewee from Algeria illustrated this reality:

> Quotation 49: "In Algeria, there are rural areas with poor internet connections, so AI tools can't be used everywhere. But in private schools, where students have better resources, I give them tasks that they can approach using tools like ChatGPT." (T.14, Algeria)

Pedro et al. (2019), in a UNESCO report, similarly warn that, as a disruptive technology, AI risks exacerbating existing educational inequalities, particularly among marginalised and disadvantaged groups. Addressing this requires not only investment in infrastructure but also policies that ensure equitable access across gender, race, age, disability, and other demographic factors. Yet, while debates in the Global North often centre on technological innovation and competitive advantage, equity concerns are frequently sidelined. A more inclusive, globally oriented approach to AI adoption is needed—one that balances innovation with fairness and accessibility (see Chapter 5 for further discussion).

Privacy and security concerns, cited by 35.9% of educators, represent another key barrier to GenAI adoption in TESOL. Teachers also expressed apprehensions about protecting student data, addressing algorithmic bias, and ensuring compliance with institutional and legal frameworks. As Floridi and Cowls (2019) argue, the ethical use of AI depends on balancing innovation with accountability and trust, guided by principles of beneficence, non-maleficence, autonomy, justice, and explicability. These principles highlight many of the same issues raised by educators in this study. One interviewee reflected:

> Quotation 50: "In terms of privacy, I don't fully trust these tools because I believe they store user data, which is concerning." (T.12, Cyprus)

A particular source of concern lies in the reliance of many GenAI tools on cloud-based platforms. Uddagiri and Isunuri (2024) identify several critical risks, including potential exposure of sensitive student information through data breaches, challenges with informed consent, and vulnerabilities that can compromise user security. The possibility of de-anonymisation, where supposedly anonymised data is reconstructed to reveal personal details, further complicates privacy protections. Additionally, the emergence of synthetic data, such as deepfakes, raises new risks of impersonation and misinformation, which educators must remain vigilant against.

A lack of appropriate tools tailored to educators' specific teaching contexts was also reported by 33.3% of respondents. This challenge relates to TAM's construct of perceived usefulness, as educators are less likely to adopt tools they perceive as irrelevant or ineffective for their unique instructional needs. Current GenAI platforms are largely designed for general educational purposes, and their integration into specialised fields like TESOL remains in its early stages. Ulla and Teng (2024) note that while AI presents opportunities for TESOL, its use is still largely experimental, with educators navigating untested practices for effective implementation. Similarly, Davoodifard and Eskin (2024) emphasise that GenAI's role in second language education is still emerging, requiring more research to tailor these tools effectively to TESOL contexts. Godwin-Jones (2024) further argues that while GenAI can support language learning, current models are not yet optimised for the complex linguistic and cultural needs of TESOL learners.

Resistance from students or institutions was the least frequently cited barrier, identified by 20.5% of educators. Nevertheless, its impact on adoption should not be underestimated. Institutional policies and student attitudes can significantly influence TESOL educators' intentions to integrate AI into their teaching practices. For example, a study by Islam et al. (2024) found that approximately 74.8% of English as a Foreign Language (EFL) teachers in Bangladeshi universities felt that existing institutional policies were inadequate for addressing the challenges posed by AI in education, potentially hindering their willingness to adopt AI tools. Similarly, de la Vall and Faundez (2024) explored the attitudes of university language teachers towards a pre-designed language learning system incorporating AI-based voice recognition. The findings revealed that instructors' perceptions of the system's ease of use, usefulness and enjoyment significantly impacted their acceptance and intention to use the AI tool in their courses. Student attitudes also play a critical role. Barrett and Pack (2023) reported that positive student perceptions of GenAI's usefulness encouraged educators to adopt these tools in English language teaching, whereas negative student attitudes, often stemming from ethical concerns, deterred adoption.

Overall, these barriers, ranging from limited training and resources to concerns about privacy, contextual fit, and resistance, demonstrate that while GenAI offers significant opportunities for TESOL, its effective integration depends on sustained professional development, equitable access, and supportive institutional and cultural frameworks.

3.7 Conclusion

This chapter has examined the current state of GenAI in TESOL, exploring its applications for teaching practices, adoption trends, and emerging challenges. The findings show that GenAI is transforming language education by supporting lesson planning, assessment, and learner engagement, with many educators recognising its potential to enhance efficiency and personalise instruction. At the same time, barriers such as limited training, inequitable access, privacy concerns, and questions about TESOL-specific relevance continue to constrain its use. While educators value GenAI's ability to automate tasks and foster engagement, concerns remain about over-reliance, ethical implications, and widening digital inequalities.

Viewed through theoretical lenses, these insights provide a deeper understanding of the complexities of GenAI integration. Social constructivism highlights opportunities for scaffolding and personalised support but it also reveals risks of encouraging individual rather than collaborative learning. The Ethical Use of Technology framework underscores concerns around privacy, bias, and misinformation, while Critical Theory draws attention to equity gaps between well-resourced and resource-constrained contexts. The Technology Acceptance Model (TAM) helps explain adoption patterns, with ease of use and perceived usefulness central to uptake, but limited training and guidance emerging as persistent barriers.

In sum, GenAI offers significant potential to support innovation in TESOL, yet its benefits depend on professional development, critical oversight, and policies that ensure equitable and ethical integration. The next chapter builds on these themes, turning to practical applications of GenAI in supporting the four core language skills, reading, writing, listening, and speaking, alongside intercultural communication skills. It also offers concrete strategies to help educators integrate these tools into their teaching in purposeful and pedagogically sound ways.

References

Abd Algani, Y., & Shine, M. (2025). Using generative artificial intelligence models (GAIM) as digital assistants for enhancing motivation and retention proficiency of mathematics undergraduates. *Research Journal in Translation, Literature, Linguistics, and Education (RJTLLE), 1*(1), 39–55. https://doi.org/10.64120/rgvf1v66

Al-Zahrani, A. M., & Alasmari, T. M. (2025). A comprehensive analysis of AI adoption, implementation strategies, and challenges in higher education across the Middle East and North Africa (MENA) region. *Education and Information Technologies*, 1–51. https://doi.org/10.1007/s10639-024-13300-y

Anis, M., & Khan, R. (2023). Integrating multimodal approaches in English language teaching for inclusive education: A pedagogical exploration. *Universal Journal of Educational Research, 2*(3), 241–257.

Barrett, A., & Pack, A. (2023). Not quite eye to AI: Student and teacher perspectives on the use of generative artificial intelligence in the writing process. *International Journal of Educational Technology in Higher Education, 20*(1), 59. https://doi.org/10.1186/s41239-023-00427-0

Begian-Lewis, K. M., & Hart, C. J. (2024). Finding time for creativity in higher education writing through generative AI. In *Impacts of generative AI on creativity in higher education* (pp. 47–68). IGI Global. https://doi.org/10.4018/979-8-3693-2418-9.ch003

Belda-Medina, J., & Calvo-Ferrer, J. R. (2022). Using chatbots as AI conversational partners in language learning. *Applied Sciences, 12*(17), 8427. https://doi.org/10.3390/app12178427

Bernardi, M. L., Capone, R., Faggiano, E., & Troilo, F. (2024). Teachers exploring the potential of generative AI in mathematics teaching. In *Proceedings of the 17th ERME topic conference MEDA4* (pp. 89–96). Università degli studi di Bari Aldo Moro.

Bloom, B. S. (1984). The 2 sigma problem: The search for methods of group instruction as effective as one-to-one tutoring. *Educational Researcher, 13*(6), 4–16. https://doi.org/10.3102/0013189x013006004

Carbonell, J. R. (1970). AI in CAI: An artificial-intelligence approach to computer-assisted instruction. *IEEE transactions on man-machine systems, 11*(4), 190–202. https://doi.org/10.1109/tmms.1970.299942

Carbonell, J. R., & Collins, A. M. (1974). Natural semantics in artificial intelligence. *American Journal of Computational Linguistics.*

Catania, F., Spitale, M., Cosentino, G., Garzotto, F. (2021. Onversational agents to promote children's verbal communication skills. In: Følstad, A., *et al.* Chatbot research and design. CONVERSATIONS 2020. Lecture notes in computer science 12604. Springer. doi:https://doi.org/10.1007/978-3-030-68288-0_11.

Clark-Fookes, T. (2025). To fear or not to fear: Generative artificial intelligence in drama education. *Research in Drama Education: The Journal of Applied Theatre and Performance, 30*(1), 117–123. https://doi.org/10.1080/13569783.2024.2401335

Cukurova, M., Kralj, L., Hertz, B., & Saltidou, E. (2024). *Professional development for teachers in the age of AI*. European Schoolnet.

Davis, F. D. (1989). Perceived usefulness, perceived ease of use, and user acceptance of information technology. *MIS Quarterly*, 319–340. https://doi.org/10.2307/249008

Davoodifard, M., & Eskin, D. (2024). Exploring the role of generative AI in second language education: Insights for instruction, learning, and assessment: Introduction to the forum. *Studies in Applied Linguistics and TESOL, 24*(1), 21–33. https://doi.org/10.52214/salt.v24i1.12863

de la Vall, R. R. F., & Faundez, C. V. (2024). Foreign language teacher's attitudes towards a pre-designed language learning system. *Digital Education Review, 45*, 222–231. https://doi.org/10.1344/der.2024.45.222-231

Department for Education. (2024, January 24). *Generative AI in education: Educator and expert views report* (Report No. RR1402). GOV.UK. https://assets.publishing.service.gov.uk/media/65b8cd41b5cb6e000d8bb74e/DfE_GenAI_in_education_-_Educator_and_expert_views_report.pdf

Diliberti, M., Schwartz, H. L., Doan, S., Shapiro, A. K., Rainey, L., & Lake, R. J. (2024). Using artificial intelligence tools in K–12 classrooms. *RAND.* https://doi.org/10.7249/rra956-21

Ding, L., & Zou, D. (2024). Automated writing evaluation systems: A systematic review of Grammarly, Pigai, and criterion with a perspective on future directions in the age of generative artificial intelligence. *Education and*

Information Technologies, 29(11), 14151–14203. https://doi.org/10.1007/s10639-023-12402-3

Doshi, A.R., & Hauser, O. (2023). Generative artificial intelligence enhances creativity but reduces the diversity of novel content. Available at SSRN: https://doi.org/10.2139/ssrn.4535536.

Floridi, L. (2023). AI as agency without intelligence: On ChatGPT, large language models, and other generative models. *Philosophy & technology, 36*(1), 15. https://doi.org/10.1007/s13347-023-00621-y

Floridi, L., & Cowls, J. (2022). A unified framework of five principles for AI in society. *Machine learning and the city: Applications in architecture and urban design*, 535–545. https://doi.org/10.2139/ssrn.3831321

Advisor, F. (2024, June 6). *Artificial intelligence in education: Teachers' opinions on AI in the classroom.* Forbes Advisor. Retrieved from https://www.forbes.com/advisor/education/it-and-tech/artificial-intelligence-in-school/

Fryer, L., & Carpenter, R. (2006). Bots as language learning tools. *Language Learning & Technology, 10*(3), 8–14. https://doi.org/10.64152/10125/44068

Godwin-Jones, R. (2022). Partnering with AI: Intelligent writing assistance and instructed language learning. *Language Learning & Technology, 26*(2), 5–24. https://doi.org/10.10125/73474

Godwin-Jones, R. (2024). Distributed agency in language learning and teaching through generative AI. *Language Learning & Technology, 28*(2), 5–31. https://doi.org/10.64152/10125/73570

Heikkilä, M. (2023, August 8). *AI language models are rife with different political biases.* MIT Technology Review. https://www.technologyreview.com/2023/08/07/1077324/ai-language-models-are-rife-with-political-biases

Innaci, D. L., & Jona, P. H. (2024). I in second language learning: Leveraging automated writing assistance tools for improving learners' writing task assessment. *Jamal Academic Research Journal: An Interdisciplinary, 5*(1). https://doi.org/10.1016/j.jslw.2007.07.001

Islam, M., Hasan, M. M., & Mahmud, R. (2024). EFL teachers' perceptions of AI'S impact on academic integrity and pedagogy in Bangladeshi universities. *Language Literacy: Journal of Linguistics, Literature, and Language Teaching, 8*(2), 564–579. https://doi.org/10.30743/ll.v8i2.10082

Jensen, C. J. D., & Cadierno, T. (2024). Differences in mobile-assisted acquisition of receptive and productive vocabulary knowledge: A case study using Mondly. *Language Learning Journal, 52*(3), 255–270. https://doi.org/10.1080/09571736.2022.2108123

Jeon, J., Lee, S., & Coronel-Molina, S. M. (2024). Rethinking AI bias in speech-recognition chatbots for ELT. *ELT Journal, 78*(4), 435–445. https://doi.org/10.1093/elt/ccae035

Jubier, M. M., Al-Rawe, M. F. A., & Algaithi, A. (2024). Effect of EditGPT on the learners' autonomy and learning anxiety. *International Journal of Learning, Teaching and Educational Research, 23*(8), 369–390. https://doi.org/10.26803/ijlter.23.8.19

Karpouzis, K., Pantazatos, D., Taouki, J., & Meli, K. (2024). Tailoring education with GenAI: A new horizon in lesson planning [Preprint]. *arXiv*. doi:https://doi.org/10.48550/arXiv.2403.12071.

Khan, R., Bhaduri, S., Mackenzie, T., Paul, A., KJ, S., & Sen, I. (2024, August). Path to personalization: A systematic review of GenAI in engineering education. In *KDD AI4Edu Workshop*.

Kim, N. J., & Kim, M. K. (2022, March). Teacher's perceptions of using an artificial intelligence-based educational tool for scientific writing. In *Frontiers in education* (Vol. 7, p. 755914). Frontiers Media SA. https://doi.org/10.3389/feduc.2022.755914

Kim, J., Yu, S., Detrick, R., & Li, N. (2025). Exploring students' perspectives on generative AI-assisted academic writing. *Education and Information Technologies, 30*(1), 1265–1300. https://doi.org/10.1007/s10639-024-12878-7

Koltovskaia, S. (2020). Student engagement with automated written corrective feedback (AWCF) provided by Grammarly: A multiple case study. *Assessing Writing, 44, Article 100450*. https://doi.org/10.1016/j.asw.2020.100450

Koraishi, O. (2023). Teaching English in the age of AI: Embracing ChatGPT to optimize EFL materials and assessment. *Language Education & Technology (LET Journal), 3*(1), 55–72.

Kreminski, M. (2024). The dearth of the author in AI-supported writing. *arXiv*. doi:https://doi.org/10.48550/arXiv.2404.10289.

Lazic, D., Thompson, A., Pritchard, T., & Tsuji, S. (2020). Student preferences: Using Grammarly to help EFL writers with paraphrasing, summarizing, and synthesizing. In K. Frederiksen, S. Larsen, L. Bradley, & S. Thouësny (Eds.), *CALL for widening participation: Short papers from EUROCALL 2020* (pp. 183–189). Research-publishing.net. doi:10.14705/rpnet.2020.48.1186.

Lee, S.-M., Wang, X., Park, I., et al. (2024). It feels so real! Situated authentic language learning in immersive virtual reality. *Education and Information Technologies, 29*(18), 24023–24045. https://doi.org/10.1007/s10639-024-12807-8

Li, P., ping, & Wang, B. (2023). Artificial intelligence in music education. *International Journal of Human–Computer Interaction, 40*(16), 4183–4192. https://doi.org/10.1080/10447318.2023.2209984

Li, Q., Zhang, J., & Cai, W. (2024). Utilizing ChatGPT to implement differentiated instruction. *International Journal of Chinese Language Teaching, 5*(1), 74–89. https://doi.org/10.46451/ijclt.20240106

Liu, Z. (2023). Cultural bias in large language models: A comprehensive analysis and mitigation strategies. *Journal of Transcultural Communication, 3*(2), 224–244. https://doi.org/10.1515/jtc-2023-0019

Loewen, S., Isbell, D. R., & Sporn, Z. (2019). The effectiveness of app-based language instruction for developing receptive linguistic knowledge and oral communicative ability. *Foreign Language Annals, 52*(3), 514–536. https://doi.org/10.1111/flan.12454

MacIntyre, P., & Gregersen, T. (2012). Affect: The role of language anxiety and other emotions in language learning. In S. Mercer, S. Ryan, & M. Williams (Eds.), *Psychology for language learning: Insights from research, theory and practice* (pp. 103–118). Palgrave Macmillan. https://doi.org/10.1057/9781137032829_8

Marzuki, W., Rusdin, U., Darwin, D., & Indrawati, I. (2023). The impact of AI writing tools on the content and organization of students' writing: EFL teachers' perspective. *Cogent Education, 10*(2), 2236469. https://doi.org/10.1080/2331186X.2023.2236469

MIT Sloan Teaching & Learning Technologies. (2025). Addressing AI hallucinations and bias. MIT Sloan Teaching & Learning Technologies., from https://mitsloanedtech.mit.edu/ai/basics/addressing-ai-hallucinations-and-bias/. Accessed December 16th, 2024.

Murray, M. D. (2023). *Artificial intelligence for learning the law: Generative AI for academic support in law schools and universities* (SSRN Electronic Journal). doi:https://doi.org/10.2139/ssrn.4564227.

Nicoletti, L., & Bass, D. (2023, June 14). Humans are biased. *Generative AI is even worse.* Bloomberg Technology + Equality. https://www.bloomberg.com/graphics/2023-generative-ai-bias

Nikolic, S., Daniel, S., Haque, R., Belkina, M., Hassan, G. M., Grundy, S., & Sandison, C. (2023). ChatGPT versus engineering education assessment: A multidisciplinary and multi-institutional benchmarking and analysis of this generative artificial intelligence tool to investigate assessment integrity. *European Journal of Engineering Education, 48*(4), 559–614. https://doi.org/10.1080/03043797.2023.2213169

Nyaaba, M., Wright, A., & Choi, G. L. (2024). Generative AI and digital neocolonialism in global education: Towards an equitable framework. *arXiv*. doi:https://doi.org/10.48550/arXiv.2406.02966.

Ozer, O. (2024). AI language models: A breach of academic integrity in online language learning. *Studies in Language Assessment, 13*(1), 237–262. https://doi.org/10.58379/ezys5680

Pettersson, J., Hult, E., Eriksson, T., & Adewumi, T. (2024). Generative AI and teachers—For us or against us? *A case study. arXiv.* https://doi.org/10.48550/arXiv.2404.03486

Pinkwart, N. (2016). Another 25 years of AIED? Challenges and opportunities for intelligent educational technologies of the future. *International Journal of Artificial Intelligence in Education, 26*(2), 771–783. https://doi.org/10.1007/s40593-016-0099-7

Qassrawi, R. M., ElMashharawi, A., Itmeizeh, M., & Tamimi, M. H. (2024). AI-powered applications for improving EFL students' speaking proficiency in higher education. *Assessment, 8*(9), 1–15. https://doi.org/10.30564/fls.v6i5.6966

Redecker, C. (2017). *European framework for the digital competence of educators: Dig Comp Edu* (No. JRC107466). Joint Research Centre (Seville site). doi:https://doi.org/10.2760/159770.

Self, J. (Ed.). (1988). *Artificial intelligence & human learning: Intelligent computer-aided instruction.* Routledge.

Streitz, N. A. (1988). Mental models and metaphors: Implications for the design of adaptive user-system interfaces. In H. Mandl & A. Lesgold (Eds.), *Learning issues for intelligent tutoring systems* (pp. 164–186). Springer. https://doi.org/10.1007/978-1-4684-6350-7_8

Uddagiri, C., & Isunuri, B. V. (2024). Ethical and privacy challenges of generative AI. In S. A. Shylaja & M. S. Gaur (Eds.), *Generative AI: Current trends and applications* (pp. 219–244). Springer Nature Singapore. https://doi.org/10.1007/978-981-97-8460-8_11

UNESCO. (2023). *Global education monitoring report 2023: Technology in education—A tool on whose terms?* Target 4.A: Education facilities and learning environments. United Nations Educational, Scientific and Cultural Organization (UNESCO). https://gem-report-2023.unesco.org/

Ulla, M. B., & Teng, M. F. (2024). Generative artificial intelligence (AI) applications in TESOL: Opportunities, issues, and perspectives. *TESOL Journal*. https://doi.org/10.58304/ijts.20240301

Varsik, S. and L. Vosberg (2024), The potential impact of artificial intelligence on equity and inclusion in education. *OECD Artificial Intelligence*

Papers, No. 23, OECD Publishing, Paris. doi:https://doi.org/10.1787/15df715b-en.

Vesselinov, R., & Grego, J. (2012). Duolingo effectiveness study. City University of New, 28(1–25).

Vygotsky, L. S. (1978). *Mind in society: The development of higher psychological processes*. Harvard University Press.

Wan, Q., Hu, S., Zhang, Y., Wang, P., Wen, B., & Lu, Z. (2024). "it felt like having a second mind": Investigating human–AI co-creativity in prewriting with large language models. *Proceedings of the ACM on human-computer interaction, 8*(CSCW1). *Art, 84*, 1–26. https://doi.org/10.1145/3637361

Wang, H., & Dang, A. (2024). Enhancing L2 writing with generative AI: A systematic review of pedagogical integration and outcomes. *Preprint.* doi:https://doi.org/10.13140/RG.2.2.19572.16005.

Wardat, Y., Tashtoush, M. A., AlAli, R., & Jarrah, A. M. (2023). ChatGPT: A revolutionary tool for teaching and learning mathematics. *EURASIA journal of mathematics, science and technology. Education, 19*(7), em2286. https://doi.org/10.29333/ejmste/13272

Weizenbaum, J. (1966). ELIZA—A computer program for the study of natural language communication between man and machine. *Communications of the ACM, 9*(1), 36–45. https://doi.org/10.1145/365153.365168

Wenger, E. (1987). *Artificial intelligence and tutoring systems*. Morgan Kaufmann.

Xiao, C., Xu, S. X., Zhang, K., Wang, Y., & Xia, L. (2023). Evaluating reading comprehension exercises generated by LLMs: A showcase of ChatGPT in education applications. In *Proceedings of the 18th Workshop on Innovative Use of NLP for Building Educational Applications (BEA 2023)* (pp. 610–625). Association for Computational Linguistics. https://aclanthology.org/2023.bea-1.52/

Xiao, F., Zhao, P., Sha, H., Yang, D., & Warschauer, M. (2024). Conversational agents in language learning. *Journal of China Computer-Assisted Language Learning, 4*(2), 300–325. https://doi.org/10.1515/jccall-2022-0032

Yin, L., & Guo, R. (2024). An artificial intelligence-based interactive learning environment for music education in China: Traditional Chinese music and its contemporary development as a way to increase cultural capital. *European Journal of Education*. https://doi.org/10.1111/ejed.12858

Zhai, C., Wibowo, S., & Li, L. D. (2024). The effects of over-reliance on AI dialogue systems on students' cognitive abilities: A systematic review. *Smart Learning Environments, 11*(1), 28. https://doi.org/10.1186/s40561-024-00316-7

Zhang, S., Shan, C., Lee, J. S. Y., Che, S., & Kim, J. H. (2023). Effect of chatbot-assisted language learning: A meta-analysis. *Education and Information Technologies, 28*(11), 15223–15243. https://doi.org/10.1007/s10639-023-11805-6

Zhang, Z., & Chang, Y. (2024, October). Leveraging generative AI to enhance engineering education at both low-level and high-level study. In *2024 Fall ASEE Mid-Atlantic Section Conference*. doi:https://doi.org/10.18260/1-2%2D%2D49450.

4

Practical Applications of GenAI in TESOL

4.1 Introduction

GenAI is reshaping TESOL by offering adaptive, interactive, and personalised learning experiences. Unlike earlier applications of AI in education (AIED), such as rule-based Computer-Assisted Language Learning (CALL) or Intelligent Tutoring Systems (ITS), today's GenAI tools can generate human-like text, provide real-time feedback, and adapt instruction to learners' needs (Alsofyani & Barzanji, 2025; Czerkawski, 2024; Yang & Jiang, 2024). These developments, building on earlier milestones, represent a significant shift (see Chapter 2), with recent advances in natural language processing and machine learning enabling more sophisticated forms of language acquisition, practice, and assessment.

Reflecting this shift, TESOL educators are already adopting GenAI to support their teaching, with one educator highlighting its potential to enhance personalisation:

> Quotation 1: "So, it cannot be taken as it is. You need to study very well your students' needs. What is it I need to focus on? It could be sometimes an abstract concept, and then you just need to make it easier, simplify it to students. We know that they have different learning styles.

C. Savvidou, *AI-Powered Language Teaching*,
https://doi.org/10.1007/978-3-032-14502-4_4

So sometimes visualization. So, I may give the concept to any GenAI and then ask for a visualization, sometimes diagrams." (T.8, Qatar)

One educator commented on the efficiency of real-time support in lessons:

Quotation 2: "I use forms quizzes quite a bit. I'll put a text into ChatGPT, and it generates a bunch of questions. I adapt them to what I need, but it gives me a starting point. Also, with Microsoft 365, I use tools like Reading Progress, which analyses student recordings. It tells them if they've missed a word, pronounced something wrong, or skipped something. I use that a lot in class." (T.10, Cyprus)

Similarly, another described how GenAI promotes inclusivity:

Quotation 3: "First of all, it will personalize the learning experience for students. AI is interactive, so it can engage with each student individually, giving them a personalized learning experience. This is especially helpful for students who are introverted or shy and don't want to interact with their teachers. So, yes, the interactive nature of AI is very beneficial. (T.2, China)

While another educator emphasised scalability in large classes and online education:

Quotation 4: "For example, we have a QR code for students to scan at the start of class to register their attendance. The system collects data on their homework submissions, participation, and performance in discussions. It even grades quizzes and tests, making it easier for teachers to access the grades at the end of the semester." (T.5, China)

Theoretically, GenAI can be situated within established SLA frameworks introduced in Chapter 2, including Krashen's (1992) Input Hypothesis, Vygotsky's (1978) sociocultural theory, Swain's (2005) Output Hypothesis, and Task-Based Language Teaching (Ellis, 2017; Long, 1985, 2014; Nunan, 2004; Prabhu, 1987). Together, these perspectives highlight its potential to provide adaptive input, scaffold guided interaction, prompt meaningful output, and generate authentic communicative tasks. These theoretical foundations frame the discussion that follows. This chapter examines how GenAI supports five key areas of TESOL: listening, reading, speaking, writing and intercultural communication. Table 4.1 provides an overview of the core functionalities of GenAI tools that will be explored.

4.2 Theories of SLA and GenAI

GenAI aligns with several established SLA frameworks, many of which were outlined in Chapter 2.5. From an input perspective, it provides adaptive reading passages and personalised listening exercises that reflect Krashen's (1992) principle of comprehensible input at "*i* + *1*." For example, GenAI can generate adaptive reading materials and scaffolded listening tasks that adjust to learners' proficiency (Chen et al., 2022). Its interactive features align with Vygotsky's (1978) sociocultural theory, positioning GenAI as a mediating tool within the Zone of Proximal Development that supports guided interaction and collaborative learning. Chatbots and collaborative writing platforms illustrate how such scaffolding can promote both support and autonomy (Lege et al., 2024). Swain's (2005) Output Hypothesis is also relevant, as learners can produce, test, and refine language through interaction with AI-generated feedback—for instance, revising essay drafts in response to targeted suggestions. Finally, Task-Based Language Teaching (Ellis, 2017; Long, 1985, 2014; Nunan, 2004; Prabhu, 1987) is extended through GenAI's capacity to simulate authentic communicative tasks such as interviews or debates, offering meaningful practice in real-world contexts. While these SLA frameworks provide the theoretical foundation for understanding GenAI in TESOL, its impact also depends on how it is integrated into pedagogical approaches.

Table 4.1 Key functionalities of GenAI tools across language skills

Skill area (section)	GenAI functionalities
Listening (4.4)	• Text-to-speech with adjustable speed and accents • Real-time transcription and error identification • Scenario-based simulations and gamified tasks • Feedback on listening strategies and performance • Exposure to varied accents and speech patterns
Reading (4.5)	• Adaptive text generation and simplification • Vocabulary scaffolding and guided summarisation • AI-generated comprehension tasks and quizzes • Annotation and visualisation tools for complex texts • Tools for critical reading and bias detection
Speaking (4.6)	• Real-time pronunciation and prosody feedback • Role-play, dialogue, and fluency practice • AI avatars and conversational agents • Speech transcription with error tracking • Low-anxiety practice environments
Writing (4.7)	• Adaptive prompts and idea generation • Real-time grammar, style, and vocabulary feedback • Paraphrasing, summarisation, and revision tools • Collaborative writing and peer-review simulations • Support for academic writing and referencing
Intercultural Communication (4.8)	• Simulations of cross-cultural dialogues • Multi-accent speech synthesis for global Englishes • Feedback on pragmatics, politeness, and speech acts • AI-assisted role-plays for cultural reflection • Storytelling and projects with intercultural themes

4.3 Pedagogical Approaches and GenAI

The integration of GenAI into language education aligns with a range of pedagogical approaches, including communicative language teaching, task-based learning, experiential learning, and flipped learning models, each of which emphasises engagement and skill development. By leveraging GenAI, educators can create authentic and context-rich environments that promote communicative competence and meaningful practice opportunities.

For example, in Taiwan, educators used ChatGPT to design content that emphasised key language structures (e.g., prepositions for young learners). These were visually reinforced through text-to-image tools such as Bing Image Creator and PlaygroundAI.com, and then embedded into audio-visual narratives using ClipChamp, where text-to-speech and background music produced immersive digital storybooks. This approach demonstrates how GenAI can support communicative and multimodal learning while adapting to diverse contexts (Yeh, 2024).

Generative AI Chatbots (GACs) are increasingly used to support Task-Based Language Teaching (TBLT) by designing authentic, real-world tasks. Examples include simulated job interviews (Borg et al., 2022; Lee et al., 2024), debate practice (Ejaz & Jamil, 2024), and collaborative storytelling (Cheung & Shi, 2024). By generating dynamic prompts, providing contextualised vocabulary support, and analysing learner responses, GenAI facilitates task-oriented learning environments that foster meaningful language use.

In experiential learning, GenAI enables immersive practice through AI-generated role-play scenarios and multilingual chatbots. Learners can interact with AI personas that mimic real, historical, or fictional characters (Terzić et al., 2023). Virtual exchanges and video chatbots, such as 'Call Annie,' allow learners to engage in authentic conversations with AI avatars, offering immediate and constructive feedback (Wan & Moorhouse, 2024).

GenAI also strengthens flipped learning models, where learners engage with content before class and apply knowledge interactively during lessons. Research indicates that flipped learning outperforms traditional methods in improving English proficiency, knowledge, and skills

(Afzali & Izadpanah, 2021; Vitta & Al-Hoorie, 2023). By combining pre-class GenAI-generated materials with in-class communicative tasks, educators promote active engagement and higher levels of interaction between teachers and students.

Beyond individual learning, GenAI supports collaborative learning environments, enhancing peer interaction, cooperative writing, and community-driven discussions. A study of university EFL learners (Chen, 2024) found that GenAI chatbot-supported collaborative note-taking (AI-CNT) and significantly improved EFL learners' interaction compared to traditional didactic methods, increasing achievement, self-efficacy, and reducing anxiety. Similarly, ChatGPT has been used to support cooperative writing, offering implicit and explicit writing mediation to enhance academic writing (Fathi & Rahimi, 2024). Tools like Google Docs and Gemini provide additional structures for group collaboration (Jinowat et al., 2024), while conversational agents also improve online collaborative writing (OCW), by encouraging opinion sharing, concept explanation, and analysis (Hu et al., 2025). Peer-review platforms, like Reviewriter, further support collaboration, offering synchronous and asynchronous feedback (Su et al., 2023).

Finally, GenAI-driven forums and virtual communities enable students to engage in real-time debates, cross-cultural exchanges, and AI-generated discussions. Case studies show how such environments support storytelling across linguistic backgrounds (Emerson, 2024) and collaborative problem-solving tasks (Richter & Langesee, 2024).

The following section explores in more depth the functionalities of GenAI, examining practical approaches, activities, and case studies that enhance the teaching of specific language skills, beginning with receptive skills before moving to productive and intercultural competencies. Examples of GenAI resources are included, but these are illustrative only, given the rapid pace of technological development.

4.4 GenAI for Teaching Listening Skills

When used thoughtfully, GenAI can enhance a range of listening skills, including comprehension, inference, interactional competence, and metacognitive awareness. A pedagogically grounded workflow can support this integration through five interrelated components (see Fig. 4.1).

First, GenAI can generate adaptive listening materials, tailoring audio passages to learners' proficiency levels and interests, often with built-in glosses and highlighted transcripts that draw attention to key vocabulary. Second, active listening practice can be supported by AI-generated comprehension questions and summarisation tools, which promote deeper engagement with input. Third, listening analysis and feedback allows GenAI to identify problem areas (e.g., missed details, unclear inferences) and provide corrective strategies through annotated transcripts or visual cues. Fourth, learners refine their skills through targeted practice, adjusting audio speed and focusing on prosodic features such as stress, intonation, and connected speech. Finally, AI-enhanced listening

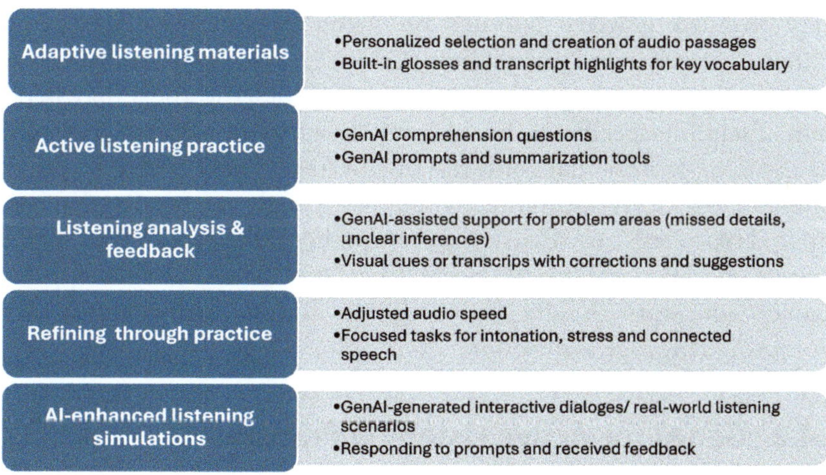

Fig. 4.1 Key components for planning GenAI-integrated listening instruction

simulations can immerse learners in interactive, scenario-based experiences where they respond to prompts, receive feedback, and practice in contexts that mirror authentic communication.

4.4.1 GenAI Adaptive Listening Materials

GenAI enables TESOL educators to create customised listening materials that align with learners' language proficiency levels, age groups, and specific educational objectives. For beginner learners, GenAI tools can generate audio passages characterised by slower speech rates, simplified language, and clear articulation, often supplemented with transcripts or visual supports to enhance understanding. In contrast, intermediate and advanced learners can access more complex, authentic listening resources, such as simulated dialogues, academic lectures, or professional discussions, delivered at natural speech speeds. GenAI systems can dynamically adapt content based on learner performance, for instance, by reducing audio speed or simplifying linguistic structures when comprehension challenges are detected.

To further scaffold listening, GenAI can pre-teach essential vocabulary through glossary pop-ups or warm-up activities. For younger learners, AI-generated interactive narratives that integrate audio and visual elements can foster engagement, while older learners may benefit from discipline-specific audio content designed to simulate real-world academic or professional contexts. In all cases, GenAI is able to provide differentiated, level-appropriate input, effectively supporting Krashen's Input Hypothesis by delivering comprehensible input that slightly exceeds the learner's current proficiency level ($i + 1$). This approach enables educators to efficiently address diverse learner needs while promoting language acquisition.

4.4.2 GenAI for Active Listening Practice

TESOL educators can use GenAI tools to transform listening practice into a more interactive and learner-centred experience using tools such as Duolingo, Babbel or Rosetta Stone. By integrating real-time comprehension questions within audio passages, these tools prompt learners to process and respond to content as they listen. Similarly, using customisable AI tools such as GPT-4 or Google's Speech-to-Text, educators can use these tools to tailor questions to learners' proficiency levels, ranging from simple factual queries (e.g., "What colour is the car?") for young beginners to more complex inferential or summary-based prompts for advanced learners.

After each segment, learners may be asked to summarise content orally or in writing, reinforcing comprehension and retention. Adolescents and adults can use chatbots for follow-up questions that require clarifying or restating information, thus enhancing fluency and active recall. For younger learners, gamified listening tasks, such as puzzles or questions embedded in AI-generated narratives, make practice engaging. Teachers can also assign self-paced activities, allowing students to pause, repeat, and interact with comprehension checks, transforming passive listening into a dynamic, participatory process.

4.4.3 Listening Analysis and Feedback

After completing listening tasks, GenAI tools can help educators provide immediate, detailed analysis of learner performance. For instance, the use of GenAI applications, such as Duolingo Max, ELSA Speak or Google's Read Along, Speakable, etc., can indicate whether difficulties arise from vocabulary gaps, misinterpretation of details, or missed inference cues. Advanced GenAI applications, such as Listenwise Premium and LingQ, can monitor learner progress by various listening skills such as main point, inferencing, vocabulary, etc.

Feedback can be adapted to learner age and level. In younger learners, GenAI might provide positive reinforcement and corrective feedback in simple, encouraging language ("Try listening to that part again"), while older students can receive text-based analysis with direct references to transcript lines they misunderstood. Moreover, GenAI tools such as ChatGPT (with voice mode) allow students to ask follow-up questions, such as "Why was my answer wrong?" or "Can you explain that part again?", facilitating reflection and deeper understanding. This feedback cycle supports both formative assessment and learner autonomy, enabling students to recognise and address weaknesses effectively.

4.4.4 Refining Listening Through Practice

Refining listening skills often requires targeted and focused practice, both of which can be greatly enhanced with GenAI applications. Educators can use GenAI tools that allow learners to replay difficult audio segments with adjustments such as slower speeds or clearer enunciation, offering repeated exposure to challenging content. For lower-proficiency or young learners, GenAI applications such as YouGlish allow listeners to hear words and phrases embedded in authentic contexts and with different accents, asking them to mimic and repeat specific sounds, stress patterns, or intonation features.

Advanced learners benefit from tools such as FluentU, which integrates authentic texts emphasising connected speech, idioms, and collocations. GenAI can also direct attention to discourse markers, transitions, and logical connectors in extended texts, strengthening comprehension of complex spoken discourse. Importantly, learners can set personal listening goals, such as improving lecture comprehension or exposure to different accents, making practice highly individualised and context-specific.

4.4.5 AI-Enhanced Listening Simulations

The final capacity in this workflow involves immersive, AI-enhanced listening simulations that replicate real-world listening environments. TESOL educators can use tools, such as ChatGPT (Voice Mode) or Duolingo Max (GPT-4 Roleplay), that generate interactive dialogues, where students listen to an audio scenario, such as a doctor's consultation or business meeting, and then respond to AI-generated comprehension or inference questions. Young learners can engage in story-based simulations, where GenAI narrates a story and prompts them to identify characters, sequence events, or solve a mystery based on audio clues. Adolescents might participate in simulations that require them to respond to spoken instructions, such as AI-guided interviews, campus tour simulations or emergency response drills in a virtual environment. For adult learners, GenAI can create professional simulations like job interviews or conference calls, helping them practice understanding specialised vocabulary and fast-paced speech. After each simulation, AI-generated feedback addresses comprehension accuracy and responsiveness. These activities consolidate listening comprehension while training learners to process information under pressure, and bridging classroom practice with authentic communicative demands.

4.4.6 Case Studies

Building on the pedagogical potential of GenAI tools for L2 listening instruction, this section turns to an examination of recent studies that address their practical implementation. These case studies provide insights into how GenAI applications align with the pedagogical workflow and examine how they may support the use of adaptive listening materials, active engagement with input, structured feedback, iterative refinement through practice, and AI-enhanced simulations.

In Japan, Dizon (2020) conducted a quasi-experimental study with 37 university-level EFL learners using Amazon's Alexa as an Intelligent Personal Assistant (IPA). Over ten weeks, students in the experimental group engaged in weekly 12-minute sessions of individual interaction with Alexa. Although the study reported significant improvements in speaking proficiency, no measurable gains were found in listening comprehension. Dizon (2023) attributes this to Alexa's limited input recognition, particularly difficulties processing accented speech, and the indirect nature of its feedback. This underscores a broader issue that GenAI tools must provide not only exposure to input but also structured, targeted feedback if they are to effectively enhance listening skills.

A similar study by Hsu et al. (2023) explored Alexa's role in supporting L2 listening and speaking among 40 Taiwanese university students. Participants in the experimental group undertook 45-minute sessions involving both structured and open-ended interactions with

Alexa over six weeks. Although no statistically significant differences in listening comprehension were found when compared to the control group, learners reported increased confidence and reduced anxiety during listening tasks. These affective benefits are noteworthy, suggesting that GenAI may indirectly support listening development by lowering affective filters and sustaining motivation, even if comprehension gains are not immediately visible.

Further exploring IPA use, Yang et al., (2022a, 2022b) examined the impact of Google Assistant on autonomous second language learning (ASLL) among 34 Taiwanese EFL learners. While both experimental groups demonstrated improvement in speaking, only those who received weekly teacher-guided evaluation forms made significantly greater progress. Listening comprehension outcomes, however, did not differ significantly between groups. These findings emphasise the necessity of teacher mediation and scaffolding if GenAI tools are to move beyond surface engagement and meaningfully impact listening comprehension.

In contrast to IPA-based applications, Runge et al. (2024) developed an AI-driven interactive listening simulation designed to assess interactional competence, including turn-taking, adaptation to communicative purposes, and negotiation of social meaning. Using GPT-3 to generate scenario-based dialogues, the task required test-takers to navigate full conversational sequences through response selection. Although the format did not include spoken production, the task effectively measured communicative listening while minimising cognitive load from reading. Importantly, the model retained a human-in-the-loop to monitor and validate AI-generated content, ensuring quality control. Despite limitations, such as variability in dialogue quality and the absence of spoken output, this approach illustrates the potential of GenAI for creating scalable, adaptive, and contextually rich listening simulations.

Taken together, these studies demonstrate both the potential and current limitations of GenAI in L2 listening instruction. While benefits are clear in terms of affective outcomes (e.g. increased confidence and reduced anxiety) and speaking practice, improvements in listening comprehension remain inconsistent. These findings suggest that effective integration of GenAI requires careful integration with pedagogical frameworks that prioritise interactive input, structured feedback, and sustained practice, with teachers playing a central role in guiding and contextualising learners' use of these tools.

4.5 GenAI for Teaching Reading Comprehension

Integrating GenAI into reading instruction requires a structured approach to support the diverse skills involved in reading, from decoding and fluency to comprehension, vocabulary development, and critical analysis. When used purposefully, GenAI can personalise reading materials, adapt texts to different proficiency levels, and provide real-time vocabulary scaffolding to meet learners' diverse needs.

GenAI tools can improve reading comprehension by generating adaptive comprehension questions, summarisation tools, and inference-making exercises that encourage deeper engagement with texts. Additionally, GenAI can support reading fluency and awareness of text structure by providing pronunciation feedback for reading aloud, sentence reordering tasks. Importantly, GenAI applications cater to different age groups, offering interactive phonics stories for young learners, critical reading and analytical tasks for teenagers, and academic and professional reading support for adults. Figure 4.2 outlines the key components of GenAI-supported reading instruction for learners across various proficiency levels.

4.5.1 AI-Generated Adaptive Reading Materials

TESOL educators can use GenAI to personalise reading materials by adjusting text complexity based on students' proficiency levels, age, and interests. GenAI can simplify, reword, or generate texts, ensuring that learners engage with content that challenges them without overwhelming

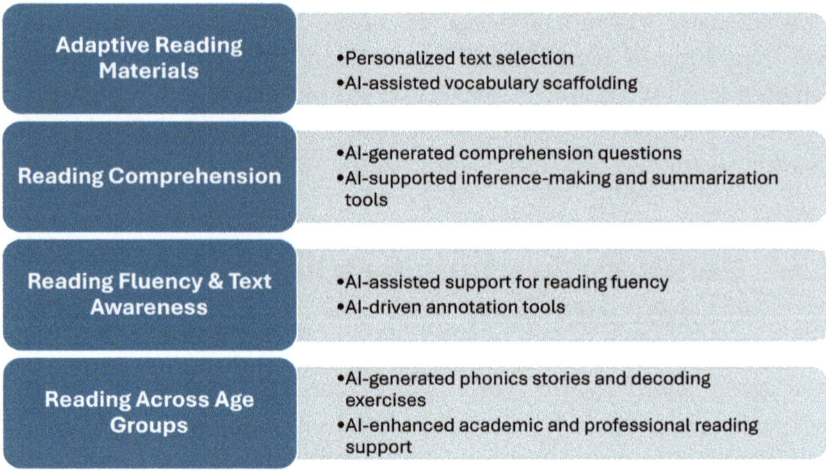

Fig. 4.2 Key components for planning GenAI-integrated reading instruction

comprehension; in other words, it can offer learners comprehensive input (referred to as "$i + 1$").

In addition, GenAI supports vocabulary development by offering real-time scaffolding. Learners can access instant definitions, contextual explanations, and example sentences for unfamiliar words, while teachers can generate interactive word lists and quizzes to reinforce retention. To create a more immersive reading experience, students can engage with AI-powered reading assistants, which provide text summarisation, real-time text adaptations, highlighting key terms, and simplifying advanced passages into more digestible versions.

4.5.2 GenAI for Reading Comprehension and Analysis

Integrating GenAI into reading lessons enables teachers to dynamically adapt comprehension activities to meet student needs. GenAI tools can generate personalised questions that test main-idea identification, inference-making, and critical thinking, adjusting follow-ups based on learners' responses. It can also provide guided reading prompts that encourage prediction, summarisation, and tone analysis, supporting deeper engagement with texts. In addition, TESOL educators can use AI-powered summarisation tools to help students compare their own summaries with AI-generated versions, encouraging reflection, revision, and self-evaluation. GenAI can further scaffold analytical tasks by suggesting text structures for students to examine, enabling them to see how arguments are built, transitions function, and key ideas are emphasised in different genres of writing.

4.5.3 GenAI for Developing Reading Fluency and Text Structure Awareness

To develop reading fluency, TESOL educators can encourage learners to practice reading aloud with AI-assisted pronunciation tools that provide real-time feedback on stress, intonation, and pacing. This allows students to use AI-powered auditory tools to refine their spoken reading skills while improving comprehension. GenAI tools can also improve students' awareness of text structure, helping them analyse how sentences connect to form coherent paragraphs. For example, learners can work with AI-generated sentences to reconstruct jumbled texts and develop better understanding of logical progression and cohesion. Additionally, GenAI-powered annotation tools can help students highlight key ideas, track character development, and analyse rhetorical devices, reinforcing critical reading strategies through interactive engagement.

4.5.4 GenAI for Reading Across Different Age Groups

Age-appropriate integration of GenAI tools ensures reading instruction meets diverse learner needs. For young learners, TESOL educators can integrate GenAI phonics stories that provide interactive, audio-supported reading exercises to build foundational literacy skills. GenAI-powered storytelling platforms allow young readers to explore narratives with highlighted words, embedded comprehension questions, and gamified reading challenges. For teenagers, GenAI can be used to develop critical reading skills through bias detection tasks, persuasive text analysis, and interactive annotation of argumentative essays. GenAI texts designed around teenage interests, such as social media discourse or current events, can engage learners in meaningful ways. For adult learners, GenAI reading tools can assist with academic and professional literacy, offering automated summarisation, citation generation, and document analysis to support research and workplace communication. GenAI reading tools can also help professionals navigate industry-specific texts, interpret legal or technical documents, and improve their ability to read complex materials more efficiently.

4.5.5 Case Studies

Building on the different capabilities of GenAI for supporting reading in the TESOL classroom, recent empirical studies have investigated its use in areas such as reading materials, comprehension, fluency, and awareness of text structure. These studies also highlight how applications vary across age groups. Overall, the findings point to promising outcomes, while also underscoring limitations and the continuing need for teacher mediation of these tools.

Several studies highlight the value of GenAI in adapting texts to learners' proficiency levels. Xin (2024) analysed three EFL teachers' interactions with ChatGPT, finding that it was primarily used for text modification and prompt generation. Teachers emphasised its time-saving benefits and capacity to personalise reading materials. Similarly, Day et al. (2025) tested various LLMs and prompting strategies to simplify 60 informational texts from Grade 12 down to lower grade levels. While the study successfully reduced text complexity, statistical analysis also revealed that different applications and prompting methods struggled to maintain accuracy and keyword integrity at lower reading levels. Nevertheless, the authors propose a generalisable evaluation framework for future text-simplification research.

Another study by Liu and Wang (2024) examined the effects of GenAI tools on critical thinking in English literature classes among 90 EFL learners in China. For an 8-week period, students in an experimental group used a variety of GenAI tools, including ChatGPT 3.5, SummarizBot, Quillionz and Bodoudou, to help them create mind maps, generate and answer questions on a text, create interactive quizzes and participate in debates. Findings showed that the use of these tools significantly improved students' critical analysis skills, suggesting that they can play a crucial role in developing higher-order reading abilities.

Other studies have explored the integration of GenAI technologies in improving reading comprehension. Nguyen et al. (2024) investigated 10 Chinese EFL teachers' perspectives on using Quillionz, an AI-powered platform for generating EFL reading comprehension quizzes. While teachers valued the time-saving aspect, they noted issues with question quality and relevance. Additionally, the quality of AI-generated questions was sometimes perceived as lower than those created by human instructors. In Malaysia, Sudin and Swanto (2024) found that GenAI-personalised texts significantly improved reading comprehension, particularly for lower- and intermediate-level learners. Similarly, Kim (2024) reported that Korean EFL learners using ChatGPT showed improved main-idea identification, outperforming a control group. In the context of independent learning, Liu et al. (2024) examined AI-mediated informal digital learning among 867 Chinese EFL learners, each averaging 50 + hours of autonomous study using GPT-based tools. The study found that AI-supported learning enhanced reading comprehension by providing personalised feedback and adaptive learning paths. Additionally, learners used AI to parse quotes and analyse source texts, improving their ability to interpret and synthesise information effectively.

Recent studies also highlight the potential of GenAI for developing reading fluency. For example, a study by Alazemi (2024) investigated the impact of GenAI-assisted formative assessment on 80 EFL students' reading comprehension development in a Kuwaiti secondary school. The research demonstrated that using Nearpod, an AI interactive platform, teachers were able to generate interactive materials for the experimental group that would test students' reading skills, provide immediate feedback, and significantly improve students' reading fluency. Additionally, Sidwell et al. (2024) examined ChatGPT's potential in generating oral reading fluency (ORF) probes, which are essential for reading assessment, intervention, and progress monitoring. ORF probes measure correct words per minute (WCPM) of reading to help assess fluency. The study highlighted the limited availability of ORF probes and proposed that GenAI can address this gap by creating customisable, grade-specific passages tailored to improving learners' fluency. Another study by Rashid et al. (2024), looking into reading fluency, examined whether Large Language Models (LLMs) like ChatGPT-3.5 could generate educational content with readability features comparable to human-authored texts. Researchers compared 300-word, 8th-grade level passages written by humans and ChatGPT-3.5, analysing reading speed, comprehension, and qualitative factors such as familiarity, interest, and perceived quality. Results showed that ChatGPT-generated passages were read faster and led to better comprehension than human-written texts, though concerns remained about text quality and authenticity.

In relation to read-along technologies, research (Abimanto & Sumarsono, 2024) highlights the effectiveness of the Google Read Along application. Based on a sample of 70 students at a university in Indonesia, divided into a control and experimental group, findings showed that the application significantly improved the pronunciation skills of the experimental group with an average N-Gain score of 65.73%.

Recent research demonstrates the impact of GenAI technologies on teaching reading and vocabulary to young learners in TESOL. Wen et al. (2025) tested ARCHe, a GenAI system that scores student sentences and recommends learning strategies, with 140 Singaporean primary students. Results showed gains in vocabulary and reading performance, with positive learner attitudes. Additionally, Hsu et al. (2024) explored the integration of GenAI image recognition technology with self-regulated learning strategies for English vocabulary development among 47 primary-aged learners. Findings showed that students using GenAI-supported image recognition tools made greater gains in vocabulary acquisition and reading comprehension compared to those relying on traditional optical recognition tools.

Among adolescents, Sudin and Swanto (2024) and Yan et al. (2025) highlighted GenAI's role in improving comprehension and guiding learners through complex visual information, promoting integrated reading skills. Recent research highlights the importance of GenAI for adult English as an Additional Language (EAL) learners. Creely et al. (2025) explored attitudes towards generative AI in EAL education, revealing enthusiasm among adult learners but hesitancy among educators, particularly for beginners. The study emphasises the need for comprehensive professional development and integration of AI literacy in learning programmes for adult migrants and refugees. Similarly, Xu et al. (2022) investigated the effectiveness of web-based text structure instruction for adult EFL learners. Their findings demonstrated significant positive effects on reading comprehension, particularly for higher-order skills like inferential and evaluative comprehension.

Across these studies, three consistent outcomes emerge. First, GenAI enhances comprehension and fluency, with learners producing stronger reading outcomes when GenAI tools provide scaffolding and feedback. Second, GenAI motivates engagement by making reading more interactive and adaptive to individual needs. Finally, while GenAI shows strong potential for vocabulary development and higher-order skills like critical analysis, issues remain with accuracy, cultural appropriateness, and the potential for over-reliance.

4.6 GenAI for Teaching Speaking and Pronunciation

Integrating GenAI into speaking and pronunciation instruction requires a structured approach that maximises its benefits while retaining essential human interaction. When used effectively, GenAI has the potential to improve oral proficiency, pronunciation accuracy, and speaking confidence by providing real-time feedback and interactive practice. Figure 4.3 outlines the key components of GenAI-integrated speaking instruction, with examples of how educators can implement these tools across different proficiency levels.

4.6.1 GenAI Speaking Prompts

Teachers can design structured activities using AI-generated prompts to develop learners' oral proficiency. For pronunciation, tools such as

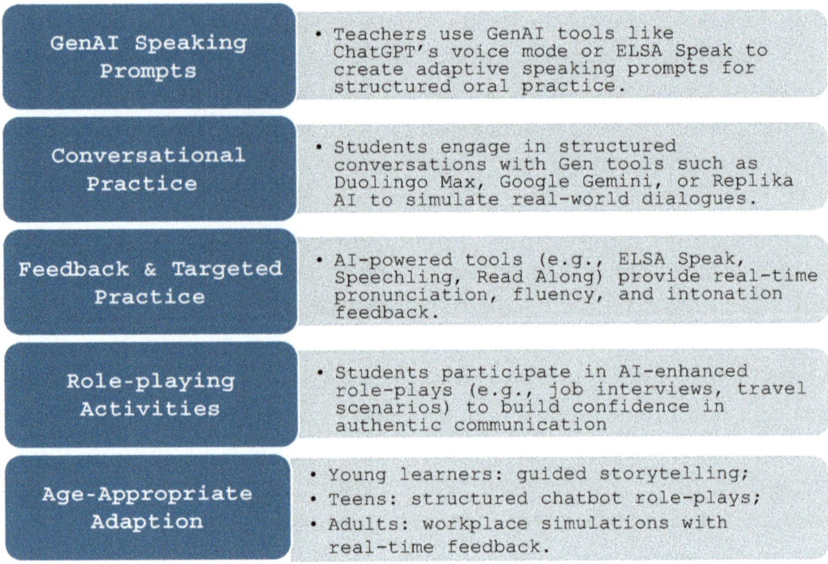

Fig. 4.3 Key components for planning GenAI-integrated speaking instruction

ChatGPT's voice mode or ELSA Speak can generate phoneme-specific drills, enabling students to repeat and refine challenging sounds. For structured speech development, progressive tasks can be scaffolded: in a presentation class, for instance, students might begin with a short prompt such as "Introduce yourself in two sentences," then move to "Give a two-minute summary of your favourite book" and finally attempt a full-length speech.

To reduce speaking anxiety, teachers can use chatbots as virtual conversation partners for role-playing scenarios, such as "You are ordering food at a restaurant. Respond naturally to the waiter's questions." These low-stakes interactions encourage fluency by removing the pressure of peer or teacher evaluation. Teachers can also train students to use GenAI for self-monitoring by asking targeted questions such as, "How can I make my explanation clearer?".

Crucially, teachers should balance AI-assisted speaking activities with peer discussions and live presentations to encourage learners to develop real-world communication skills.

4.6.2 GenAI Conversational Practice

In TESOL classrooms, structured GenAI conversations can support the development of fluency, accuracy, and real-time interaction. Tools such as ChatGPT's voice mode, Duolingo Max, or Google Gemini allow students to simulate authentic dialogues. For instance, in a lesson on travel vocabulary, learners might practice booking a hotel room with a chatbot acting as a receptionist, receiving immediate AI-generated responses before rehearsing the same scenario with a peer.

Additionally, teachers can use tools such as Speak AI to record and transcribe student speech, providing pronunciation feedback and data visualisation that track student progress over time. Independently, students can extend their learning beyond the classroom to practice spontaneous speaking with tools like Replika AI, which mimics human conversation and adapts responses based on learner input. For advanced learners, platforms like Talkpal AI provide topic-based prompts for academic discussions and debates, encouraging critical thinking and spontaneous language use.

By combining AI-assisted conversations with peer interaction and teacher mediation, educators can ensure that GenAI supports communicative competence while maintaining the collaborative and social dimensions of language learning.

4.6.3 GenAI Feedback and Targeted Practice

TESOL educators can use GenAI-powered speech analysis tools to help students refine pronunciation, fluency, and intonation through real-time feedback. In the classroom, teachers can use AI-driven pronunciation software like ELSA Speak, Speechling, and Microsoft's Azure Speech Services to assess students' speech patterns. For instance, during a pronunciation drill, ELSA Speak can analyse learners' stress, rhythm, and articulation, highlighting mispronunciations and providing corrective feedback.

For younger learners, tools like Google's Read Along offer phonics-based correction by evaluating spoken words and reinforcing sound–letter correspondences. Interviews with educators also report success with Microsoft 365 Reading Progress, which provides automated analysis of student recordings. As one teacher from Cyprus explained:

> Quotation 5: "Also, with Microsoft 365, I use tools like Reading Progress, which analyses student recordings. It tells them if they've missed a word, pronounced something wrong, or skipped something. I use that a lot in class." (T10, Cyprus)

In group activities, apps such as Say It: English Pronunciation enable learners to compare their speech with native-speaker models and make phonetic adjustments based on AI recommendations. Independent learners can also benefit from Speak AI, which provides real-time analysis and personalised feedback to support self-directed practice. Advanced learners preparing for job interviews or exams like IELTS or TOEFL can benefit from using tools such as SmallTalk2Me, which evaluates oral responses based on coherence, accuracy, and pronunciation. Together, these AI-driven applications deliver personalised, adaptive feedback that complements classroom instruction, empowers learners to practice autonomously, and reinforces pronunciation development.

At the same time, educators should remain cautious: many AI pronunciation tools prioritise "standard" English accents, which may unintentionally underrepresent the diversity of global English varieties. As such, teachers play a crucial role in contextualising feedback and ensuring learners develop confidence in using English across varied accents and communication contexts.

4.6.4 GenAI Role-Playing Activities

Teachers can make use of GenAI-enhanced role-playing activities to help students practice real-world communication skills by simulating authentic social and professional interactions. In the classroom, teachers can use ChatGPT's role-play mode for guided dialogues such as booking a hotel room, handling a job interview, or making a complaint in a store.

Similarly, platforms like Duolingo Max (powered by GPT-4 Roleplay) enable learners to converse with AI-generated characters across travel, work, and daily life scenarios, with responses adapting dynamically to student input.

Teachers can also integrate immersive, story-driven platforms, such as Google Gemini or AI Dungeon, which encourage learners to sustain conversations across multiple turns and practice spontaneity in dialogue. These activities can be scaffolded through AI-mediated group role-plays, where students first interact with GenAI before practicing with peers, ensuring they gain confidence prior to live discussions.

Similarly, for independent learning, students can use tools such as SmallTalk2Me, which provides AI-driven mock interviews and professional communication role-plays, helping learners prepare for IELTS Speaking exams or workplace interactions. Such AI-enhanced role-playing tools offer low-pressure, adaptive speaking practice and encourage self-directed speaking development.

At the same time, teachers remain central in framing these role-playing activities to ensure they are pedagogically purposeful, culturally relevant, and aligned with learning objectives.

4.6.5 GenAI-Assisted Speaking Across Different Age Groups

In TESOL instruction, GenAI-assisted speaking activities can be adapted to different age groups, ensuring age-appropriate engagement and skill development.

For young learners, teachers can use AI-driven storytelling apps like Google's Read Along, where students listen to AI-generated stories and practice repeating or responding to comprehension questions aloud. These tools provide phonics-based pronunciation support and interactive speaking exercises that make language learning fun.

For teenagers, teachers can integrate GenAI chatbots like ChatGPT or Duolingo Max Roleplay to create real-world conversational scenarios, such as ordering food, giving directions, or discussing social issues.

Students can first practice with GenAI, then participate in peer role-plays, reinforcing fluency and confidence.

For adult learners, GenAI business communication tools like SmallTalk2Me or VirtualSpeech can help students practice workplace interactions, such as delivering presentations, negotiating deals, or preparing for job interviews. These tools allow adults to simulate professional dialogues, receiving instant feedback on pronunciation, tone, and coherence.

By aligning GenAI-assisted speaking activities with learners' developmental stages, educators can maximise engagement and ensure that practice remains meaningful, relevant, and pedagogically appropriate.

4.6.6 Case Studies

Studies in TESOL are increasingly documenting how GenAI-assisted tools support learners' speaking proficiency, motivation, and confidence across diverse contexts.

GenAI is also being integrated into fluency-building and conversational practice, where a growing body of research highlights its potential to improve speaking competence, reduce anxiety, and increase learner engagement. For example, Qiao and Zhao (2023) compared AI-generated speaking practice via Duolingo's AI features with peer-led practice among 93 Chinese college EFL students. Using IELTS speaking band criteria, the AI group showed significant post-test gains in fluency, coherence, vocabulary, and pronunciation. Similarly, Han (2020) studied 44 middle school EFL learners using a voice-based chatbot (Echodot) for conversational prompts. Results showed improved speaking competence and reduced anxiety, with learners reporting positive attitudes towards AI practice. Yang et al. (2022a, 2022b) developed Ellie, a task-based AI chatbot for 314 Korean elementary school students, which significantly increased speaking turns (~9.6 per session) and task completion (88%). Students valued the conversational practice but noted occasional misunderstandings. In higher education, Qassrawi et al. (2024) found that 66 EFL undergraduates using Google Assistant across a semester made notable improvements in fluency and interactive communication, while also reporting enjoyment in self-directed practice.

Another function of GenAI tools relates to their capacity to provide feedback and pronunciation support. Dennis (2024) investigated an AI speech recognition programme, Speechling, for pronunciation training. In the study, 25 Thai EFL learners were trained to use the tool and were then given a pre and post-test designed to measure their pronunciation proficiency. The study found significant improvements in learners' pronunciation accuracy and overall speaking skills after the AI-assisted training. Mean speaking scores rose substantially (e.g. from 3.28 to 7.12 out of 20 on one rating scale), and 88% of students reported the GenAI feedback was effective in improving their pronunciation. Similarly, Hoang et al. (2023) introduced Mission Fluent, an AI pronunciation chatbot, to 60 Vietnamese vocational college students. The chatbot group outperformed a non-AI control group, with students appreciating real-time error detection. Guan et al. (2024) compared two self-study groups of 47 Chinese undergraduates, one with one group interacting with an IELTS teacher and the other with the AI interpreter Lucy. Both groups improved, but the AI-supported learners demonstrated notable gains in oral proficiency, showing the potential of GenAI to complement traditional instruction. Overall, these studies demonstrate that GenAI pronunciation tools can significantly enhance oral proficiency and accuracy.

Other research shows that GenAI tools such as chatbots can serve as roleplay interlocutors, supporting simulated real-world conversations. For example, Sim et al. (2025) examined 40 Korean university EFL learners (aged 18–21) in a task-based pragmatics study and found that ChatGPT roleplays facilitated the practice of speech acts such as requests and refusals, with learners reporting that the interactions felt authentic and useful for real-life communication. Similarly, Lee and Davis (2024) studied 89 Korean university students using AI avatars (SoulMachines) in role-play scenarios such as interviews and travel dialogues. Participants reported increased confidence, motivation, and reduced anxiety compared to traditional classes. Additionally, a study by Kang (2022) compared the effects of interacting with two different interlocutors—an artificial intelligence (AI) avatar and a native speaker (NS) of English—on ESL learners' speaking ability and affective outcomes. The study, involving 61 US college-level ESL students, found that practice with AI avatars led to significant improvements in accuracy, fluency, coherence, and interaction, particularly among lower-proficiency learners. In addition, AI avatars helped lower learners' anxiety and increase motivation, highlighting their potential for providing stress-free, adaptive speaking practice.

These case studies collectively show that GenAI strengthens speaking instruction in TESOL by improving fluency, pronunciation, and confidence. AI-generated prompts encourage low-stakes practice, feedback tools provide personalised error correction, and role-play platforms simulate authentic communication. However, while GenAI is a valuable pedagogical tool, it cannot replace human instruction. Over-reliance on GenAI may limit learners' ability to independently self-correct, and AI-generated interactions may lack cultural context requiring teacher guidance. Furthermore, AI tools vary in accuracy, and errors may reinforce incorrect usage if not monitored. As such, GenAI should be implemented strategically, with teachers ensuring that it complements rather than replaces authentic communication and human interaction.

4.7 GenAI for Teaching Writing Skills

Effectively integrating GenAI into writing classrooms requires carefully planned workflows that complement, rather than replace, human instruction. Therefore, the aim for TESOL educators is to use GenAI as a supportive tool across the stages of the writing process. Figure 4.4 outlines an example of a research-informed workflow illustrating how TESOL educators can possibly integrate GenAI while maintaining pedagogical control.

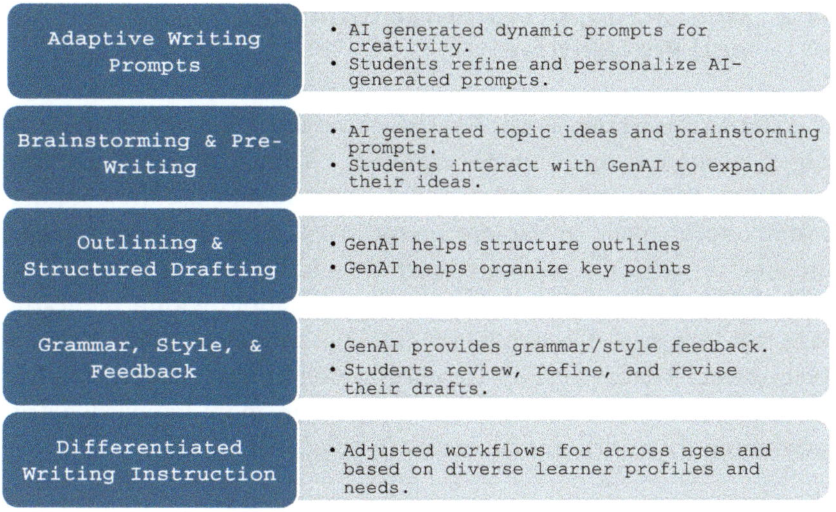

Fig. 4.4 Key components for planning GenAI-integrated writing instruction

4.7.1 Adaptive AI-Generated Prompts to Foster Creativity

Teachers can use GenAI to generate prompts tailored to learners' proficiency levels, interests, and objectives. Research shows that AI-generated prompts can stimulate motivation and idea generation while adapting task complexity for different learners (Wang & Dang, 2024). This was also reflected in classroom practice, with one teacher commenting in the survey: "For a writing unit, I utilised an AI tool to create tailored prompts based on each student's proficiency level and interests" (Survey participant). Such examples illustrate how GenAI supports engagement and differentiation, though teacher supervision remains essential to ensure that prompts align with curriculum requirements and age-appropriate content.

4.7.2 GenAI-Supported Brainstorming and Pre-Writing

At the brainstorming stage, GenAI can pose open-ended questions, suggest scenarios, or provide examples, helping students overcome 'writer's block' and expand their ideas. Learners may use these inputs to create concept maps or explore perspectives, while teachers encourage students to critically evaluate outputs rather than accepting them passively. In this way GenAI functions as a scaffold within the learner's Zone of Proximal Development (ZPD), consistent with Vygotsky's Sociocultural Theory (1978). Recent research further supports this view, showing that students using GenAI engage in more knowledge-driven questioning than with human tutors (Cheng et al., 2025).

4.7.3 GenAI-Assisted Outlining and Drafting

Once ideas are developed, GenAI can assist in generating outlines, grouping ideas, and suggesting logical structures for essays or narratives. During drafting, students compose their own work while consulting GenAI for phrasing or elaboration when needed, with teachers guiding students to preserve authenticity and avoid over-reliance. In this way, the first draft remains student-owned but benefits from GenAI's scaffolding.

4.7.4 AI-Based Grammar, Style, and Feedback Mechanisms

During revision, AI-powered tools provide instant feedback on grammar, style, and clarity, with detailed explanations and alternatives (Kurt & Kurt, 2024). Beyond grammar, GenAI supports style and coherence, allowing students to ask follow-up questions like, "Why is this unclear?" or "How can I rephrase this formally?" This interactive process fosters reflection and deeper learning (Song & Song, 2023). Teachers should train students to critically evaluate GenAI feedback by making sure that revisions genuinely improve the text, rather than create superficial corrections.

4.7.5 Differentiated AI-Assisted Writing Instruction Across Age Groups

Effective GenAI integration in TESOL requires age-appropriate approaches. Young learners need guided use, with teachers facilitating whole-class brainstorming or vocabulary games. For instance, an AI-generated prompt for children might involve cartoon characters, with young learners drawing a picture and writing a few sentences, with the GenAI suggesting one additional detail to scaffold emergent writing, such as prompting a child to describe a character's feelings.

Adolescents, with greater language proficiency, can use GenAI more independently for brainstorming and feedback. They might self-edit drafts with AI grammar checkers, with teachers reviewing revisions to build accountability and digital literacy. Educators must stress ethical AI use, ensuring students critically evaluate AI-generated suggestions rather than relying on them uncritically.

Adult learners, including university students and professionals, can engage with AI as a peer-like tool for writing refinement. They may use GenAI to improve business emails or research summaries, then discuss AI feedback in class. This demographic benefits from GenAI's ability to provide immediate, on-demand assistance given their busy schedules; it enables practice and improvement outside class time with less teacher dependency (Song & Song, 2023).

Across all age groups, GenAI should enhance, not replace, human instruction. Teachers remain responsible for setting goals, encouraging discussions, and ensuring academic integrity. Differentiated workflows allow GenAI to be heavily moderated for children, skill-building for teens, and productivity-enhancing for adults, making it a versatile support tool for teaching writing.

4.7.6 Case Studies

Research in TESOL is increasingly documenting the impact of GenAI-assisted writing instruction across various classroom settings. Studies show gains in writing proficiency, engagement, and self-efficacy when

GenAI is effectively integrated. Below are several key case studies illustrating these findings.

Research in higher education shows GenAI tools enhance academic writing. A quasi-experimental study by Hwang et al. (2023) in Taiwan found that EFL students using AI feedback significantly outperformed those relying solely on teacher feedback. GenAI's personalised, 24/7 assistance helped students refine essays, improving clarity and organisation. Similarly, Chang et al. (2021) reported that students in China using AI grammar checkers (e.g., Grammarly) produced higher-quality writing, reinforcing GenAI's role in improving accuracy and coherence. In Indonesia, Utami et al. (2023) found that AI not only improved writing quality but also boosted engagement and motivation. Students were more involved in revising, likely due to GenAI making the process more interactive and less isolating. Collectively, these findings suggest that, with proper guidance, GenAI can effectively support EFL writing instruction in higher education.

Research shows GenAI benefits younger EFL learners by improving writing skills, motivation, and confidence. Song and Song (2023) found that Chinese high school students using GenAI feedback wrote more accurate and complex sentences while also experiencing a boost in self-efficacy. AI's instant support reduced anxiety, encouraging students to write more freely. Similarly, Nazari et al. (2021) studied Iranian high school learners and found that those using AI for drafting and revision outperformed a non-AI group in writing. Teachers noted higher engagement, as students actively revised and enjoyed the process. These studies highlight how GenAI's immediacy and interactivity can make writing less daunting and more motivating for adolescents.

In multilingual classrooms, GenAI tools help differentiate support. Li et al. (2023) studied an afterschool programme for low-income Chinese language learners, where ChatGPT acted as a writing tutor by adjusting input complexity to individual proficiency levels. Over time, students showed notable improvements in sentence structure and vocabulary. While research on K-12 learners is still in early stages, these cases suggest GenAI can be successfully integrated with younger learners, provided content is carefully moderated and tasks are age-appropriate.

Beyond academic writing, GenAI has been explored in creative and professional domains. Ippolito et al. (2022) studied Wordcraft, an AI-powered text editor, showing that it helped writers overcome writer's block by generating alternative storylines and prompts, such as "What happens next?" Results showed that it boosted creative output, helping writers explore diverse storylines and maintain momentum when writing. While these were proficient writers rather than students, the insight translates to the classroom. GenAI can act as a creative partner, encouraging learners to experiment with language and ideas in ways they might not alone. In classroom contexts, Woo et al. (2025) explored GenAI-assisted collaborative story writing with secondary EFL students. Students used ChatGPT to generate sentences for their stories, primarily to overcome writer's block and develop their stories. The study found a positive correlation between academic achievement and GenAI use. However, it is noteworthy that students from lower-achieving schools often struggled to use GenAI creatively, perhaps due to lack of knowledge of AI and/or English, often resulting in incomplete drafts. Overall, the findings highlight the importance of teacher guidance in helping students effectively construct prompts for GenAI.

Another emerging area is GenAI-supported peer review. McGuire et al. (2024) studied how graduate students used ChatGPT to simulate peer review of research papers. Students used structured prompts requesting AI feedback on key sections, including introduction clarity, research objectives, theoretical alignment, findings, practical implications, and APA formatting. Findings showed how GenAI provided detailed, diplomatic feedback, helping students refine their writing and analytical skills. Students reported that this practice not only improved their drafts but also enhanced their ability to offer critique in future work, suggesting a broader role for GenAI in developing evaluative and metacognitive skills.

Across these case studies, three consistent findings emerge. First, GenAI integration enhances writing proficiency, enabling learners to produce more accurate, complex, and coherent texts. Second, it increases engagement and motivation by making writing feel more interactive and less solitary. Third, GenAI contributes to self-efficacy, providing learners with a "safety net" that reduces anxiety and encourages practice. That said, researchers also caution that the use of GenAI requires clear guidelines: students and teachers must be aware of the potential pitfalls (such as over-reliance on AI, or ethical issues like plagiarism). Furthermore, while AI-generated collaborative writing and peer review are promising, they work best when integrated with human interaction, not as a replacement.

4.8 GenAI in Teaching Intercultural Communication Skills

When applied strategically, GenAI tools can enhance the teaching of intercultural communication (IC) in TESOL by creating dynamic, context-sensitive, and age-appropriate learning environments. Their integration can be organised around three core areas: AI-enabled intercultural communication training, exposure to global English varieties, and age-differentiated intercultural learning.

The process often begins with AI-generated cultural scenarios and simulated dialogues, which immerse learners in diverse, contextually rich situations that demand culturally appropriate responses. These interactions can be tailored to reflect authentic social practices such as greetings, requests, or apologies across different cultures, helping learners understand implicit norms, politeness strategies, and speech acts in cross-cultural communication.

Complementing this, learners benefit from exposure to global English varieties, with GenAI offering access to multiple English dialects and accents, encouraging listening flexibility and sociolinguistic awareness. This exposure supports AI-enhanced negotiation tasks, where learners practice managing turn-taking, indirectness, or conflict resolution across cultural boundaries. Such simulations not only build linguistic skills but also cultivate intercultural sensitivity and adaptability.

These components can be tailored to different learner age groups. For young learners, AI-assisted cultural storytelling can introduce global themes through interactive narratives, fostering early intercultural awareness in accessible and engaging ways. For teenagers, GenAI can support

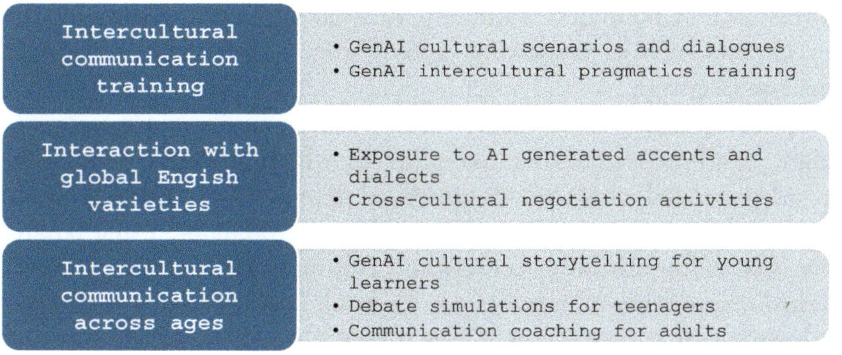

Fig. 4.5 Key components for planning GenAI-integrated intercultural communication instruction

cross-cultural debate simulations and collaborative projects, encouraging perspective-taking, argumentation, and critical reflection on cultural norms. For adult learners, GenAI applications can provide business-oriented coaching, such as role-play scenarios involving workplace norms, email tone, or culturally sensitive negotiation practices. These experiences align with the professional and academic needs of adult TESOL learners while promoting intercultural competence. Figure 4.5 illustrates these core components and how GenAI can be applied to support intercultural communication development across TESOL contexts and learner profiles.

4.8.1 GenAI for IC Communication Training

GenAI tools offer significant potential for the teaching of intercultural pragmatics by enabling learners to engage with simulated dialogues grounded in culturally specific contexts. Platforms such as ChatGPT or character-based dialogue generators (e.g., Character.AI or Gemini) can produce role-play scenarios that reflect endless possible real-world intercultural encounters, such as workplace etiquette in Germany, small talk in Japan, expressing disagreement in Korea, or gift-giving in Arab cultures. Such scenarios can provide a foundation for pragmatic instruction, helping learners understand how culture shapes communicative norms such as politeness, formality, turn-taking, and the ways in which speech acts such as requesting, apologising, or refusing, are expressed through language.

For intermediate or advanced adult learners, an AI-supported activity might involve intercultural role-plays in which students interact with an AI-generated character designed to represent a culturally specific persona. The learners' task is to complete the exchange using language that is both linguistically accurate and culturally appropriate. Afterward, GenAI can provide metapragmatic feedback (e.g., noting over-directness or insufficient politeness), which is then discussed in peer groups under teacher guidance. This mirrors Ishihara and Cohen's (2021) model of explicit pragmatic instruction, which emphasises noticing, reflection, and consciousness-raising.

For lower-level or younger learners, educators can generate AI story scaffolds which can introduce pragmatic norms in simpler terms. For instance, a child-friendly chatbot (e.g. ChatGPT with custom instructions, StoryWizard.ai or Book Creator) could guide learners through a story where characters solve misunderstandings caused by different greeting customs. Learners might then write alternative endings to show improved cultural understanding. In both contexts, teacher mediation is crucial to ensure that learners recognise cultural variation and avoid overgeneralised stereotypes, an issue commonly associated with AI-generated cultural representations (Godwin-Jones, 2024a).

4.8.2 GenAI Interaction with Global English Varieties

Exposure to global English varieties is vital in preparing learners for authentic intercultural communication, particularly in international academic, business, or social settings where non-native varieties dominate. For advanced secondary or adult learners, one possible activity is a GenAI-mediated negotiation simulation in which teams represent different cultural stakeholders (e.g., a German engineering firm, a Brazilian distributor, a Chinese supplier, etc.). Each team interacts with an AI character embodying a distinct negotiation style, such as high-context indirectness or low-context explicitness, and which require learners to adapt their tone, sequencing, and politeness strategies.

GenAI models trained on diverse corpora can simulate a range of dialects and accents, providing learners with realistic input, extending beyond standard RP varieties. Tools such as Speechling, Amazon Polly, and SpeechGen.io can model Indian, South African, or Filipino English, while ElevenLabs can approximate regional UK accents (e.g., Geordie, Cockney, Scouse) when provided with input samples. Such resources allow learners to practice listening to diverse varieties of English, respond in real-time, and reflect on how accent influences comprehension. Teachers might then prompt reflection: "What assumptions did you make about this speaker? How did the accent affect your understanding?" Such reflection tasks promote critical intercultural awareness, as advocated by Byram (1997), and may help deconstruct linguistic prejudice.

4.8.3 GenAI for Intercultural Communication Across Age Groups

Differentiating intercultural communication tasks by age group is critical to ensuring that learning is developmentally appropriate and meaningful. GenAI tools allow educators to customise content complexity, tone, and cultural framing to suit diverse learner profiles, from early learners to professionals. For young learners, GenAI-supported cultural storytelling (using tools such as Book Creator, StoryWizard.ai) can introduce intercultural awareness through simple, interactive narratives. Stories might feature children from different cultural backgrounds navigating shared experiences (e.g., first day at school, holiday traditions). Learners can identify cultural similarities and differences, draw illustrations of scenes, or role-play the dialogue. Such tasks build empathy, perspective-taking, and vocabulary, which are all skills shown to be interrelated in early language learning (Emen & Aslan, 2019).

For teenagers, GenAI facilitates cross-cultural debate simulations on culturally relevant issues (e.g., "Should school uniforms be mandatory?" or "What makes a good apology?"). By presenting culturally diverse perspectives, GenAI tools challenge learners to consider how values influence communication styles. This allows learners to critically analyse how cultural background influences opinions, reasoning, and communication styles. This not only enhances argumentative discourse skills but also fosters awareness of how values influence communication. Educators can design activities in which students use AI research assistants to gather culturally diverse perspectives, participate in structured debates, and reflect on AI-generated feedback that highlights rhetorical strategies, tone, and cultural appropriateness.

For adult learners who are preparing for professional environments, GenAI resources can simulate common workplace interactions such as writing polite follow-up emails, managing miscommunications, or participating in international team meetings. Educators can present learners with AI-generated business dilemmas and guide them in crafting appropriate responses through email, chat, or spoken dialogue, allowing for targeted instruction in intercultural business communication. GenAI platforms can provide feedback on tone appropriateness, clarity, and cultural fit by aligning with established intercultural business communication models. Particularly, Hofstede's (2001) Cultural Dimensions Theory offers a framework for understanding how cultural values influence communication styles, including aspects like power distance and individualism versus collectivism. For example, students might role-play how a manager delivers feedback in a high power-distance culture (e.g., Malaysia) versus a low power-distance culture (e.g., Denmark), encouraging them to reflect on tone and levels of formality and directness.

4.8.4 Case Studies

Empirical research supports the use of AI-driven tools in facilitating intercultural pragmatics instruction through authentic role-play and metapragmatic feedback. Dai et al. (2025) outline the integration of GenAI into a university-level English language programme in Japan through the TEAI (Teaching English with AI) project. This design-based initiative centres on the use of AI-generated intercultural scenarios to simulate professional clinical communication. Example scenarios included interactions with a Vietnamese construction worker with a rib injury, a retired Macedonian teacher presenting with a chest infection, and a young Burmese pregnant woman with limited English proficiency. These AI-generated characters were developed to reflect culturally distinct communication styles in healthcare, enabling learners to practice delivering sensitive information, managing communicative misunderstandings, and applying culturally appropriate politeness strategies. Due to institutional resource constraints, such as the inability to hire professional actors, the use of GenAI offered a scalable and accessible alternative. Following each interaction, learners completed reflective questionnaires designed to elicit responses across behavioural, cognitive, and social dimensions of the communicative experience. Although the study does not present formal empirical data or a defined participant sample, it provides practice-based insights that demonstrate how GenAI can facilitate the development of pragmatic awareness through contextualised, culturally responsive simulations. These findings align with Ishihara and Cohen's (2021) model of pragmatic instruction, which emphasises noticing, reflection, and consciousness-raising as key to intercultural communicative competence. However, while Dai et al. (2025) offer a valuable pedagogical model, the study is limited by its lack of empirical validation and serves only as a proof-of-concept rather than a fully validated instructional model.

Godwin-Jones (2024b) expands on this as he notes that cultural bias in training data often reflects Western, industrialised, male-oriented norms that can result in culturally inappropriate outputs. For example, Naous et al. (2023), in testing LLM completions in culturally sensitive scenarios, found that one model recommended alcohol consumption immediately after Islamic prayer, a response that not only demonstrates cultural insensitivity but also underscores the limitations of GenAI training data in capturing diverse sociocultural norms.

A growing body of research on AI-powered text-to-speech (TTS) and speech recognition tools highlights both the potential and the challenges of applying GenAI to intercultural pragmatics. Amin (2024) found that learners using AI-powered text-to-speech (TTS) applications reported improved awareness of intonation, politeness markers, and culturally sensitive phrasing. Similarly, Dennis (2024) observed that

AI speech recognition tools enhanced learners' confidence in spoken interactions by providing real-time feedback on appropriateness and fluency, although the study focused more on affective outcomes than on nuanced pragmatic development. Meanwhile, Badlani et al. (2023) introduced a sophisticated multi-accented TTS model capable of generating speech that simulates different speaker identities, offering potential for customised intercultural roleplay. However, this tool has yet to undergo classroom-based validation with language learners.

Collectively, these studies suggest that GenAI technologies may support the development of intercultural pragmatics, particularly when used to simulate diverse interactional norms and highlight cultural variation in speech acts, politeness strategies, or turn-taking. Yet significant limitations remain: few studies measure learners' ability to transfer pragmatic skills from AI-mediated tasks to authentic contexts, and most rely on scripted exchanges rather than dynamic, co-constructed discourse. Without teacher mediation, there is also a risk that learners may misinterpret AI-generated input or reinforce essentialist views of culture.

Another area currently being explored for its potential to develop intercultural competence among language learners is that of GenAI storytelling tools. It is already shown that using digital storytelling tools to support language expression and identify exploration can positively influence learners' attitudes towards their own cultural heritage (Liang et al., 2024). Building on this, Cheung and Shi (2024) explored how undergraduate students in Hong Kong collaborated with asylum-seeking children to co-create digital stories in both written and podcast formats. While GenAI tools were employed to assist in the storytelling process, students maintained critical engagement, ensuring the narratives authentically represented the children's experiences. The study found that this approach not only enhanced students' creative capacities but also promoted linguistic, digital, and cultural awareness, offering a meaningful platform for interaction between ESL learners and culturally diverse communities. However, the researchers also noted that GenAI often reproduced narratives rooted in Western cultural norms, misaligning with the children's realities. The study therefore emphasised the crucial role of the teacher in adapting and critically filtering AI-generated content to ensure culturally relevant and ethical storytelling practices.

The opportunities and risks of GenAI storytelling are highlighted in a study by Zheng and Stewart (2024). The study, conducted at a university in China, asked EFL students to engage with ChatGPT-generated moral dilemma stories as part of a classroom-based intervention designed to foster intercultural awareness. The Chinese context is significant, as it allowed learners from a collectivist cultural background to critically engage with narratives that often reflect Western, individualist value systems. One such moral dilemma involved a man who considered giving up a high-paying job to pursue his passion for music while also taking care of his ageing parents. The GenAI version framed the dilemma around personal fulfilment and career autonomy, implicitly prioritising individual aspiration over family obligation. In contrast, students highlighted the importance of filial piety and social responsibility, proposing alternative versions of the story that emphasised compromise, shared caregiving, or culturally appropriate decision-making strategies. This reframing process helped students recognise how moral reasoning is shaped by cultural norms and how such values are embedded in language use. While the activity effectively promoted intercultural reflection and metapragmatic awareness, the authors noted limitations in ChatGPT's tendency to reproduce WEIRD (Western, Educated, Industrialised, Rich, and Democratic) perspectives. Without explicit teacher mediation, these cultural assumptions risk being accepted uncritically. So, while GenAI storytelling can serve as a powerful tool for developing intercultural competence, the study demonstrates that it requires thoughtful implementation, teaching learners how to navigate and critique the cultural narratives that GenAI tools reproduce.

As previously discussed, the study by Dai et al. (2025) offers a convincing example of how GenAI can be applied to support intercultural competence among adult EFL learners, particularly in professional communication contexts. The researchers developed AI-mediated scenarios that simulate culturally diverse workplace interactions, enabling learners to practice pragmatic strategies such as tone adaptation, clarification, and culturally sensitive explanations. One such scenario involved a healthcare professional communicating with a Vietnamese factory worker with a rib injury and required the learner to adapt their language for clarity while also navigating cultural expectations related to authority, politeness, and patient–provider relationships. This approach highlights GenAI's potential to generate authentic, context-rich dialogues that reflect real-world intercultural challenges faced by adults in professions. However, the study raises concerns mentioned in earlier research Zheng and Stewart (2024), regarding the dominance of WEIRD (Western, Educated, Industrialised, Rich, and Democratic) cultural norms in AI-generated content. This further highlights that while GenAI can efficiently generate diverse scenarios, it may still reproduce cultural stereotypes or fail to fully capture the dynamic and affective aspects of intercultural encounters. As such, the researchers warn against uncritical reliance on AI outputs and stress the importance of teacher mediation to ensure that learning materials are both accurate and culturally responsive.

4.9 Implementation Challenges and Considerations

In response to the pedagogical and infrastructural challenges associated with GenAI integration, several European initiatives are actively working to support educators and institutions. The European Union (EU) is advancing GenAI in language education through projects that prioritise transparency, accessibility, and inclusivity. One key initiative is the OpenEuroLLM project, funded with €20.6 million from the Digital Europe Programme, which seeks to develop open-source Large Language Models (LLMs) for all EU languages, ensuring linguistic diversity and equitable access (European Commission, 2025, February 3).

Complementary projects address different aspects of implementation. For instance, the Artificial Intelligence and English Language Teaching: Preparing for the Future project (Edmett et al., 2024) investigates AI's pedagogical impact on TESOL, while the (Em)powered by AI initiative (Media & Learning Association, 2024) focuses on creating adaptive and accessible teaching materials. At the tertiary level, the ADMIT project (Erasmus+, 2024) examines frameworks for GenAI integration in higher education, and the 'Teaching in the AI Age' course (ITC International, 2024) provides targeted professional training on the ethical and effective use of AI in language classrooms.

Together, these initiatives demonstrate the EU's commitment to addressing the challenges of GenAI adoption by promoting pedagogically sound, ethically grounded, and inclusive practices that are accessible across diverse educational contexts.

Despite these initiatives, several systemic barriers continue to limit effective GenAI implementation. In this study, many educators highlighted a lack of professional development focused specifically on GenAI literacy, including how to evaluate AI outputs, align them with curricular goals, and safeguard academic integrity. Institutions therefore need sustained, context-sensitive training to build teacher confidence and technical competence, and while initiatives such as 'Teaching in the AI Age' (ITC International, 2024) offer promising support, their reach remains limited.

Institutional policy and governance form a second area of challenge. Universities and schools must develop coherent policies on data management, authorship, and the responsible use of AI-generated materials. The ADMIT project provides a foundation for such frameworks, yet adoption across institutions remains uneven, particularly in institutions with limited administrative capacity. Without clear governance structures, uncertainty about accountability and quality assurance can inhibit experimentation with new AI-based pedagogies. The broader ethical implications of these governance challenges are examined in Chapter 5.

Chapter 5 also examines a third challenge concerning equity of access. Differences in infrastructure, funding, and linguistic representation create disparities in who benefits from GenAI. Open-access projects such as OpenEuroLLM aim to address these gaps by promoting linguistic diversity and open availability, but their long-term viability will depend on sustained collaboration among policymakers, researchers, and developers.

Curricular alignment and institutional readiness also determine the pace of GenAI adoption. Many language programmes lack the flexibility to integrate emerging technologies quickly, especially where accreditation standards and assessment systems remain tied to pre-AI models of learning. Updating these frameworks requires both leadership commitment and evidence from classroom-based research on the pedagogical value of GenAI tools. The implications of these issues for teacher education and professional development are explored further in Chapter 6.

All in all, these initiatives illustrate both the promise and the limitations of current efforts. The European projects outlined above offer useful models of coordinated action, showing how large-scale, multilingual initiatives can support responsible GenAI innovation. At the same time, they highlight that implementation in TESOL is as much an organisational and policy challenge as a technological one. Sustainable adoption will depend on connecting teacher training with infrastructure and clear governance. These structural considerations also provide a foundation for the ethical issues examined in the next chapter.

4.10 Conclusion

This chapter examined the practical applications of GenAI in TESOL, demonstrating its potential to enhance language teaching and learning across multiple domains. GenAI supports personalised instruction, provides immediate feedback, and offers scalable solutions for diverse learner groups, from young children to adult professionals. The integration of GenAI aligns with established theories of second language acquisition and supports various pedagogical approaches, including task-based, communicative, experiential, and flipped learning models.

Empirical evidence reviewed throughout this chapter shows that GenAI tools can significantly improve student engagement, motivation, and proficiency across the core language skills—listening, reading, speaking, and writing—as well as intercultural communication. These tools offer differentiated support, facilitating inclusive practices for learners with diverse needs and backgrounds. However, their effectiveness depends on careful instructional design and sustained teacher mediation.

At the same time, GenAI raises important concerns. Issues such as algorithmic bias, over-reliance on automated feedback, and threats to data privacy highlight the need for critical implementation strategies. Educators must be equipped with the digital literacy and pedagogical skills required to use GenAI ethically and effectively. Moreover, disparities in access to AI technologies risk exacerbating educational inequities, particularly in under-resourced contexts.

Encouragingly, institutional initiatives are emerging to address these challenges. The European Union, for instance, is advancing several strategic projects—including OpenEuroLLM, ADMIT, and (Em)powered by AI—that promote transparent, multilingual, and pedagogically aligned GenAI integration in education. These projects reflect a broader recognition of GenAI's transformative potential and the need to integrate it within equitable and inclusive frameworks.

These considerations lead directly into the focus of the next chapter, which examines the ethical dimensions of GenAI in TESOL. Key issues include data privacy, algorithmic bias, intellectual property, and the sociocultural implications of AI integration. The discussion extends beyond classroom practice to consider the ethical responsibilities of teachers, institutions, policymakers, AI developers, and international bodies. In doing so, the chapter aims to articulate a framework for the responsible and sustainable use of GenAI in language education.

References

Abimanto, D., & Sumarsono, W. (2024). Improving English pronunciation with AI speech-recognition technology. *Acitya: Journal of Teaching and Education, 6*(1), 146–156. https://doi.org/10.30650/ajte.v6i1.3810

Afzali, Z., & Izadpanah, S. (2021). The effect of the flipped classroom model on Iranian English foreign language learners: Engagement and motivation in English language grammar. *Cogent Education, 8*(1), 1870801. https://doi.org/10.1080/2331186x.2020.1870801

Alazemi, A. F. T. (2024). Formative assessment in artificial integrated instruction: Delving into the effects on reading comprehension progress, online academic enjoyment, personal best goals, and academic mindfulness. *Language Testing in Asia, 14*(1), 44. https://doi.org/10.1186/s40468-024-00319-8

Alsofyani, A. H., & Barzanji, A. M. (2025). The effects of ChatGPT-generated feedback on Saudi EFL learners' writing skills and perception at the tertiary level: A mixed-methods study. *Journal of Educational Computing Research, 63*(2), 431–463. https://doi.org/10.1177/07356331241307297

Amin, E. A.-R. (2024). EFL students' perception of using AI text-to-speech apps in learning pronunciation. *Migration Letters, 21*(3), 887–903. https://migrationletters.com/index.php/ml/article/view/6905,

Bachiri, Y. A., Mouncif, H., Bouikhalene, B., & Hamzaoui, R. (2024). Integrating AI-based speech recognition technology to enhance reading assessments within Morocco's TARL program. *Turkish Online Journal of Distance Education, 25*(4), 1–15. https://doi.org/10.17718/tojde.1335062

Badlani, R., Valle, R., Shih, K. J., Santos, J. F., Gururani, S., & Catanzaro, B. (2023). Multilingual multiaccented multispeaker TTS with RADTTS. *arXiv preprint* arXiv:2301.10335. https://doi.org/10.21437/interspeech.2023-2330

Borg, M., Bengtsson, J., Österling, H., Hagelborn, A., Gagner, I., & Tomaszewski, P. (2022, May). Quality assurance of generative dialog models in an evolving conversational agent used for Swedish language practice. In *Proceedings of the 1st International Conference on AI Engineering: Software Engineering for AI* (pp. 22–32). https://doi.org/10.1145/3522664.3528592

Byram, M. (1997). 'Cultural awareness' as vocabulary learning. *Language Learning Journal, 16*(1), 51–57. https://doi.org/10.1080/09571739785200291

Chang, T. S., Li, Y., Huang, H. W., & Whitfield, B. (2021, March). Exploring EFL students' writing performance and their acceptance of AI-based automated writing feedback. In *Proceedings of the 2021 2nd International Conference on Education Development and Studies* (pp. 31–35). https://doi.org/10.1145/3459043.3459065

Chen, M. R. A. (2024). The AI chatbot interaction for semantic learning: A collaborative note-taking approach with EFL students. *Language Learning & Technology*, *28*(1), 1–25.https://doi.org/10.64152/10125/73586

Chen, X., Meurers, D., & Rebuschat, P. (2022). ICALL offering individually adaptive input: Effects of complex input on L2 development. *Language Learning & Technology*, *26*(1), 1–21. https://doi.org/10.64152/10125/73496

Cheng, Y., Fan, Y., Li, X., Chen, G., Gašević, D., & Swiecki, Z. (2025). Asking generative artificial intelligence the right questions improves writing performance. *Computers and Education: Artificial Intelligence, 8*, 100374.

Cheung, L. M. E., & Shi, H. (2024). Co-creating stories with generative AI: Reflections from undergraduate students of a storytelling service-learning subject in Hong Kong. *Australian Review of Applied Linguistics, 47*(3), 259–283. https://doi.org/10.1075/aral.24101.che

Creely, E., Barnes, M., Tour, E., Henderson, M., Waterhouse, P., Pena, M. A., & Patel, S. V. (2025). Exploring attitudes to generative AI in education for English as an additional language (EAL) adult learners. *ReCALL*, 1–17. https://doi.org/10.1017/s0958344024000314

Czerkawski, B. C. (2024). Designing language learning experiences with generative AI tools. In *AI in language teaching, learning, and assessment* (pp. 324–341). IGI Global Scientific Publishing. https://doi.org/10.4018/979-8-3693-0872-1.ch015

Dai, D. W., Suzuki, S., & Chen, G. (2025). Generative AI for professional communication training in intercultural contexts: Where are we now and where are we heading? *Applied Linguistics Review, 16*(2), 763–774. https://doi.org/10.1515/applirev-2024-0184

Day, S. L., Cirica, J., Clapp, S. R., Penkova, V., Giroux, A. E., Banta, A., Bordeau, C., Mutteneni, P., & Sawyer, B. D. (2025). Evaluating GenAI for simplifying texts for education: Improving accuracy and consistency for enhanced readability. *arXiv preprint* arXiv:2501.09158. https://doi.org/10.48550/arXiv.2501.09158

Dennis, N. K. (2024). Using AI-powered speech recognition technology to improve English pronunciation and speaking skills. *IAFOR Journal of Education, 12*(2), 107–126. https://doi.org/10.22492/ije.12.2.05

Dizon, G. (2020). Evaluating intelligent personal assistants for L2 listening and speaking development. *Language Learning & Technology*, 24(1), 16–26. 10125/44705.

Dizon, G. (2023). Affordances and constraints of intelligent personal assistants for second-language learning. *RELC Journal, 54*(3), 848–855. https://doi.org/10.1177/00336882211020548

Edmett, A., Ichaporia, N., Crompton, H., & Crichton, R. (2024). *Artificial intelligence and English language teaching: Preparing for the future* (2nd ed.). British Council. https://doi.org/10.57884/78EA-3C69

Ejaz, R. U., & Jamil, M. B. (2024). Integrating generative AI into technology-mediated task-based language teaching (TMTBLT) for enhancing English language learning in Pakistan. *Pakistan Languages and Humanities Review, 8*(4), 390–401. https://doi.org/10.47205/plhr.2024(8-IV)36

Ellis, R. (2017). Task-based language teaching. In *The Routledge handbook of instructed second language acquisition* (pp. 108 –125). Routledge. https://doi.org/10.4324/9781315676968-7

Emen, M., & Aslan, D. (2019). The relationship between perspective taking skills and language development in preschool children. *Journal of Education and Educational Development*, *6*(1), 25–42. https://doi.org/10.22555/joeed.v6i1.2159

Emerson, N. (2024). AI-enhanced collaborative story writing in the EFL classroom. *Technology in Language Teaching & Learning*, *6*(3), 1764–1764. https://doi.org/10.29140/tltl.v6n4.1764

Erasmus+. (2024). *ADMIT: Generative AI and large language models in higher education*.https://r3beccaf.wordpress.com/2024/02/13/generative-ai-and-large-language-models-in-higher-education-admit/

European Commission. (2025, February 3). *Pioneering AI project awarded for opening large language models for European languages. European Commission.* https://digital-strategy.ec.europa.eu/en/news/pioneering-ai-project-awarded-opening-large-language-models-european-languages

Fathi, J., & Rahimi, M. (2024). Utilising artificial intelligence-enhanced writing mediation to develop academic writing skills in EFL learners: a qualitative study. *Computer Assisted Language Learning*, 1–40. https://doi.org/10.1080/09588221.2024.2374772

Godwin-Jones, R. (2024a). Distributed agency in language learning and teaching through generative AI. *Language Learning & Technology*, *28*(2), 5–31. https://doi.org/10.64152/10125/73570

Godwin-Jones, R. (2024b). Generative AI, pragmatics, and authenticity in second language learning. *Virginia Commonwealth University, verfügbar unter* https://arxiv.org/pdf/2410.14395, *letzter Zugriff am*, *15*, 25. https://doi.org/10.48550/arXiv.2410.14395

Guan, L., Zhang, E. Y., & Gu, M. M. (2024). Examining generative AI–mediated informal digital learning of English practices with social cognitive theory: A mixed-methods study. *ReCALL*, 1 –17. https://doi.org/10.1017/S0958344024000259

Han, D. E. (2020). The effects of voice-based AI chatbots on Korean EFL middle school students' speaking competence and affective domains. *Asia-pacific Journal of Convergent Research Interchange*, *6*(7), 71–80. https://doi.org/10.47116/apjcri.2020.07.07

Hoang, N. T., Han, D. N., & Le, D. H. (2023). Exploring Chatbot AI in improving vocational students' English pronunciation. *AsiaCALL Online Journal*, *14*(2), 140–155. https://doi.org/10.54855/acoj.231429

Hofstede, G. (2001). *Culture's consequences: Comparing values, behaviors, institutions, and organizations across nations* (2nd ed.). Sage Publications.

Hsu, H. L., Chen, H. H. J., & Todd, A. G. (2023). Investigating the impact of the Amazon Alexa on the development of L2 listening and speaking skills. *Interactive Learning Environments, 31*(9), 5732–5745.https://doi.org/10.1080/10494820.2021.2016864

Hsu, T. C., Chang, C., & Jen, T. H. (2024). Artificial intelligence image recognition using self-regulation learning strategies: Effects on vocabulary acquisition, learning anxiety, and learning behaviours of English language learners. *Interactive Learning Environments, 32*(6), 3060–3078. https://doi.org/10.1080/10494820.2023.2165508

Hu, W., Tian, J., & Li, Y. (2025). Enhancing student engagement in online collaborative writing through a generative AI-based conversational agent. *The Internet and Higher Education, 65*, Article 100979. https://doi.org/10.1016/j.iheduc.2024.100979

Hwang, W. Y., Nurtantyana, R., Purba, S. W. D., Hariyanti, U., Indrihapsari, Y., & Surjono, H. D. (2023). AI and recognition technologies to facilitate English as foreign language writing for supporting personalization and contextualization in authentic contexts. *Journal of Educational Computing Research, 61*(5), 1008–1035. https://doi.org/10.1177/07356331221137253

Ippolito, D., Yuan, A., Coenen, A., & Burnam, S. (2022). Creative writing with an AI-powered writing assistant: Perspectives from professional writers [Preprint]. *arXiv*. https://doi.org/10.48550/arXiv.2211.05030

Ishihara, N., & Cohen, A. D. (2021). *Teaching and learning pragmatics: Where language and culture meet* (2nd ed.). Routledge. https://doi.org/10.4324/9781003168188

ITC International. (2024). *Teaching in the AI Age*. Erasmus+ training courses. https://www.itc-international.eu/erasmusplus/teaching-in-the-ai-age-2026-new

Jinowat, N., Unapang, J., Kangsawiwat, T., & Sapai, P. (2024, May). Fostering critical writing excellence: Leveraging Google Gemini and collaborative online writing with Google Docs. In *International Workshop on Learning Technology for Education Challenges* (pp. 349–363). Springer Nature Switzerland. https://doi.org/10.1007/978-3-031-61678-5_25

Kang, H. (2022). Effects of artificial intelligence (AI) and native speaker interlocutors on ESL learners' speaking ability and affective aspects. *Multimedia-Assisted Language Learning, 25*(2), 9–43. https://doi.org/10.15702/mall.2022.25.2.9

Kim, R. (2024). Effects of ChatGPT on Korean EFL learners' main-idea reading comprehension via top-down processing. *Language Research, 60*(1), 83–108. https://doi.org/10.30961/lr.2024.60.1.83

Krashen, S. (1992). The input hypothesis: An update. In *Linguistics and language pedagogy: The state of the art* (pp. 409–431).
Kurt, G., & Kurt, Y. (2024). Enhancing L2 writing skills: ChatGPT as an automated feedback tool. *Journal of Information Technology Education: Research, 23*, Article 24. https://doi.org/10.28945/5370
Lee, L. K., Chan, E. H., Tong, K. K. L., Wong, N. K. H., Wu, B. S. Y., Fung, Y. C., Fong, E. K. S., Hou, U. L., & Wu, N. I. (2024, July). Utilizing virtual reality and generative AI chatbot for job interview simulations. In *2024 International Symposium on Educational Technology (ISET)* (pp. 209–212). IEEE). https://doi.org/10.1109/ISET61814.2024.00048
Lee, Y. J., & Davis, R. O. (2024). A case study of implementing generative AI in university's general English courses. *Contemporary Educational Technology, 16*(4), ep533. https://doi.org/10.30935/cedtech/15218
Lege, R., Bonner, E., & Aikawa, T. (2024). Pecha, a language practice peer: Guiding language learning interactions through large language models. *Technology in Language Teaching & Learning, 6*(3), 1716–1716. https://doi.org/10.29140/tltl.v6n3.1716
Li, X., Li, B., & Cho, S. J. (2023). Empowering Chinese language learners from low-income families to improve their Chinese writing with ChatGPT's assistance afterschool. *Languages, 8*(4), Article 238. https://doi.org/10.3390/languages8040238
Liang, X., Mat Said, S. H., & Wei, L. (2024). Influences of digital native storytelling on foreign language learners' native cultural awareness. *Forum for Linguistic Studies, 6*(6), 1073–1087. https://doi.org/10.30564/fls.v6i6.7100
Liu, G. L., Darvin, R., & Ma, C. (2024). Exploring AI-mediated informal digital learning of English (AI-IDLE): A mixed-method investigation of Chinese EFL learners' AI adoption and experiences. *Computer Assisted Language Learning*, 1–29. https://doi.org/10.1080/09588221.2024.2310288
Liu, W., & Wang, Y. (2024). The effects of using AI tools on critical thinking in English literature classes among EFL learners: An intervention study. *European Journal of Education, 59*(4), Article e12804. https://doi.org/10.1111/ejed.12804
Long, M. (2014). *Second language acquisition and task-based language teaching*. John Wiley & Sons.
Long, M. H. (1985). A role for instruction in second language acquisition: Task-based language teaching. In K. Hyltenstam & M. Pienemann (Eds.),

Modeling and assessing second language acquisition (pp. 77–99). Multilingual Matters.

McGuire, A., Qureshi, W., & Saad, M. (2024). A constructivist model for leveraging GenAI tools for individualized, peer-simulated feedback on student writing. *International Journal of Technology in Education (IJTE), 7*(2), 326–352. https://doi.org/10.46328/ijte.639

Media & Learning Association. (2024). *(Em)powered by AI: Education Empowered by Generative AI*. https://media-and-learning.eu/subject/artificial-intelligence/education-empowered-by-generative-ai

Naous, T., Ryan, M. J., Ritter, A., & Xu, W. (2023). Having beer after prayer? Measuring cultural bias in large language models. *arXiv*. https://doi.org/10.48550/arXiv.2305.14456

Nazari, N., Shabbir, M. S., & Setiawan, R. (2021). Application of artificial intelligence powered digital writing assistant in higher education: randomized controlled trial. *Heliyon, 7*(5). https://doi.org/10.1016/j.heliyon.2021.e07014

Nguyen, T. L., Nguyen, H. L., & Le, D. H. (2024, November). Teachers' perspectives on AI-driven Quillionz for generating EFL reading comprehension quizzes. In *Proceedings of the AsiaCALL International Conference* (Vol. 6, pp. 20–34). AsiaCALL. https://doi.org/10.54855/paic.2462

Nunan, D. (2004). Task-based language teaching. *Cambridge University Press*. https://doi.org/10.1017/cbo9780511667336

Prabhu, N. S. (1987). *Second language pedagogy*. Oxford University Press.

Qassrawi, R. M., ElMashharawi, A., Itmeizeh, M., & Tamimi, M. H. (2024). AI-powered applications for improving EFL students' speaking proficiency in higher education. *Assessment, 8*(9), 1–15. https://doi.org/10.30564/fls.v6i5.6966

Qiao, H., & Zhao, A. (2023). Artificial intelligence-based language learning: Illuminating the impact on speaking skills and self-regulation in Chinese EFL context. *Frontiers in Psychology, 14,* Article 1255594. https://doi.org/10.3389/fpsyg.2023.1255594

Rashid, M. M., Atilgan, N., Dobres, J., Day, S., Penkova, V., Küçük, M., Clapp, S. R., & Sawyer, B. D. (2024, September). Humanizing AI in education: A readability comparison of LLM and human-created educational content. In *Proceedings of the Human Factors and Ergonomics Society Annual Meeting* (Vol. 68, No. 1, pp. 596–603). SAGE Publications. https://doi.org/10.1177/10711813241261689

Richter, T. T., & Langesee, L. M. (2024). Supporting virtual learning and international academic visits with AI. *IDIMT-2024: Changes to ICT, Management, and Business Processes through AI*. https://doi.org/10.35011/IDIMT-2024-141

Runge, A., Attali, Y., LaFlair, G. T., Park, Y., & Church, J. (2024). A generative AI-driven interactive listening assessment task. *Frontiers in Artificial Intelligence, 7*, 1474019. https://doi.org/10.3389/frai.2024.1474019

Sidwell, M. D., Bonner, L. W., Bates-Brantley, K., & Wu, S. (2024). Utilizing text-generative AI for creating oral reading fluency probes. *Intervention in School and Clinic, 60*(2), 119–125. https://doi.org/10.1177/10534512241235896

Sim, S., Kim, Y., & Ku, K. (2025). Exploring generative AI as a roleplay interlocutor in L2 task-based pragmatics learning: Comparing ChatGPT-learner and technology-mediated peer interactions. *TESOL Quarterly*. https://doi.org/10.1002/tesq.70010

Song, C., & Song, Y. (2023). Enhancing academic writing skills and motivation: Assessing the efficacy of ChatGPT in AI-assisted language learning for EFL students. *Frontiers in Psychology, 14*, 1260843. https://doi.org/10.3389/fpsyg.2023.1260843

Su, X., Wambsganss, T., Rietsche, R., Neshaei, S. P., & Käser, T. (2023, July). Reviewriter: AI-generated instructions for peer review writing. In *Proceedings of the 18th workshop on innovative use of NLP for building educational applications (BEA 2023)* (pp. 57–71). https://doi.org/10.18653/v1/2023.bea-1.5

Sudin, V. D. K., & Swanto, S. (2024). Enhancing ESL learners reading comprehension and motivation via AI-generated personalised reading texts. *International Journal on E-Learning Practices (IJELP), 7*(1). https://doi.org/10.51200/ijelp.v7i1.5440

Swain, M. (2005). The output hypothesis: Theory and research. *Handbook of research in second language teaching and learning.* Lawrence Erlbaum Associates.

Terzić, I., Drobnjak, A., & Botički, I. (2023). Designing educational personas using generative AI. In *The 31st International Conference on Computers in Education* (pp. 961–963). https://doi.org/10.58459/icce.2023.1488

Utami, S. P. T., Andayani, Winarni, R., & Sumarwati. (2023). Utilization of artificial intelligence technology in an academic writing class: How do Indonesian students perceive?. *Contemporary Educational Technology*, 15(4), ep450. https://doi.org/10.30935/cedtech/13419

Vitta, J. P., & Al-Hoorie, A. H. (2023). The flipped classroom in second language learning: A meta-analysis. *Language Teaching Research, 27*(5), 1268–1292. https://doi.org/10.1177/1362168820981403

Vygotsky, L. S. (1978). *Mind in society: The development of higher psychological processes*. Harvard University Press.

Wan, Y., & Moorhouse, B. L. (2024). *Using Call Annie as a generative artificial intelligence speaking partner for language learners*. Advance online publication. https://doi.org/10.1177/00336882231224813

Wang, H., & Dang, A. (2024). Enhancing l2 writing with generative ai: A systematic review of pedagogical integration and outcomes. *Preprint*. https://doi.org/10.13140/RG.2.2.19572.16005

Wen, Y., Chiu, M., Guo, X., & Wang, Z. (2025). AI-powered vocabulary learning for lower primary school students. *British Journal of Educational Technology, 56*(2), 734–754. https://doi.org/10.1111/bjet.13537

Woo, D. J., Guo, K., & Susanto, H. (2025). Exploring EFL students' prompt engineering in human–AI story writing: An activity theory perspective. *Interactive Learning Environments, 33*(1), 863–882. https://doi.org/10.1080/10494820.2024.2361381

Xin, J. J. (2024). Investigating EFL teachers' use of generative AI to develop reading materials: A practice and perception study. *Language Teaching Research*, 1–30. https://doi.org/10.1177/13621688241303321

Xu, Z., Wijekumar, K., Lin, S., Yang, X., & Nan, B. (2022). Web-based text structure instruction on ELLs' high-order reading comprehension skills. *Reading Psychology, 43*(3–4), 211–231. https://doi.org/10.1080/02702711.2022.2094037

Yan, L., Martinez-Maldonado, R., Jin, Y., Echeverria, V., Milesi, M., Fan, J., Zhao, L., Alfredo, R., Li, X., & Gašević, D. (2025). The effects of generative AI agents and scaffolding on enhancing students' comprehension of visual learning analytics. *Computers & Education*, 105322. https://doi.org/10.1016/j.compedu.2025.105322

Yang, C. T. Y., Lai, S. L., & Chen, H. H. J. (2022a). The impact of intelligent personal assistants on learners' autonomous learning of second language listening and speaking. *Interactive Learning Environments, 32*(5), 2175–2195. https://doi.org/10.1080/10494820.2022.2141266

Yang, F., & Jiang, L. (2024). Research on generative artificial intelligence facilitating oral business English teaching in higher vocational schools. In *Modern Management based on Big Data V* (pp. 573–580). IOS Press. https://doi.org/10.3233/faia240294

Yang, H., Kim, H., Lee, J. H., & Shin, D. (2022b). Implementation of an AI chatbot as an English conversation partner in EFL speaking classes. *ReCALL, 34*(3), 327–343. https://doi.org/10.1017/s0958344022000039

Yeh, H. C. (2024). Revolutionizing language learning. *Educational Technology & Society, 27*(3), 335–353. https://doi.org/10.46328/ijte.732

Zheng, Y. D., & Stewart, N. (2024). Improving EFL students' cultural awareness: Reframing moral dilemmatic stories with ChatGPT. *Computers and Education: Artificial Intelligence, 6*, Article 100223. https://doi.org/10.1016/j.caeai.2024.100223

5

Ethical Considerations in GenAI Integration in TESOL

5.1 Introduction

When confronted with emerging technologies, TESOL educators frequently express concern over their lack of Technological Pedagogical Content Knowledge (TPACK), which hinders their ability to meaningfully integrate digital tools into language instruction (Mishra & Koehler, 2006; Tseng et al., 2022). Such concerns are also echoed by educators for this study who feel underprepared for integrating GenAI into their practice.

> Quotation 1: "I don't feel prepared enough as a teacher to use it. I don't think I have the right tools or knowledge yet." (T.11, Cyprus)

However, the challenges posed by GenAI extend beyond questions of pedagogical readiness. Integration of the technology into practice requires deeper ethical and moral considerations, raising questions about fairness, authorship, and trust. As GenAI becomes more prevalent in TESOL classrooms, educators are not only having to adapt technically but also having to confront its potentially disruptive implications for surveillance, autonomy, and its impact on their own professional roles

C. Savvidou, *AI-Powered Language Teaching*,
https://doi.org/10.1007/978-3-032-14502-4_5

and identities in language teaching and learning (Lan, 2024; Zawacki-Richter et al., 2019). The rapid integration of GenAI into educational contexts therefore demands sustained critical attention to the ethical dimensions of its use in TESOL. As such, fairness, privacy, equity, and accountability are no longer peripheral issues, but central to pedagogical and institutional decision-making. Addressing these concerns requires a more systematic examination of how GenAI is reshaping the TESOL landscape and the ethical responsibilities that arise from its use.

The previous chapter examined the pedagogical integration of GenAI in TESOL, highlighting its capacity to enhance learner engagement, differentiation, and proficiency across the development of second language skills. It illustrated how GenAI tools can support inclusive, communicative, and task-based learning, while also warning against risks such as bias, and overreliance. Importantly, it also highlighted that educators' use of GenAI depends not only on planning, design and instruction, but also on teacher readiness, ethical reflection, and institutional support. This chapter builds upon that foundation by turning explicitly to the ethical considerations that form the basis for responsible use of GenAI in TESOL.

The foundations of this discussion, draw on three complementary frameworks. First, critical digital pedagogy, rooted in the emancipatory work of Paulo Freire (1970), challenges educators to consider how GenAI mediates learning, structures pedagogical relationships, and either reinforces or resists social and linguistic inequities (Köseoğlu et al., 2023; Selwyn et al., 2020). Second, the responsible AI framework offers guiding principles—such as human agency and oversight, technical robustness and safety, privacy and data governance, transparency, diversity, non-discrimination and fairness; societal and environmental well-being, and accountability—that provide a structured basis for institutional and professional reflection (Dignum, 2019; Moniz & Escartín, 2023) and the European Commission's Ethics Guidelines for Trustworthy AI (European Commission, 2019). Finally, posthuman theory adds a more radical perspective by interrogating the shifting boundaries between human and non-human agency, questioning assumptions of autonomy, authorship, and control in human–AI relations. Together, these three perspectives support a critical discussion of GenAI in TESOL that situates ethical concerns not just at the level of pedagogy, but also in relation to power, agency, and identity.

This chapter also presents empirical data gathered for this book that asked TESOL educators to evaluate a range of ethical concerns. These quantitative patterns are further contextualised by interview data, which provide deeper insight into the ethical dimensions of GenAI in classroom practice, particularly around questions of authorship, assessment integrity, teacher autonomy, and the risks of over-dependence on AI.

The remainder of this chapter is organised thematically to offer a structured and in-depth examination of the ethical dimensions of GenAI integration in TESOL. The following section outlines the conceptual and regulatory frameworks that underpin responsible AI use, drawing on both theoretical principles and emerging international policy developments. It moves on to address key ethical concerns which are examined through the lens of responsible AI principles and informed by empirical insights from survey and interview data. The final section brings together these findings, highlighting recurring themes and practitioner concerns. In sum, this chapter provides a critical and comprehensive foundation for ethical engagement with GenAI in TESOL.

5.2 Conceptual and Normative Frameworks

As GenAI becomes more embedded in TESOL practice, its use must be grounded in a clear ethical and theoretical framework. This section outlines three key strands: critical digital pedagogy, which highlights power, inclusion, and human agency; the responsible AI framework, which provides normative guidance for ethical AI design and use; and the global policy landscape, including initiatives such as the EU AI Act and UNESCO's ethics recommendations. Together, these foundations offer a lens for assessing the ethical implications of GenAI in TESOL.

5.2.1 Critical Digital Pedagogy: Humanising Technology Use

If we are to understand education as a relational and emancipatory process, then the ethical integration of GenAI in TESOL must be grounded in pedagogical traditions that prioritise dialogue, relationality, and social justice (Freire, 1970). Freire's conception of pedagogy as a dialogic, co-intentional act positions learners as active participants in knowledge creation, rather than merely passive recipients of instruction. In TESOL, this principle challenges the reduction of language education to algorithmic outputs and instead calls for approaches that empower learners, respect linguistic and cultural identities, and preserve the pedagogical value of human interaction.

Building on the work of Freire (1970), Köseoğlu et al. (2023) extend critical pedagogy into digital contexts, emphasising that meaningful technology use must be humanising, reflexive, and inclusive. Digital tools should not be viewed as neutral, but, rather, as part of a pedagogy that focuses on learner voice, cultural identity, and co-construction of knowledge. In TESOL classrooms, such a perspective asks educators to consider how GenAI might be used to develop or limit multilingual expression, and whether its use supports or suppresses learners' diverse rhetorical and cultural practices. In other words, does GenAI support the development of students' diverse linguistic expression and communication styles, or does it marginalise language use and their cultural voices?

One way of adapting critical pedagogy to AI is through the Pacific model of Talanoa—a dialogic, relational practice rooted in Tongan, Samoan, and Fijian knowledge systems (see Schofield, et al., 2023). Talanoa emphasises storytelling, empathy, and trust as ways of humanising technology and resisting dehumanising, data-driven models of education. Applied to TESOL, this perspective suggests that GenAI could support rather than override learner agency. For example, chatbots and other AI tools can be framed not simply as providers of information but as partners in dialogic interaction, where transparency, openness, and collaborative knowledge-building are prioritised. In this way, Talanoa provides a lens for evaluating whether GenAI applications align with values of respect and reciprocity, rather than reinforcing hierarchical or extractive uses of technology.

Although these ideas (Köseoğlu et al., 2023) are not a direct address to language learning, the emphasis on relational pedagogy, cultural responsiveness, and ethical reflexivity is highly relevant to TESOL. These principles resonate with the challenges of multilingual classrooms, where GenAI must be framed as a sociotechnical system adapted to uphold inclusion, value diverse linguistic repertoires, and support learner voice.

In parallel, Wiliamson et al. (2023) provide a critical lens for understanding how AI systems are reshaping education, highlighting three interrelated dynamics. The first, 'automation' refers to the increasing use of AI to perform pedagogical functions such as assessment, feedback, and even content generation. In TESOL contexts, this includes tools that automatically grade written texts or generate corrective feedback which may improve efficiency but risk minimising the teacher's dialogic role and reducing language learning to language recognition. Second, 'platformisation,' describes the reliance on centralised commercial platforms. In TESOL, this is evident in the widespread use of proprietary language learning platforms, such as Grammarly, Duolingo and ChatGPT trained on large, English-dominant corpora, which are often scraped from academic, journalistic, or commercial sources. These sources tend to privilege standard American or British English varieties and formal over informal, colloquial uses. As a result, these tools may reinforce dominant language norms often treating regional varieties and informal registers as incorrect, even when contextually appropriate. Third, 'datafication' transforms learning into streams of measurable data, enabling predictive analytics and surveillance that may reinforce deficit views of learners. In the TESOL classroom, this includes tracking students' writing errors, participation time, or linguistic accuracy in AI-mediated activities, which can lead to reductive judgements about learner proficiency. Such metrics often fail to capture pragmatic competence, intercultural communication skills, or non-standard yet effective language strategies.

Overall, these critiques highlight the need for a reflexive, context-sensitive approach to the use of GenAI in TESOL recognising that educational technologies are never neutral but reflect and reshape power relations, cultural values, and institutional agendas. These critiques point to the importance of moving beyond abstract concerns to consider how responsibility for GenAI use can be structured and shared.

5.2.2 A Framework for Responsible AI Use

Dignum (2019) defines responsible artificial intelligence as a framework grounded in the distributed nature of responsibility across all actors involved in the development and use of AI systems. Rather than locating accountability in a single developer or institution, ethical responsibility is shared among designers, policymakers, educators, and end-users, through participatory processes that ensure AI systems align with human values. For TESOL, this model offers a foundation for engaging with GenAI in ways that respect linguistic diversity, uphold educational equity, and reinforce the agency of educators and students in shaping ethical practice.

As the deployment of GenAI tools in education accelerates, the need for structured, principle-based ethical guidance becomes increasingly urgent. This is not a new response, however; even before the rise of GenAI, the European Commission (2019) (see Fig. 5.1), proposed a comprehensive framework for 'trustworthy AI,' outlining seven core principles intended to guide the design, use, and regulation of AI systems. When considered in relation to TESOL, these principles can be understood as follows: (1) Human agency and oversight means that educators must remain central in pedagogical decision-making, even when AI tools are integrated. (2) Technical robustness and safety protects learners from unreliable or harmful outputs, particularly in high-stakes contexts, such as language assessment. (3) Privacy and data governance safeguards sensitive learner data, which may reveal personal or cultural information. (4) Transparency allows both teachers and students to understand how AI-generated feedback or evaluations are produced. (5) Diversity, non-discrimination, and fairness requires systems to accommodate varied Englishes and multilingual identities, avoiding bias against non-standard forms. (6) Societal and environmental well-being encourages the development of AI tools that support inclusive, accessible, and sustainable language education. Finally, (7) accountability ensures that responsibility for AI-driven decisions—such as grading, placement, or content generation—remains clearly defined and open to review.

These seven principles underpin the ethical analysis in the remainder of this chapter. Ethical issues—including bias, fairness, and representation (5.3); privacy, consent, and data protection (5.4); academic integrity and misuse (5.5); and equity, access, and the digital divide (5.6)—are examined through a practice-oriented approach to the use of GenAI in TESOL.

Fig. 5.1 Interrelationship of the seven requirements of trustworthy AI (*Source* European Commission (2019). *Ethics guidelines for trustworthy AI.* High-Level Expert Group on Artificial Intelligence. https://ec.europa.eu/futurium/en/ai-alliance-consultation/guidelines/1.html)

It should be noted that while the European Commission's (2019) Ethics Guidelines for Trustworthy AI predate the rapid uptake of large language models in education (notably from 2022 onwards), they remain highly relevant as they articulate enduring principles that are directly applicable to TESOL. However, their pre-LLM origin means they do not fully address recent challenges around authorship, learner autonomy, and assessment raised by GenAI, which calls for an updated application in this context.

5.2.3 Policy Frameworks: Global and National Contexts

Building on the ethical foundations of critical digital pedagogy and responsible AI principles, attention now shifts to the global and national policy frameworks that shape the governance of AI in education. While theoretical models highlight the importance of human agency, cultural responsiveness, and shared accountability, policy frameworks provide the regulatory scaffolding through which these values are put into practice, including in TESOL contexts.

The UNESCO Recommendation on the Ethics of Artificial Intelligence (2021) sets out global commitments that are highly relevant to TESOL. Its emphasis on protecting human rights, dignity, and equality ensures that GenAI tools respect diverse linguistic identities and avoid reinforcing dominant ideologies. The principle of promoting cultural diversity and inclusiveness aligns with TESOL's commitment to plurilingualism and intercultural competence, while equitable access and benefit-sharing highlight the risks of deepening inequality in under-resourced contexts. Importantly, the recommendation calls for multi-stakeholder dialogue, advocating for the participation of educators, learners, developers, and policymakers in co-creating ethical AI applications.

Complementing UNESCO's recommendations, the OECD AI Principles (OECD, 2019, 2024) provide a widely recognised, non-binding framework for trustworthy AI use. These principles articulate five core values: (1) inclusive growth and sustainable development; (2) respect for human rights and democratic values; (3) transparency and explainability; (4) robustness, security, and safety; and (5) accountability. While the principles closely align with UNESCO's commitments, they remain voluntary and general, meaning their application to language education depends on institutional will and local policy translation. Their broad scope often lacks the specificity needed for TESOL, where issues such as language ideology, learner identity, and intercultural communication require more targeted ethical guidance.

At the regional level, the EU AI Act (The European Parliament & Council of the European Union, 2024) introduces a binding, risk-based classification system for AI. Education is categorised as a "high-risk" domain, due to AI's influence on teaching, assessment, and access to opportunity. Consequently, developers and institutions deploying AI in TESOL—such as tools for writing assistance, translation, or assessment—are subject to strict requirements for transparency, bias mitigation, human oversight, and user rights. The Act also promotes best practices in accountability, inclusivity, and accessibility. However, its compliance demands may place heavier burdens on smaller or under-resourced TESOL institutions, while general-purpose, open-source AI tools widely used in classrooms may not always fall under the high-risk designation.

Finally, broader data protection laws such as the General Data Protection Regulation (GDPR) (European Union, 2016) provide essential safeguards around privacy, consent, and access. Yet, while GDPR offers protection of personal data, it falls short in addressing AI-specific challenges such as algorithmic opacity, contextual bias, and automated surveillance. In TESOL, these concerns are particularly concerning, since learners' spoken and written language may reveal personal, cultural, or context-specific information that goes beyond traditional notions of privacy, creating risks of misrepresentation, exploitation, or misuse.

These frameworks demonstrate the importance of developing enforceable regulations for education in general. They also highlight the pressing need for TESOL-specific ethical guidelines that build on the strengths of existing policy but are responsive to the sociolinguistic diversity of learners, the mediating role of teachers, and the risks of bias in GenAI outputs.

5.3 Bias, Fairness, and Representational Ethics

The issue of bias in GenAI tools is a significant ethical concern in TESOL, particularly as these tools are increasingly becoming embedded in language teaching and assessment. In this context, bias refers to systematic patterns of unfairness or inaccuracy in AI outputs that reflect inequalities in training data or algorithmic design. Such biases can reinforce dominant linguistic norms, marginalise diverse identities, and perpetuate stereotypes that shape how language is taught, learned, and assessed.

Linguistic bias in GenAI is frequently evident in the preference for standardised English varieties, particularly native-speaker norms of American or British English. While educators have often reported this anecdotally, recent research provides empirical confirmation. Fleisig et al. (2024) found that GPT-3.5 and GPT-4 systematically defaulted to Standard American English, even when prompted to engage with regionally specific dialects such as African American English, Indian English, or Nigerian English. Their findings showed a measurable disadvantage in responses to non-standard dialect prompts, with lower comprehension accuracy (−9%), a higher incidence of stereotyping (+19%), and a more condescending tone (+15%) compared to standard forms.

This aligns with UNESCO's and IRCAI (2024) observations that some GenAI systems associate non-standard Englishes with informal or inappropriate contexts, further marginalising their use in educational discourse. Such patterns raise ethical concerns within TESOL, where World Englishes and culturally situated language practices are increasingly recognised as pedagogically valid. Thus, without intervention, GenAI risks reinforcing prescriptive norms rather than supporting inclusive, context-sensitive language learning.

Cultural bias was also identified as a recurring concern among interview participants. Participants described their concerns that GenAI tools might fail to recognise or properly interpret culturally specific references, particularly from non-Western or Indigenous contexts. This omission reflects the Western centrism of many AI training datasets, with consequences for TESOL learners. When learners' lived realities are excluded from educational materials, they risk being further marginalised, reinforcing feelings of exclusion and limiting opportunities for culturally responsive teaching. This sentiment was expressed by one of the educators:

> Quotation 1: "I'm teaching in China. There may be political or ideological sensitivities around what is considered acceptable information, especially with Western AI tools like ChatGPT. What's acceptable in one country might not be in another, and there could be a clash between certain facts or beliefs. For example, Western perspectives on certain political topics might not align with Chinese perspectives, which could cause issues. There might also be cultural biases that don't align with the students' experiences or expectations." (T.5, China)

This concern is supported by empirical research which demonstrates that cultural bias in GenAI systems systematically privileges English-speaking or Western perspectives, marginalising non-Western and Indigenous worldviews. A comprehensive study by Tao et al. (2024) evaluated five GPT models against nationally representative cultural values data from the Inglehart–Welzel model, finding that their outputs closely align with values from English-speaking and Protestant European countries rather than global cultural norms. This pattern was evident across a diverse sample of 107 countries, highlighting the Western-centric training bias embedded in these models.

While gender bias was not specifically addressed by participants in the study, the literature has identified it as a recurring issue in AI outputs, particularly in AI-generated outputs that defaulted to stereotypical gender roles—for instance, associating leadership or technical expertise with men and caregiving with women. While less overt than linguistic bias, such patterns can subtly shape learner expectations about social norms and communicative behaviour, especially in contexts where language learning is also tied to cultural acculturation. One participant also expressed such concerns.

> Quotation 2: "I take those concerns very seriously. A few years ago, there was a famous case involving gender bias in translation between English and Turkish. Even though the pronoun in Turkish is gender-neutral, AI was introducing gender biases, like translating "he is a doctor" and "she is a nurse." It sparked a lot of discussion." (T.1, United States)

Moreover, research has demonstrated that large language models (LLMs), including those used in TESOL contexts, exhibit measurable gender biases that can affect learner perceptions and outcomes. Kotek et al. (2023) found that LLMs are three to six times more likely to associate traditionally male professions such as "doctor" or "engineer" with male pronouns, while female-typed roles like "nurse" or "teacher" are disproportionately assigned female pronouns—even in gender-neutral prompts. This occupational stereotyping persists across multiple languages and is especially problematic in AI-generated writing prompts, dialogues, and translation tasks common in TESOL instruction.

Similarly, UNESCO and IRCAI (2024) documented how some LLMs systematically associate female names with domestic or emotional concepts and male names with career-oriented or analytical terms, reinforcing stereotypical gender norms. Research in AI-assisted machine translation has also highlighted systemic gender bias. Ghosh and Caliskan (2023) found that when translating from gender-neutral languages such as Tagalog or Bengali into English, LLMs frequently defaulted to masculine pronouns, effectively erasing non-binary or gender-ambiguous expressions. These tendencies not only undermine the accuracy and inclusivity of AI-mediated language learning but also risk reinforcing implicit gender norms for learners engaging with GenAI in educational contexts.

These concerns are further reflected in survey data from TESOL educators. In response to the question: "Do you believe generative AI systems have biases that could impact language learning (e.g., gender, race, or cultural biases)?" (see Fig. 5.2), nearly half the respondents answered "Yes" (46.2%), indicating widespread awareness of bias as a pressing pedagogical issue. Additionally, 35.9% selected "Unsure," suggesting that many educators may suspect the presence of bias but lack strategies to identify or address it. Only 17.9% responded "No,"

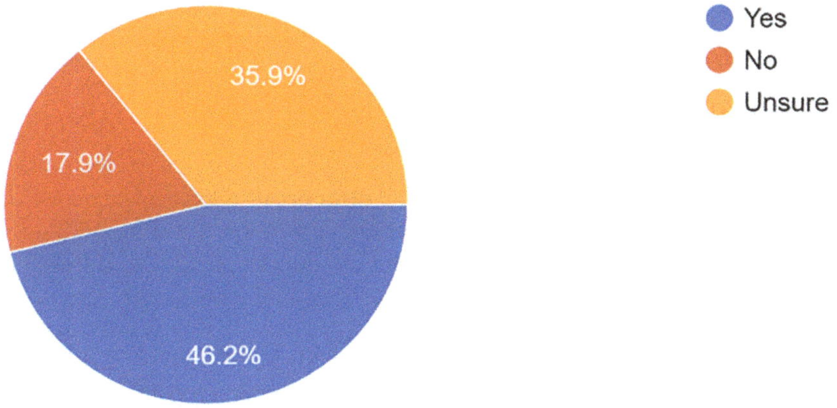

Fig. 5.2 Educators' perceptions that bias in GenAI could impact language learning

reflecting a minority view that GenAI systems do not pose bias-related risks to language learning.

This distribution suggests the need for greater training and institutional guidance on identifying and mitigating bias in GenAI tools. The high proportion of "Unsure" responses also highlights a potential gap in AI literacy among TESOL practitioners, reinforcing the importance of developing educators who can critically engage with GenAI tools in culturally and linguistically diverse classrooms.

Despite the risks associated with linguistic, cultural, and gender bias, educators in this study demonstrated reflective strategies to mitigate such effects. Rather than adopting AI uncritically, many reported using these tools selectively and adaptively. A common approach involved reviewing and modifying AI-generated content before introducing it to students, ensuring that it was both culturally appropriate and aligned with learners' needs. As one educator explained:

> Quotation 3: "I use ChatGPT to generate some ideas or make the classes more engaging. but I tailor it to the level and context of my students. So, I use it in a limited way to adapt materials." (T. 10, Cyprus)

Other educators highlighted institutional support such as professional development as key in promoting more culturally sensitive practices. For example, one participant recounted:

> Quotation 4: "We had a professional development workshop, we spoke about DALL-E, which is generating pictures because lots of teachers are taking videos or pictures from the Internet which are not suitable. They have lots of cultural considerations, and all content should be culturally appropriate. Even from a religious perspective, it should be appropriate." (T.8, Qatar)

Another recurring theme was the importance of framing GenAI outputs as suggestions rather than authoritative answers, helping to preserve learner agency and originality.

> Quotation 5: "Students got value from it, but I emphasized that AI can't replace their voice in writing. AI can assist in research, but students' voices are what matter in their work. That's the advice I'd give—use AI as an assistant but remind students that their voice is irreplaceable." (T. 6., Japan)

Another theme was the promotion of critical digital literacy. Some educators described the need to explicitly teach students to question the neutrality of AI systems, fostering reflection on how linguistic and cultural norms are embedded in algorithmic outputs.

> Quotation 6: "They need to be able to assess the information AI provides, as it can generate hallucinations or inaccurate content. Students often find it convenient and may blindly trust the information, thinking they're saving time and effort. This is a problem, and it comes down to training. We as teachers need to be trained in using AI tools ourselves, and then we need to train our students to use them judiciously." (T. 9, Cyprus)

Several educators highlighted not only classroom-level strategies but also the pressing need for institutional and policy-level responses to guide ethical AI use in TESOL. One educator expressed concern about the absence of top-down direction, noting:

> Quotation 7: "There seems to be a lack of policy—a lack of guidelines from the top. It's obviously a technological tool developed by these massive companies, but there doesn't seem to be any mediator between them and us. It feels like it's being generated from the bottom up, and everybody I've spoken to seems to be figuring it out on their own." (T. 8, Qatar)

This sense of decentralised adoption highlights the need for formal frameworks and clearer institutional guidelines, alongside transparent documentation from AI developers regarding the cultural assumptions embedded in their systems. As Jandrić and Ford (2022) argue, algorithmic systems are not neutral but reproduce existing social prejudices because their training data reflect dominant cultural attitudes. Without coordinated support, educators are left to navigate these complexities independently, potentially exacerbating inequities across TESOL contexts.

These findings strongly resonate with principles for ethical AI in education, particularly diversity, transparency, and accountability, as well as international policies such as the EU AI Act, UNESCO's Recommendation on the Ethics of AI, and the OECD AI Principles. While these frameworks stress inclusive, bias-aware, and transparent AI use, many GenAI tools commonly used in TESOL remain under-regulated. This highlights the critical role of educators in actively identifying and addressing bias through informed, ethical classroom practices.

Based on the findings, several key recommendations emerge for TESOL professionals seeking to engage with GenAI ethically and effectively. First, educators should encourage critical engagement by framing GenAI outputs as suggestions rather than definitive answers. This helps learners identify potential bias and reflect on issues of linguistic and cultural diversity. Second, teachers are advised to localise content by reviewing and adapting AI-generated materials to align with learners' cultural contexts and to avoid defaulting to standardised English norms that may exclude or marginalise non-dominant varieties. Third, the integration of AI literacy into language curricula is essential—not only to familiarise students with GenAI's capabilities and limitations but also to develop critical thinking and learner agency. Fourth, there is a pressing need for ongoing professional development, enabling educators to recognise bias in AI tools and to implement pedagogically sound responses, particularly in relation to global Englishes and inclusive teaching practices. Finally, educators and institutions should advocate for transparency, prioritising the use of GenAI systems that disclose how outputs are generated and encouraging developers to adopt documentation tools such as model cards and data sheets. Taken together, these practices support a more equitable, informed, and context-sensitive integration of GenAI in TESOL.

5.4 Privacy, Consent, and Data Governance

GenAI tools depend on vast datasets, including real-time user inputs, to function and improve. In TESOL settings, this often involves the collection and processing of sensitive learner data such as writing samples, personal reflections, and cultural or linguistic identifiers. Such data is deeply tied to learner identity, making privacy a fundamental ethical concern and not just a technical or regulatory one.

Because of this, the use of GenAI in language education raises critical questions about consent, data ownership, and the potential for surveillance. Language learning inherently involves self-expression, and if learner data is unprotected or repurposed without consent, it risks breaching trust and undermining inclusive, supportive pedagogy. To evaluate these risks, the European Commission's (2019) Ethics Guidelines for Trustworthy AI provide a foundation for addressing these risks, particularly the principles of privacy and data governance, technical robustness and safety, and accountability.

In TESOL, these principles are especially urgent because learner outputs—essays, reflections, recordings, and cultural narratives—are inherently personal and identity-linked. LLMs, such as GPT-3 and GPT-4, are trained on vast corpora of text (Brown et al., 2020; OpenAI, 2023), and while their ability to provide personalised feedback and generate tasks has clear pedagogical benefits, it also raises risks if sensitive data is stored, reused, or exposed without safeguards.

Without strong data governance, this information may be stored, reused, or exposed in ways that compromise learner privacy and autonomy. To mitigate these risks, the European Commission's (2019) Ethics Guidelines for Trustworthy AI provide a normative framework to address these risks. The principle of privacy and data governance stresses transparent data collection and informed consent. Technical robustness and safety call for reliable systems with protections against misuse. Accountability demands that institutions and educators share responsibility for ethical deployment and data management.

Despite the availability of such guidelines, empirical research on how they are applied in TESOL remains limited. Survey and interview data gathered for this book indicate that concerns around data privacy, informed consent, and potential surveillance are widely shared among educators, but concrete strategies for addressing them are often absent. The fast pace of GenAI development continues to outstrip institutional policy responses, leaving many teachers to make complex ethical decisions independently. This decentralised adoption risks exacerbating inequities across contexts, particularly where teacher preparedness or access to ethically governed tools varies.

Because language education is closely tied to identity, inadequate data protection can undermine learner trust and participation in the use of GenAI tools. As such, a proactive, policy-informed approach that is grounded in institutional guidance, educator training, and transparent AI tool design is needed to ensure that GenAI supports, rather than weakens, ethical language learning.

5.4.1 Educator Perceptions of Data Privacy

Concerns around data privacy in TESOL are not solely theoretical but are widely shared among educators. In response to one survey question, which asked, "How concerned are you about privacy issues related to generative AI tools in TESOL?", a clear majority of participants expressed varying degrees of apprehension. Specifically, 33.3% reported being very concerned, 51.3% were somewhat concerned, and only 15.4% stated they were not concerned. Taken together, 84.6% of respondents clearly

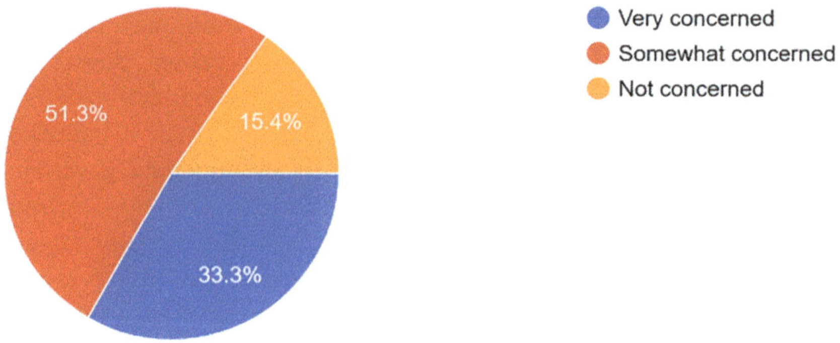

Fig. 5.3 Educators' level of concern about privacy issues in GenAI tools in TESOL

expressed at least moderate concern about the privacy implications of using GenAI in their professional practice (see Fig. 5.3).

This strong consensus reflects a broader recognition among educators that the integration of GenAI into language teaching introduces complex ethical risks, particularly in relation to how learner data is collected, stored, and potentially reused. One likely cause for this concern is the lack of clarity around data flows in many commercial GenAI tools. Most AI platforms do not make it transparent whether user inputs are stored, how they are processed, or if they are retained for model improvement or third-party use. This lack of transparency can make it difficult for teachers to confidently explain to students what happens to their data and thereby undermines informed consent and trust in the learning process.

Another important issue is the limited control educators and learners have over how student-generated data is managed, particularly in cloud-based environments or proprietary platforms. For example, students' written responses, feedback interactions, or even biometric data in speech-based tools may be stored or analysed without clear opt-in processes. In multilingual or culturally diverse classrooms, this raises concerns about how language use and identity markers are recorded, categorised, and possibly misinterpreted by AI systems.

In the absence of robust data governance protocols at institutional or national level, educators may feel that they are bearing the ethical burden alone and they make privacy-related decisions without sufficient guidance. The high level of concern reported in the survey suggests that data privacy is not just an abstract worry, but a concrete barrier to confident and responsible GenAI adoption in TESOL.

These concerns around privacy were also clearly reflected in the interview data. Several participants expressed unease about how GenAI tools store and process user input, particularly in relation to data retention and visibility. One educator remarked:

> Quotation 8: "I'm sure AI tools collect user data to build profiles, and we don't know how that information will be used in the future." (T.12, Cyprus)

They went on to link this to their concerns about the increasing use of persistent memory features in AI systems:

> Quotation 9: "AI tools now remember prompts from weeks ago… this raises privacy concerns because it means that even if you provided a prompt weeks ago, the AI can recall that information, which means it is being stored on an internal server." (T.12, Cyprus)

These insights reinforce the perception that many GenAI platforms operate with limited transparency regarding data retention and usage. Another educator similarly noted the risks associated with algorithmic profiling:

> Quotation 10: "Every time you search for something, AI tracks that information, and big data can remember your interests and push related content. This can sometimes lead to inappropriate advertisements" (T.5, China)

Together, these accounts stress the importance of greater transparency, clearer consent mechanisms, and institutional guidance on ethical data practices in TESOL contexts. They echo survey findings by highlighting the extent to which privacy concerns are grounded in real classroom experiences and practical uncertainties about how learner data is handled by AI systems.

5.4.2 Data Collection and Consent

The lack of openness in how GenAI tools collect, store, and potentially reuse learner-generated data presents significant ethical challenges in educational settings. When students input writing samples, answer prompts, or engage in AI-mediated conversations, their contributions may be logged and retained on external servers, often without their explicit knowledge. This raises serious issues around informed consent, which requires that learners are fully informed not only about the collection of their data, but also about how it will be processed, stored, and potentially shared. Importantly, learners should retain the right to withdraw consent at any time, maintaining control over their personal data. However, many GenAI applications lack clear mechanisms to ensure transparency and consent (Oye et al., 2024).

Another critical issue is the secondary use of data. Huang (2023) warns that major online educational platforms, often owned by large internet corporations, increasingly operate as data monopolies. These platforms collect vast amounts of student information, which may be extensively processed and repurposed for commercial gain without users' knowledge or consent. For example, Huang (2023) gives examples of AI platforms widely used in educational settings which include advertising services capable of tracking detailed user data such as browsing activity, IP addresses, and email information. Huang (2023) argues that such practices not only obscure how learner data is used but also restrict users' ability to control their personal information, raising serious ethical concerns about secondary data use and information privacy in educational contexts. There are concerns that incorporating learner input into future training datasets or product development pipelines will blur the boundaries between educational support and commercial data exploitation. This practice raises ethical questions about data ownership and the commodification of educational data.

In addition, the anonymisation of data is not guaranteed, as the possibility of de-anonymisation, where supposedly anonymised data is reconstructed to reveal personal details, is a serious concern (Uddagiri & Isunuri, 2024). Even when names or email addresses are removed, linguistic data can include identifiable cultural, geographic, or demographic markers that may expose students to profiling or misrepresentation. As Lison et al. (2021) explain, legal frameworks, such as the GDPR, require anonymisation to remove not only direct identifiers but also any indirect data that, when combined with background knowledge, could reasonably be used to re-identify an individual. In TESOL contexts, this is especially important because students' language inputs may include cultural references, idioms, or writing styles that can act as indirect identifiers. Advanced AI systems may use these cues to infer personal details, putting learner privacy at risk.

5.4.3 Legal and Policy Contexts

These concerns highlight the urgent need for clear legal and regulatory guidance governing the use of learner data in AI-supported educational contexts. Several legal frameworks offer protections intended to safeguard personal data, but their applicability to GenAI in educational contexts such as TESOL is still evolving.

In the European Union, the GDPR provides a strong foundation, emphasising principles of informed consent, data minimisation, and user rights, including the right to access, correct, and delete personal data. Similarly, in the United States, laws such as the Family Educational Rights and Privacy Act (FERPA) govern access to student education records though it does not address many of the AI-specific risks. More recently the EU Artificial Intelligence Act (European Parliament and Council of the European Union 2024) further reinforces the importance of data protection in education by classifying AI systems used in learning environments as high-risk. This designation subjects them to strict requirements around transparency, human oversight, and bias mitigation.

However, many GenAI tools operate across national boundaries, raising issues for enforcement and cross-border data flows. Park (2023) notes how the regulatory frameworks of the EU, Canada and Brazil follow a horizontal approach that treats AI systems uniformly based on common risks. The US, UK, and several other countries favour a more decentralised approach that aims for flexibility to address developing risks and reduce the regulatory burdens of a one-size-fits-all approach.

Added to this, existing frameworks often fail to clearly address the secondary use of learner data, especially when tools are developed by private companies rather than educational institutions. As a result, educators and administrators are frequently left without clear guidance on how to navigate these ambiguities in existing data governance frameworks. These gaps highlight the importance of aligning legal protections with principles of responsible and trustworthy AI, as discussed earlier. Without stronger provisions for transparency, accountability, and fairness, educators are left to manage unclear data practices on their own, often without institutional or regulatory support. Embedding these principles into TESOL-specific policies would help ensure that GenAI tools not only comply with existing regulations but also uphold learner rights and reflect cultural diversity in practice.

5.4.4 Pedagogical Implications and Best Practices

In the TESOL classroom, concerns over data collection and privacy extend beyond regulatory compliance and can directly affect learner trust and engagement. If students suspect that their written work or personal information is being misused, this can discourage their participation and limit the authenticity of their language use. For example, imagine a TESOL writing class where an English language learner from a refugee background avoids discussing cultural identity or migration experiences for fear that such culturally sensitive information might be stored and reshared beyond the classroom. Or consider a teenage English language learner who is facing family tensions or questioning their gender identity. Such learners may self-censor, preferring to write generic answers than express themselves authentically. Learner mistrust undermines not only their educational experience but also the communicative foundations of language teaching, which depends on openness and cultural sensitivity.

Similarly, for teachers, the use of GenAI tools introduces new responsibilities that extend beyond pedagogical suitability to include their ethical risks. This includes ensuring that learners are not compelled to use tools that compromise their privacy or expose them to unregulated data practices. Currently, there are very few options available for implementing clear opt-in policies that provide transparency and respect regarding the management and storage of learners' data.

So, what are educators to do? Best practices for ensuring privacy, data governance, and accountability in GenAI-supported TESOL classrooms draw directly from the European Commission's (2019) Ethics Guidelines for Trustworthy AI. First, educators should prioritise informed consent by clearly communicating how GenAI tools operate, what data they collect, and how learner information might be stored or reused. This includes providing students with meaningful choices to consent and, where necessary, obtaining consent from guardians. Equally important is data minimisation; educators should limit the collection of identifiable information and avoid sharing culturally sensitive or personal content with GenAI platforms. The selection of GenAI tools should also be made with care, favouring those tools with transparent data policies, secure storage, and the option to delete or anonymise student inputs. Technical robustness is another key principle; tools should be vetted for their ability to safeguard data through encryption and secure authentication. Accountability should be supported institutionally, as it is neither realistic nor fair to expect individual teachers to shoulder full responsibility for ethical GenAI use alone. This includes selecting and vetting GenAI tools for their ability to safeguard learners' data, advocating for clear institutional policies, offering professional development on data ethics, and fostering transparency with learners about how GenAI is used for teaching and assessment. Collectively, these strategies are designed to protect learner trust and ensure that GenAI integration in TESOL remains ethically grounded.

To summarise, data privacy is not a peripheral issue in GenAI-supported TESOL. It is central to ensuring the ethical, effective, and equitable integration of new technologies into language education. As

GenAI tools become more embedded in teaching and learning, TESOL professionals must learn to engage critically with the ways these systems collect, process, and retain learner data. However, this cannot be done without stronger institutional policies, enhanced teacher training, and greater learner awareness, all of which are essential for creating an ethical AI ecosystem in TESOL.

5.5 Academic Integrity and AI Misuse

The rapid integration of GenAI into language education has prompted widespread concern about its potential to undermine academic integrity, particularly in relation to plagiarism, ghostwriting, and student overreliance on automated tools. In many TESOL contexts, written assignments are central to language assessment, so these concerns are especially important. GenAI tools such as ChatGPT and GrammarlyGO can generate fluent, contextually appropriate text in seconds, making it increasingly difficult to distinguish between student-generated and AI-generated work (Alexander et al., 2023; Perkins et al., 2024). Indeed, a recent study by Georgiou (2025) found that university professors often relied on limited stylistic cues such as overly uniform sentence structures or the absence of typical learner errors to identify AI-generated writing. In settings where detection relies solely on human judgement, a combination of linguistic knowledge and contextual awareness is required.

Despite the increase in AI detection tools such as GPTZero, OpenAI's Text Classifier, and Copyleaks, recent research has raised critical concerns about their reliability in educational settings. Chaka (2023) tested five prominent AI detection systems across responses generated by ChatGPT, YouChat, and Chatsonic, including translations into German, French, Spanish, Southern Sotho and isiZulu. The results demonstrated substantial inaccuracies, particularly in multilingual contexts. For example, GPTZero failed to detect any AI-generated text when responses were translated into Southern Sotho and isiZulu, while Copyleaks showed only partial accuracy with German and French translations. These findings suggest that current AI detection tools are not yet fully capable of reliably distinguishing between human and machine-generated texts.

Complementing this, Georgiou (2024) shows that while AI-generated writing is fluent, it differs systematically from human texts. GenAI favours certain sounds (e.g., alveolar and bilabial consonants) and uses more nouns and conjunctions. Its syntax relies on modifiers and direct objects, while human writing more often uses prepositional phrases. GenAI also prefers rare, technical vocabulary, whereas human texts use simpler, frequent words that aid readability. Although Georgiou's study identifies observable distinctions between GenAI and human text, the author also suggests that these are not easily distinguishable in practice.

Such concerns are expressed by TESOL educators in the current study. In one survey question, over 85.9% of respondents expressed concern that GenAI tools may contribute to academic dishonesty. Only 7.7% indicated they were "not concerned" and 6.4% were "unsure" (see Fig. 5.4). This strong consensus reflects broader anxieties about how GenAI might facilitate plagiarism or reduce students' motivation to engage in authentic writing processes.

These findings were expanded upon in response to an open-ended question that asked educators to identify their primary ethical concerns. Many cited "plagiarism," "rampant cheating," and "lack of originality" as

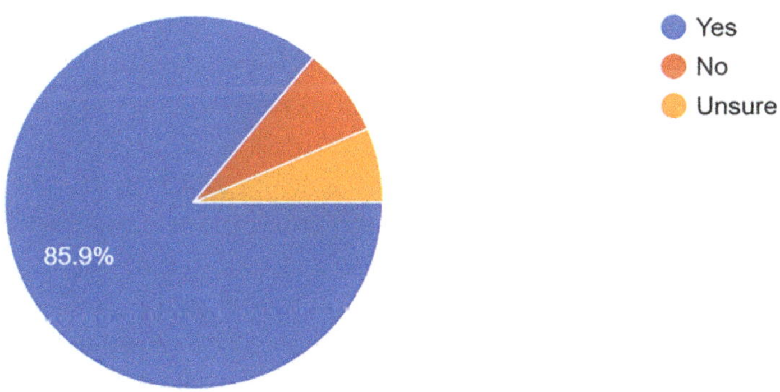

Fig. 5.4 Educators' level of concern about how GenAI might contribute to academic dishonesty

core problems, while others raised their deeper pedagogical worries that GenAI would erode students' critical thinking skills. As one participant observed:

> Quotation 11: "Replacing students' lack of critical thinking since they have easy access to anything they want and basically AI does the work for them within seconds." (Survey Participant)

Another explained:

> Quotation 12: "Students will rely too much on the available tools; it will be difficult to prove they do [their work] and difficult to motivate them to work." (Survey Participant).

These concerns reflect a changing pedagogical landscape in which algorithms are redefining how professional judgements about engagement, feedback, and assessment are made. In relation to the European Commission's (2019) Ethics Guidelines for Trustworthy AI, several principles are relevant. The principle of transparency stresses the need for clear communication about what GenAI tools are capable of, and how they are used. The principle of accountability calls for institutions—not individual teachers—to take responsibility for implementing ethical AI policies. Finally, the principle of human agency insists that learners must remain active participants in their educational journey, rather than passive recipients of algorithmic output.

In response to these principles, several pedagogical strategies for TESOL can be considered. First, promoting AI literacy is critical: TESOL educators should integrate discussions about GenAI into the curriculum, helping students understand when and how these tools can be used ethically. Second, TESOL instructors might design assignments that require process-based learning, such as annotated drafts or peer feedback, that make it more difficult to outsource work to GenAI tools. Third, institutions should invest in professional development and establish clear policies outlining the acceptable use of GenAI in assessment and instruction. Finally, educators should advocate for the development and adoption of GenAI tools that include documentation practices such as model cards, which outline how a system was trained, the data sources used (e.g., types of text, languages, sources), its known biases or limitations (e.g., poor performance on non-standard English), and its performance across different contexts or demographic groups (Mitchell et al., 2019).

Overall, these strategies reaffirm the importance of developing ethical awareness and academic integrity in TESOL classrooms. Implementing safeguards that preserve the authenticity of language learning, protect learner agency, and uphold institutional values is essential for the responsible integration of GenAI in education.

5.6 Overreliance, Autonomy, and Human-AI Balance

As noted earlier, overreliance on GenAI by both learners and educators is a major concern in TESOL, as its widespread use can unintentionally displace key elements of human-centred pedagogy. This concern was strongly reflected in the survey findings (see Fig. 5.5). From 78 respondents, 37.2% strongly agreed and 41% agreed that overreliance poses a significant risk—nearly 80% in total. By contrast, only 14.1% were neutral, and just 7.7% disagreed or strongly disagreed. These results suggest that most educators recognise a real risk that GenAI tools could displace critical aspects of language learning, such as learner autonomy and human judgement.

One of the most frequently expressed concerns among TESOL educators is the growing dependency of students on GenAI tools for language production, vocabulary acquisition, and even idea generation. While these tools can enhance engagement and provide access to resources, many educators observed that learners often bypass active language processing in favour of copying or paraphrasing AI outputs. They warned that this reliance could hinder language acquisition, critical thinking, and communicative competence.

Several educators noted that students are using GenAI to complete assignments without sufficient critical evaluation:

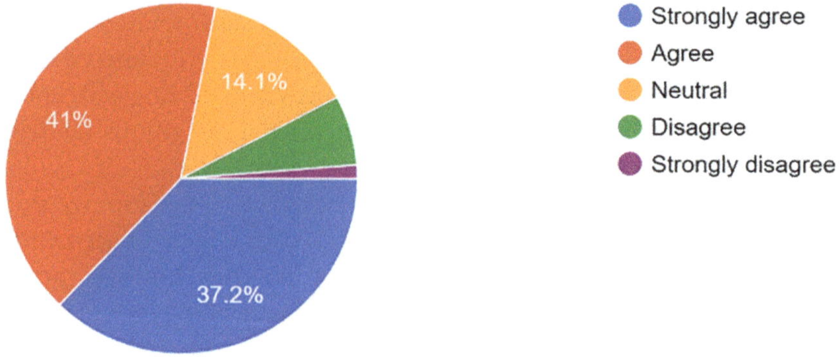

Fig. 5.5 Educators' level of concern about overreliance on GenAI tools

> Quotation 13: "Students can easily become too reliant on these tools. The problem is they don't always use them critically. AI-generated content can have issues like hallucinations or misinformation, and students need to be trained to assess the information and not blindly rely on it." (T.7, South Africa).
> Quotation 14: "Students might rely too much on AI because it provides answers very quickly, which may discourage critical thinking... If students depend too heavily on AI, they might not develop strong critical thinking skills." (T2, China).

Concerns also emerged regarding students' ability to produce original, communicative output:

> Quotation 15: "If students rely on AI too much, they might miss out on opportunities to interact in real-life situations...The goal of learning a language is to use it for communication." (T.4, China).
> Quotation 16: "Some students write essays using AI tools, and it's not always easy to detect. While using AI for ideas isn't necessarily a bad thing, the problem arises when students over-rely on it." (T.12, Cyprus).

Despite these concerns, it was also acknowledged that GenAI could offer motivational benefits by lowering affective barriers and increasing learner confidence:

> Quotation 17: "Students are motivated because AI makes it easier for them to participate... but it can also make students lazier and more dependent." (T5, China).

Concerns about overreliance extended to teachers themselves. While many valued GenAI for its time-saving features, especially in high-demand teaching environments, some warned that convenience could erode professional judgement. One teacher observed:

> Quotation 18: "Teachers are overwhelmed with lots of paperwork... At some point, they just take it as it is, whatever content is generated." (T.8, Qatar)

Continuing, they reflected on the consequence of this overreliance:

> Quotation 19: "Sometimes they take the content as it is... and later realise, oh no, that actually doesn't fit what I want to use it for." (T.8, Qatar)

Other educators stressed the risks of over-reliance on assessment and feedback:

> Quotation 20: "Teachers can use AI, like ChatGPT, for assessments, which can be helpful and efficient. But if they rely on it too much, they might not fully understand their students' progress." (T.2, China).

From these perspectives, it remains essential that GenAI remains a support, not a substitute for professional expertise. As one teacher explained:

> Quotation 21: "It should be used as assistance, but teachers and students need to critically evaluate the information it provides... AI should be handled carefully." (T.14, Algeria).

Educators also emphasised the importance of balancing GenAI's efficiency, which is often depersonalised, with a more humanistic approach to second language education, one grounded in empathy, dialogue, and learner agency. They described various strategies for maintaining this balance, including designing tasks that require interpersonal collaboration, guiding learners to revise rather than reproduce AI-generated content, and embedding digital literacy into the curriculum to develop learners' critical awareness:

> Quotation 22: "I recommend using ChatGPT as a helpful tool but not relying on it too much. It should be used as assistance… Teachers and students need to critically evaluate the information it provides. They shouldn't trust everything blindly." (T.14, Algeria).
> Quotation 23: "Students can use AI to help them learn words or complete assignments, but they need to be able to say what they've written. We have to be very careful with that." (T.10, Cyprus).

These insights reflect a pedagogical ethic that values GenAI as a support mechanism that can scaffold engagement without displacing learner identity or teacher agency.

Several educators also emphasised the importance of balancing AI with established pedagogical practices. As one teacher explained,

> Quotation 24: "We need to balance [AI] with tried-and-true teaching methods… AI is a great tool, but we need to remember that learning is a long process." (T.4, China).

Such perspectives advocate for GenAI to be treated not as a substitute, but as a resource guided by critical reflection, professional integrity, and learner-centred objectives. This orientation resonates with critical posthumanism, a philosophical approach that challenges traditional human–machine dualities and offers a framework for rethinking the boundaries of agency, authorship, and control in education.

Critical posthumanism offers a valuable theoretical lens for examining the integration of GenAI in TESOL, particularly in challenging conventional human–machine dichotomies. Rooted in post-anthropocentric thought, it reframes educational practice not as a solely human-centred endeavour but as one shaped by an "assemblage" of human and non-human actors, including learners, teachers, algorithms, and infrastructures (Bayne, 2015). Through the concept of "entanglement" (Calderwood, 2025), teaching and learning are seen as co-produced through "intra-action" (Barad, 2007). In other words, humans and GenAI technologies shape what counts as knowledge and how it is created.

This emphasis on relationality complements policy-oriented perspectives, such as the European Commission's (2019) Ethics Guidelines for Trustworthy AI, which stress human agency, transparency and accountability. Together, these approaches highlight both the philosophical and practical conditions for responsible integration of GenAI: one offers a philosophical reframing of how humans relate to technology, while the other sets out the practical and normative safeguards for their application. Considered together, they support a more reflective and responsible use of GenAI that enhances efficiency and creativity while maintaining learner voice, teacher judgement, and the relational dimensions of second language education.

5.7 Equity, Access, and the Digital Divide

The integration of GenAI in TESOL raises significant concerns around equity and access. While GenAI tools hold promise for enhancing language instruction, their benefits are known to be unevenly distributed. Disparities come from limited infrastructure, variations in digital literacy among educators and learners, and institutional resource constraints. At the core of this issue is the notion of a digital divide that influences not only who can access AI tools, but also who can meaningfully engage with them (Weng & Fu, 2025).

As discussed in earlier sections, the requirements of trustworthy AI (European Commission, 2019) stress that technological benefits must be distributed fairly, particularly in under-resourced contexts. In practice, however, GenAI adoption in TESOL remains uneven, which is reflected in the interview data.

Several educators expressed concern about disparities in infrastructure and connectivity that hinder meaningful use. In some contexts, even basic access to reliable internet or suitable devices is lacking. One educator commented:

> Quotation 25: "But there are technical challenges, such as ensuring that students have the necessary devices like computers or tablets. Phones could be used, but there are issues with phone use in classrooms." (T.12, Cyprus)

Lack of infrastructure not only limits students' access to GenAI but also restricts teachers' ability to prepare and deliver technology-supported lessons. Without institutional investment in basic technological infrastructure, there is a risk that GenAI deepens educational inequalities and widens the digital divide.

Beyond access to hardware, digital literacy emerged as a major theme. While some educators felt confident due to training opportunities, others described being unprepared. As one teacher noted:

> Quotation 26: "I've learned a lot through using the tools myself, and I've developed a sense for the patterns AI uses, especially in tools like ChatGPT. But I've also attended training. Last year, I took a 9-month seminar on technology and language education." (T.7, South Africa).

In contrast, others conveyed uncertainty and a lack of preparedness, underscoring disparities in support and institutional guidance:

> Quotation 27: "I don't feel prepared enough as a teacher to use it. I don't think I have the right tools or knowledge yet. We definitely need professional development on AI. If I knew how to incorporate it properly, like using translingual methods or other ELT approaches, I'd definitely use it." (T.11, Cyprus).

These contrasting experiences point to an uneven distribution of readiness, echoing findings by Granström and Oppi (2025), who found that teacher confidence and access to training were the strongest predictors of AI adoption among Estonian educators. Similarly, Alnasib (2023) reported that Saudi faculty showed only moderate readiness overall, with significant variation linked to resources, prior experience, and attitudes towards AI.

Student access and digital skills also vary widely. While it may once have been assumed that inherent digital nativeness translates into AI competency, recent work highlights that effective engagement with AI requires critical maturity and autonomy that cannot be assumed of so-called digital natives (Watanabe, 2024). As one educator noted:

> Quotation 28: "I've been a bit disappointed by the apathy towards new technology, especially AI. I found it exciting—being able to make quizzes or integrate AI into Google Forms—but the students didn't seem to share that excitement. I'll keep trying to introduce it, but it's been surprising how indifferent they've been." (T.6, Japan)

Another stressed affordability:

> Quotation 29: "I think the challenge would be access—maybe not everyone can access AI. Even if teachers and students use AI extensively, there might be costs involved." (T.2, China).

These insights reflect a growing need for pedagogical support and infrastructure ensuring that no student is disadvantaged by uneven access or preparation.

Some educators also raised concerns about institutional and policy-level barriers to equitable AI adoption. In some cases, policy ambiguity or lack of leadership has created confusion about what tools can be used, under what conditions, and with what pedagogical purpose:

> Quotation 30: "There's no clear directive at my university. It's up to the teacher to decide what's ethical. I'd like more uniformity and guidelines, but there's none at the moment. So I only use AI for in-class experiments and nothing that affects final grades, I'm trying to avoid any ethical gray areas." (T.6, Japan).

These challenges show how uneven infrastructure, training, and policy support can widen inequalities between well-resourced institutions and those with fewer supports.

Importantly, several educators stress that the digital divide is compounded by socio-economic, linguistic, and cultural factors, which intensifies challenges of equity and access. For example, students from lower socio-economic backgrounds may be less likely to have private access to GenAI tools outside the classroom:

> Quotation 31: "In Algeria, there are rural areas with poor internet connections, so AI tools can't be used everywhere. But in private schools, where students have better resources, I can give them tasks that they can approach using tools like ChatGPT… So, for those with access, it helps." (T.14, Algeria).

Such insights highlight the need for inclusive design in educational technology to avoid reproducing the very inequities GenAI is intended to address.

To bridge this divide, strategies include hybrid instructional models in low-tech classrooms, differentiated instruction to accommodate varied digital fluency, and collaborative learning tasks that treat GenAI as a shared rather than individual resource. At the institutional level, investment in infrastructure, expanded professional development, and policies prioritising inclusivity are essential.

Equity also involves inclusive pedagogy. Stentiford and Koutsouris (2021) describe this as a flexible, context-sensitive approach that values diversity without deficit and fosters belonging. In TESOL, GenAI can support inclusivity by simplifying texts, generating scaffolded tasks, or offering multimodal inputs for learners with different needs. Real-time translation, speech-to-text, and adaptive formats can also enhance access for multilingual, neurodivergent, or disabled learners (Kormos & Smith, 2023).

Yet challenges remain. Many GenAI tools reflect structural and representational biases in their training data (Blodgett et al., 2020) and may overlook accessibility considerations. In a study of twenty GenAI tools against the Web Content Accessibility Guidelines (WCAG), Acosta-Vargas et al. (2024) found recurring barriers such as poor image descriptions and weak keyboard navigation. It is important, therefore, that institutions must prioritise platforms that meet accessibility standards and critically review how inclusivity is operationalised.

Ultimately, inclusivity is not an inherent feature of GenAI but, rather, it is a pedagogical and institutional choice. By combining responsible tool selection, professional development, and inclusive teaching practices, TESOL educators can ensure that GenAI enhances rather than undermines equitable access to language learning.

5.8 Conclusion

The integration of GenAI in TESOL offers immense potential to enhance language learning and teaching. However, this potential comes with significant ethical risks. This chapter has discussed several of these key risks, including data privacy, academic integrity, overreliance, unequal access, and the possible marginalisation of learners with diverse needs. These risks focus attention on what it means to teach and learn languages ethically, responsively, and inclusively.

Data-related concerns emerge as particularly pressing. GenAI tools rely on vast and often opaque data infrastructures that may collect, store, and repurpose learner inputs without explicit consent or transparency. As discussed, issues such as informed consent, secondary data use, and the limits of anonymisation present real threats to learner trust and autonomy. Moreover, these risks are exacerbated by lack of clear frameworks for regulation and the transnational nature of AI platforms, making oversight and accountability difficult to enforce.

Academic integrity presents another major area of concern. The use of GenAI in second language writing and assessment raises questions about authorship, authenticity, and the pedagogical value of tasks completed with AI support. Educators highlighted the challenge of detecting plagiarism while acknowledging the limitations and inequities of existing GenAI detection tools.

Further, the risks of overreliance, by learners and educators alike, signal a growing need for critical digital literacy and pedagogical reflection. There is a belief by teachers that GenAI will lead to a kind of 'cognitive offloading' (Dawson, 2020) whereby students outsource too much of their thinking and expression to GenAI, ultimately limiting language development. Similarly, there is concern that teacher overreliance may reduce professional agency and depersonalise language teaching. Finally, there is concern that uneven access to technology, skills, and institutional support may contribute to a widening digital divide.

In response to these challenges, this chapter highlighted the European Commission's (2019) 'Ethics Guidelines for Trustworthy AI" as a values-driven framework for GenAI in TESOL, while also drawing on critical posthumanism to question traditional human–machine boundaries. Principles of privacy, accountability, human agency, and technical robustness provide useful guidance, but their application requires ongoing, context-sensitive reflection rather than rigid prescription. Responsible integration further depends on professional development and clear policies at multiple levels, supported by infrastructure and inclusive design that give educators and learners real choice over how their data and labour are used.

In sum, the ethical future of GenAI in TESOL lies not in resisting this technology, but rather, embedding it within a pedagogy of care, justice, and reflexivity. Educators are not passive adopters of technological tools but are active mediators and designers of ethical learning environments, who can advocate for inclusion and equitable practices that aim to empower learners.

Looking ahead, the following chapter examines the critical role of teacher education in shaping the ethical and effective integration of GenAI in TESOL. It explores current gaps in training, the professional development needs, and how best to equip teachers with the skills needed to navigate AI-enhanced classrooms confidently and responsibly.

References

Acosta-Vargas, P., Acosta-Vargas, G., Salvador-Acosta, B., & Jadán-Guerrero, J. (2024, June). Addressing web accessibility challenges with generative artificial intelligence tools for inclusive education. In *2024 Tenth International Conference on eDemocracy & eGovernment (ICEDEG)* (pp. 1–7). IEEE. https://doi.org/10.1109/icedeg61611.2024.10702085

Alexander, K., Savvidou, C., & Alexander, C. (2023). Who wrote this essay? Detecting AI-generated writing in second language education in higher education. *Teaching English with Technology, 23*(2), 25–43. https://doi.org/10.56297/buka4060/xhld5365

Alnasib, B. N. (2023). Factors affecting faculty members' readiness to integrate artificial intelligence into their teaching practices: A study from the Saudi higher education context. *International Journal of Learning, Teaching and Educational Research, 22*(8), 465–491. https://doi.org/10.26803/ijlter.22.8.24

Barad, K. (2007). Meeting the universe halfway: Quantum physics and the entanglement of matter and meaning. *Duke University Press*. https://doi.org/10.2307/j.ctv12101zq

Bayne, S. (2015). Teacherbot: Interventions in automated teaching. *Teaching in Higher Education, 20*(4), 455–467. https://doi.org/10.1080/13562517.2015.1020783

Blodgett, S. L., Barocas, S., Daumé Iii, H., & Wallach, H. (2020). Language (technology) is power: A critical survey of "bias" in NLPp. *arXiv preprint* arXiv:2005.14050. https://doi.org/10.18653/v1/2020.acl-main.485

Brown, T. B., Mann, B., Ryder, N., Subbiah, M., Kaplan, J., Dhariwal, P., … Amodei, D. (2020). Language models are few-shot learners. *Advances in Neural Information Processing Systems, 33*, 1877–1901. https://doi.org/10.48550/arXiv.2005.14165

Calderwood, S. J. (2025). An exploration of human and platform intra-actions in a digital teaching and learning environment. *Learning, Media and Technology, 50*(2), 263–275. https://doi.org/10.1080/17439884.2023.2285820

Chaka, C. (2023). Detecting AI content in responses generated by ChatGPT, YouChat, and Chatsonic: The case of five AI content detection tools. *Journal of Applied Learning and Teaching, 6*(2), 94–104. https://doi.org/10.37074/jalt.2023.6.2.12

Dawson, P. (2020). Cognitive offloading and assessment. In M. Bearman, P. Dawson, R. Ajjawi, J. Tai, & D. Boud (Eds.), *Re-imagining University Assessment in a Digital World* (pp. 37–48). Springer International Publishing. https://doi.org/10.1007/978-3-030-41956-1_4

Dignum, V. (2019). What is artificial intelligence? In *Responsible Artificial Intelligence: How to develop and use AI in a responsible way* (pp. 9–34). Springer International Publishing. https://doi.org/10.1007/978-3-030-30371-6_1

European Commission. (2019). Ethics guidelines for trustworthy AI. High-Level Expert Group on Artificial Intelligence. https://digital-strategy.ec.europa.eu/en/library/ethics-guidelines-trustworthy-ai

European Union. (2016). Regulation (EU) 2016/679 of the European Parliament and of the Council of 27 April 2016 on the protection of natural persons with regard to the processing of personal data and on the free movement of such data, and repealing Directive 95/46/EC (General Data Protection Regulation). *Official Journal of the European Union, L119,* 1–88. https://eur-lex.europa.eu/eli/reg/2016/679/oj

Fleisig, E., Smith, G., Bossi, M., Rustagi, I., Yin, X., & Klein, D. (2024). Linguistic bias in ChatGPT: Language models reinforce dialect discrimination. *Proceedings of the 2024 Conference on Empirical Methods in Natural Language Processing*, 13541–13564. https://doi.org/10.18653/v1/2024.emnlp-main.750

Freire, P. (1970). Pedagogy of the oppressed (MB Ramos, Trans.). *New York: Continuum, 2007*.

Georgiou, G. P. (2024). *Differentiating between human-written and AI-generated texts using linguistic features automatically extracted from an online computational tool*. arXiv preprint arXiv:2407.03646. https://doi.org/10.48550/arXiv.2407.03646

Georgiou, G. P. (2025, July 3). Key features to distinguish between human- and AI-generated texts: What university professors say [Preprint]. *OSF Preprints*. https://doi.org/10.31234/osf.io/jvytm_v2

Ghosh, S., & Caliskan, A. (2023, August). Chatgpt perpetuates gender bias in machine translation and ignores non-gendered pronouns: Findings across Bengali and five other low-resource languages. In *Proceedings of the 2023 AAAI/ACM Conference on AI, Ethics, and Society* (pp. 901–912). https://doi.org/10.1145/3600211.3604672

Granström, M., & Oppi, P. (2025, June). Assessing teachers' readiness and perceived usefulness of AI in education: An Estonian perspective. In *Frontiers in Education* (Vol. 10, p. 1622240). Frontiers. https://doi.org/10.3389/feduc.2025.1622240

Huang, L. (2023). Ethics of artificial intelligence in education: Student privacy and data protection. *Science Insights Education Frontiers, 16*(2), 2577–2587. https://doi.org/10.15354/sief.23.re202

Jandrić, P., & Ford, D. R. (2022). Postdigital ecopedagogies: Genealogies, contradictions, and possible futures. *Postdigital Science and Education, 4*, 692–710. https://doi.org/10.1007/s42438-020-00207-3

Kormos, J., & Smith, A. M. (2023). *Teaching languages to students with specific learning differences* (Vol. 18). Channel View Publications. https://doi.org/10.21832/kormos8615

Köseoğlu, S., Veletsianos, G., & Rowell, C. (Eds.). (2023). *Critical digital pedagogy in higher education.* Athabasca University Press. https://doi.org/10.15215/aupress/9781778290015.01

Kotek, H., Dockum, R., & Sun, D. (2023, November). Gender bias and stereotypes in large language models. In *Proceedings of the ACM collective intelligence conference* (pp. 12–24). https://doi.org/10.1145/3582269.3615599

Lan, Y. (2024). Through tensions to identity-based motivations: Exploring teacher professional identity in artificial intelligence-enhanced teacher training. *Teaching and Teacher Education, 151*, Article 104736. https://doi.org/10.1016/j.tate.2024.104736

Lison, P., Pilán, I., Sánchez, D., Batet, M., & Øvrelid, L. (2021, August). Anonymisation models for text data: State of the art, challenges and future directions. In *Proceedings of the 59th Annual Meeting of the Association for Computational Linguistics and the 11th International Joint Conference on Natural Language Processing (Volume 1: Long Papers)* (pp. 4188–4203). Association for Computational Linguistics. https://doi.org/10.18653/v1/2021.acl-long.323

Mishra, P., & Koehler, M. J. (2006). Technological pedagogical content knowledge: A framework for teacher knowledge. *Teachers College Record, 108*(6), 1017–1054. https://doi.org/10.1111/j.1467-9620.2006.00684.x

Mitchell, M., Wu, S., Zaldivar, A., Barnes, P., Vasserman, L., Hutchinson, B., ... & Gebru, T. (2019, January). Model cards for model reporting. In *Proceedings of the Conference on Fairness, Accountability, and Transparency* (pp. 220–229). ACM. https://doi.org/10.1145/3287560.3287596

Moniz, H., & Escartín, C. P. (2023). *Towards responsible machine translation: Ethical and legal considerations in machine translation.* Springer. https://doi.org/10.26034/cm.jostrans.2024.4731

OECD. (2019/2024). *Recommendation of the Council on Artificial Intelligence* (OECD/LEGAL/0449). OECD. https://legalinstruments.oecd.org/en/instruments/OECD-LEGAL-0449

OpenAI. (2023). *GPT-4 system card*. OpenAI. https://cdn.openai.com/papers/gpt-4-system-card.pdf

Oye, E., Frank, E., & Owen, J. (2024). Ethical considerations in AI-driven education. ResearchGate https://www.researchgate.net/publication/387275777_Ethical_Considerations_in_AI-Driven_Education

Park, S. (2023). Bridging the global divide in AI regulation: A proposal for a contextual, coherent, and commensurable framework. *Washington International Law Journal, 33*(2), 216–255. https://doi.org/10.2139/ssrn.4950781

Perkins, M., Roe, J., Postma, D., McGaughran, J., & Hickerson, D. (2024). Detection of GPT-4 generated text in higher education: Combining academic judgement and software to identify generative AI tool misuse. *Journal of Academic Ethics, 22*(1), 89–113.https://doi.org/10.48550/arXiv.2305.18081

Schofield, L., Johnstone, A., Kayes, D., & Thomas, H. (2023). Talking about nothing to talk about something. In S. Köseoğlu, G. Veletsianos, & C. Rowell (Eds.), *Critical digital pedagogy in higher education* (pp. 15–30). Athabasca University Press. https://doi.org/10.15215/aupress/9781778290015.01

Selwyn, N., Hillman, T., Eynon, R., Ferreira, G., Knox, J., Macgilchrist, F., & Sancho-Gil, J. M. (2020). What's next for Ed-Tech? Critical hopes and concerns for the 2020s. *Learning, Media and Technology, 45*(1), 1–6. https://doi.org/10.1080/17439884.2020.1694945

Stentiford, L., & Koutsouris, G. (2021). What are inclusive pedagogies in higher education? A systematic scoping review. *Studies in Higher Education, 46*(11), 2245–2261. https://doi.org/10.1080/03075079.2020.1716322

Tao, Y., Viberg, O., Baker, R. S., & Kizilcec, R. F. (2024). Cultural bias and cultural alignment of large language models. *PNAS Nexus, 3*(9), page 346. https://doi.org/10.1093/pnasnexus/pgae346

The European Parliament and the Council of the European Union. (2024). Regulation (EU) 2024/1689 of the European Parliament and of the Council of 13 June 2024 laying down harmonised rules on artificial intelligence and amending other acts (Artificial Intelligence Act). Official Journal of the European Union, L 1689. https://eur-lex.europa.eu/eli/reg/2024/1689/oj/eng

Tseng, J. J., Chai, C. S., Tan, L., & Park, M. (2022). A critical review of research on technological pedagogical and content knowledge (TPACK) in language teaching. *Computer Assisted Language Learning, 35*(4), 948–971. https://doi.org/10.1080/09588221.2020.1868531

Uddagiri, C., & Isunuri, B. V. (2024). Ethical and privacy challenges of generative AI. In S. A. Shylaja & M. S. Gaur (Eds.), *Generative AI: Current trends and applications* (pp. 219–244). Springer Nature. https://doi.org/10.1007/978-981-97-8460-8_11

UNESCO. (2021). *Recommendation on the ethics of artificial intelligence.* UNESCO. https://unesdoc.unesco.org/ark:/48223/pf0000381137

UNESCO, & IRCAI. (2024). *Challenging systematic prejudices: An investigation into gender bias in large language models.* UNESCO. https://unesdoc.unesco.org/ark:/48223/pf0000388971

Watanabe, A. (2024). Have courage to use your own mind, with or without AI: The relevance of Kant's enlightenment to higher education in the age of artificial intelligence. *Electronic Journal of e-Learning, 22*(2), 46–58. https://doi.org/10.34190/ejel.21.5.3229

Weng, Z., & Fu, Y. (2025). Generative AI in language education: Bridging divide and fostering inclusivity. *International Journal of Technology in Education, 8*(2), 395–420. https://doi.org/10.46328/ijte.1056

Williamson, B., Macgilchrist, F., & Potter, J. (2023). Re-examining AI, automation and datafication in education. *Learning, Media and Technology, 48*(1), 1–5. https://doi.org/10.1080/17439884.2023.2167830

World Wide Web Consortium (W3C). (2018). *Web Content Accessibility Guidelines (WCAG) 2.1.* https://www.w3.org/TR/WCAG21/

Zawacki-Richter, O., Marín, V. I., Bond, M., & Gouverneur, F. (2019). Systematic review of research on artificial intelligence applications in higher education—Where are the educators? *International Journal of Educational Technology in Higher Education, 16*(1), 1–27. https://doi.org/10.1186/s41239-019-0171-0

6

Teacher Education for GenAI Integration in TESOL

6.1 Introduction

As GenAI technologies become more accessible and embedded within TESOL contexts, educators are increasingly expected to critically select and integrate these tools into their teaching practices. However, this transformation is occurring with minimal guidance or support for many TESOL educators, who must navigate a shifting pedagogical landscape shaped by technologies whose implications are still only partially understood. In this context, teacher education plays a vital role for ensuring that TESOL professionals are not only technically proficient but also ethically and pedagogically prepared to engage with GenAI tools in meaningful, inclusive, and context-responsive ways.

Despite the widespread attention GenAI has received in educational discourse, current evidence suggests that there is a significant lag in how teacher education programmes are responding to these developments (Weiner et al., 2024; Zawacki-Richter et al., 2019) with many educators encountering GenAI tools through informal experimentation rather than structured professional learning. The absence of coordinated training has created challenges for teachers, including unequal access to resources, ethical dilemmas around responsible use, and difficulties

C. Savvidou, *AI-Powered Language Teaching*,
https://doi.org/10.1007/978-3-032-14502-4_6

in aligning AI tools with established pedagogical goals (Holmes et al., 2019).While some teachers show enthusiasm for using GenAI for lesson planning, feedback generation, and learner engagement, other teachers express concerns about its ability to maintain existing academic and ethical standards, and the risk of undermining teachers' professional judgement.

This chapter examines the role of teacher education in supporting TESOL professionals to use GenAI responsibly and effectively. Drawing on the survey responses from the 78 participants and interview transcripts collected from 14 TESOL educators across a range of global contexts, this chapter examines how teachers currently perceive GenAI, the types of training they have, and the professional development models they find most supportive. This discussion situates these findings within critical and posthuman frameworks that question not only the capabilities of AI tools but also the human, institutional, and ideological systems that shape their use in educational settings (Selwyn, 2019).

6.2 Situating GenAI in the Context of TESOL Teacher Education

While the integration of digital technologies into TESOL has long been a focus of research, policy, and practice (see Chapter 2), the rise of GenAI technologies constitutes an 'inflection point,' far exceeding the capabilities of earlier digital tools (Kern, 2024). Unlike previous educational technologies, which allowed for improved content delivery or administrative efficiency, GenAI tools such as ChatGPT and other large language models (LLMs), offer real-time language generation that can simulate authentic communication, create instructional materials, and respond to learner questions in real-time. While these functions have the potential to transform language teaching, they also challenge TESOL teachers' existing classroom roles, as well as traditional models of teacher knowledge and practice.

For many TESOL educators, engaging with GenAI begins from a position of uneven preparedness, marked by significant obstacles in training, resources, and institutional support. As discussed in Chapter 5, the increasing digitalisation of TESOL has widened global inequalities, especially between contexts with differing levels of infrastructure, training, and policy support (Minna, 2024). Educators also report feeling pressure to integrate digital tools effectively despite expressing their own lack of competence and confidence, limited availability of resources and professional development opportunities (Bui, 2022). Some teachers are even reluctant to reveal their use of GenAI, fearing that colleagues or institutions may view it as a threat to language learning and teaching (Barnes & Tour, 2025). Against this background, it appears that traditional ideas of 'digital literacy' based on technical proficiency and the navigation of online platforms, are no longer sufficient.

Although research in Artificial Intelligence in Education (AIED) has grown, it is mainly grounded in STEM subjects focusing on technical uses, such as prediction, assessment, and personalisation, while often overlooking pedagogical or ethical considerations (Zawacki-Richter et al., 2019). In TESOL, by contrast, what is needed is a pedagogical framework for AI literacy, that includes not only technical competence but also critical awareness and knowledge of capabilities, limitations, and ethical implications. Chiu et al., (2024) propose such a framework based on five key components: technology, impact, ethics, collaboration, and self-reflection.

To better understand these dynamics, this chapter draws on three critical theoretical perspectives that foreground ethical, pedagogical, and posthuman approaches to technology in education.

First, international frameworks developed by bodies such as UNESCO (2021) and the European Commission (2019), provide a foundation for evaluating GenAI integration. These frameworks emphasise values that must be upheld in teacher decision-making and institutional policy, such as human agency, transparency, accountability, and fairness. For example, in a secondary education TESOL context, a school might introduce GenAI tools for writing support but ensuring policies that guarantee transparency about how tools are used, maintaining teacher oversight, and limiting use during assessments.

Second, postdigital approaches encourage educators to ask who benefits from GenAI, how it reshapes classroom relationships, and what assumptions are embedded in its design (Jandrić & Ford, 2022). For

TESOL, these issues are particularly significant because language, identity, and ideology are deeply interconnected. Research shows that LLMs often default to Standard American or British English while marginalising World Englishes. For example, Fleisig et al. (2024) found that GPT-3.5 and GPT-4 produced less accurate comprehension, more stereotyping, and condescending tones—up to 25% worse—when responding to non-standard varieties such as Indian or Nigerian English. Such biases risk undermining learners' linguistic identities and reinforcing contested notions of "correct English," especially in postcolonial and Global South contexts.

Third, critical posthumanism conceptualises teaching and learning as emerging from entangled relationships between humans, technologies, and environments (Barad, 2007; Calderwood, 2025). In this view, learning to teach with GenAI is not simply about mastering new tools, but about engaging with "assemblages," i.e. the complex mix of technologies, people, environments and practices that shape the classroom, Such a view moves beyond seeing technology as just a tool and instead encourages approaches to teacher development that recognise how GenAI actively shapes what teachers do, how knowledge is valued, and how professional roles are defined.

For example, when a TESOL teacher uses GenAI to help students write essays, the tool often suggests phrases and structures that reflect Western academic writing norms. As the teacher and students work with these suggestions, they are not passive recipients of this knowledge but are encouraged to critically engage with assumptions of what is seen as "good" writing. In this way, the teacher's role shifts from not simply delivering language instruction to helping students critically evaluate the outputs of technology as part of their language learning.

Together, these perspectives stress the need for TESOL teacher education that moves beyond simply adopting AI as part of their teaching practice to developing critical understanding and ethical reasoning in a context-sensitive practice.

6.3 Current Teacher Education and Perceptions

Survey and interview data reveal how TESOL educators perceive their preparedness to use GenAI and the level of training and institutional support available to them. Overall, findings highlight significant gaps in formal training, reliance on informal learning, and a strong consensus on the need for structured professional development.

Survey data indicate a clear lack of preparation to use GenAI tools. Of the 78 respondents, only 9% reported feeling adequately trained, while 39.7% described themselves as "moderately "trained. A majority (51.3%) reported receiving no meaningful training at all. Together, these results indicate that over 90% of respondents believe that they lack sufficient preparation to engage with GenAI tools confidently (see Fig. 6.1).

Interview data contextualise these results, highlighting how the absence of structured training is compounded by inconsistent institutional support and limited training. Many educators described self-directed exploration, minimal or superficial professional development, and uncertainty about how to apply GenAI meaningfully in TESOL contexts:

> Quotation 1: "I have been experimenting and trying to use it the last few months, maybe to see how it could help me revise some material and

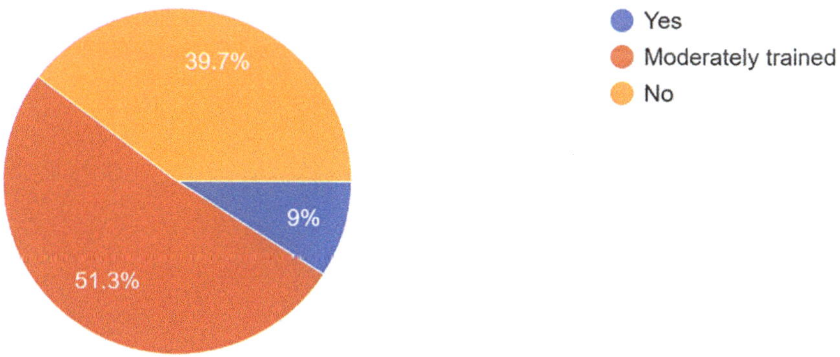

Fig. 6.1 Educators' perceptions of preparedness to use GenAI tools

> maybe make my life a bit easier with my teaching … But I'm sure there are so many things that I haven't discovered yet. I'm sure that there are many functions that I don't know, so I'm kind of trying to train myself, about that." (T.13, Greece)
> Quotation 2: "We had one workshop, but it was very basic, more like a box-ticking exercise. Everything I know, I've taught myself. I don't think any of my colleagues use AI tools in their classrooms." (T.6, Japan)

Survey findings also demonstrate strong recognition of the importance of GenAI training in teacher education. Over half of respondents (52.6%) rated training as "very important," while 39.7% considered it "somewhat important." Fewer than 8% described it as "neutral" or "unimportant," reflecting broad consensus among educators that GenAI represents a fundamental shift in the way they teach (see Fig. 6.2).

The literature also indicates that education often lags behind technological innovation due to resource limitations, institutional resistance and ethical concerns (Zawacki-Richter et al., 2019). Indeed, in TESOL research, educators emphasise that teacher training must go beyond technical skills to include critical awareness. They point to frameworks such as TPACK (Technological Pedagogical Content Knowledge) and SAMR (Substitution, Augmentation, Modification, Redefinition) as useful tools for evaluating the pedagogical relevance of GenAI (Kohnke & Zou, 2025).

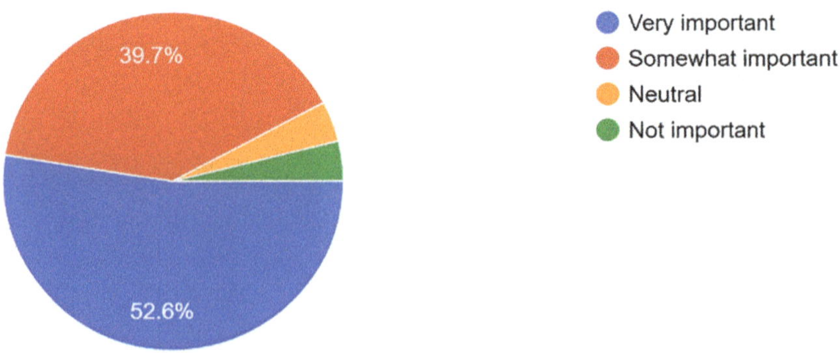

Fig. 6.2 Educators' perceptions of the importance of GenAI training in teacher education

Yet in the absence of formal provision, professional development is often left to teacher-led initiatives. Many educators reported turning to peers, social media, and collaborative exchanges for support:

> Quotation 3: "As for professional support, we usually get guidance from friends or colleagues…Some colleagues share new apps in group chats, and we exchange ideas about what works best." (T5, China)

This grassroots approach highlights teacher agency but also reinforces inequities between teachers with strong networks and others, who are left to navigate independently. Indeed, lack of formal training was repeatedly identified as a barrier to effective GenAI integration, with several participants reporting that their institutions offered little or no official support or training on AI use:

> Quotation 4: "There hasn't been formal training from the university management. Recently, my department published some AI guidelines … But we haven't had any sessions on how to practically integrate these guidelines into teaching and assessment." (T.3, China)

These training gaps also reflect regional inequalities. For example, in some educational settings, limited infrastructure and connectivity restrict opportunities:

> Quotation 5: "In Algeria, there are rural areas with poor internet connections, so AI tools can't be used everywhere. But in private schools, where students have better resources, you can give them tasks that they can approach using tools like ChatGPT." (T.14, Algeria)

Other educators expressed financial concerns that influence access to professional learning:

> Quotation 6: "Who's going to pay for those short courses? This should be something that should be funded, from, public institutions." (T.13, Greece)

Despite these barriers, educators expressed strong motivation to engage with GenAI, often to remain relevant in the face of digitally skilled students:

> Quotation 7: "It's becoming harder to catch up as students get savvier. They now know how to use AI from the beginning." (T.1, US).

Others described exploratory approaches, such as experimentation with prompts as a self-training strategy:

> Quotation 8: "Maybe I ask the same question twice or three times, not because it hasn't responded, but just to see if I change a little bit the phrasing or, I make it more specific if it would give me a different and a more effective response" (T.13, Greece)

For TESOL teacher education, there is also a need for training that equips teachers to navigate differences in politically or ideologically diverse environments:

> Quotation 9: "Regarding bias, that's also a concern because AI is trained by organizations that may have biases, such as political biases. For example, ChatGPT is not accessible in China, and China has its own AI. If you ask the same questions to an international AI and a Chinese AI, the answers might differ, which is very interesting to consider." (T.2, China)

Concerns about over-reliance on GenAI, by both students and teachers, also emerged:

> Quotation 10: "it can make students lazier and more dependent. Instead of organizing their own knowledge or translating content themselves, they often rely on AI to do it for them." (T.5, China)
> Quotation 11: "Teachers have become so over reliant that sometimes they take the content as it is. And later on, when we sit together and discuss whatever they have used, then they come to realize that actually it doesn't fit what they want to use it for. Maybe because at a certain point, teachers are overwhelmed with lots of paperwork." (T8, Qatar)

Ethical issues such as data privacy, bias, and misinformation were also raised:

> Quotation: 12: "AI tools like ChatGPT sometimes provide inaccurate information and false quotations. I've tested it multiple times, and it often gives false references. In terms of privacy, I don't fully trust these tools because I believe they store user-data, which is concerning." (T.14, Algeria)
> Quotation 13: I asked ChatGPT to describe various countries. For developed countries like Spain, Italy, and Germany, it provided very positive descriptions. But when I asked about developing countries, such as those in Africa like Ghana, the language was more negative. (T.12, Cyprus)

Finally, some educators described how GenAI is beginning to reshape their professional identities and roles.

> Quotation 14: [its] like a second voice, someone who's always there I can communicate with to come up maybe with new ideas, maybe to refine my own, or adopt the ideas and then adapt them myself based on my needs, we use as critical friend, you know, this idea of the mentor kind of role. (T.8, Qatar)

These reflections from TESOL educators express their concerns around the use of GenAI and highlight the urgent need for teacher education that equips them with not only the technical competence but also opportunities for critical, ethical, and context-sensitive knowledge required for responsible GenAI integration.

6.4 Professional Development Needs and Preferences

When asked which types of professional development would most effectively support the integration of GenAI into their teaching, the educators ($n = 78$) expressed a clear preference for structured and practical forms of support (see Table 6.1).

Table 6.1 Educators' preferences for professional development types to support their use of GenAI

Professional development type	% of Respondents
GenAI integration workshops	76.9%
Online courses or webinars	75.6%
Practical AI toolkits or resources	57.7%
Mentorship or peer collaboration	39.7%
Professional learning communities	32.1%
Other (e.g. clear institutional policies, ethics and data privacy workshops, case studies, in-school training)	2.6%

The most popular choices selected by educators include workshops (76.9%) and online courses or webinars (75.6%), highlighting the demand for systematic, guided learning opportunities that can be integrated into teachers' workloads. A second preference is the desire for practical resources. Over half of respondents (57.7%) selected toolkits or ready-to-use materials, signalling the need for annotated prompts, lesson-plan templates, and examples of classroom adaptation. A third choice reflects educators' preference for collaborative and sustained professional development, with nearly 40% favouring mentorship or peer collaboration and 32.1% valuing professional learning communities.

This preference for dialogic and reflective formats is also echoed in research by Arefian et al. (2025). In a qualitative study with pre-service EFL teachers, findings showed how collaborative reflective practice (CRP) supported by ChatGPT helped participants connect theory to practice, sharpen critical thinking, and engage in meaningful professional dialogue. In their model, weekly group meetings with peers and teacher educators created a reflective cycle in which GenAI was positioned not only as a resource generator but also as a collaborative partner. This suggests that GenAI training is most effective when it is social, dialogic, and situated.

Interview data reinforces these findings, with TESOL educators expressing a strong desire for training that is not only accessible but also pedagogically relevant, ethically grounded, and contextually appropriate. As one educator commented:

> Quotation 15: "I know how to lesson plan, I need to learn how to integrate AI into my teaching." (T.11, Cyprus)

Alongside practical needs, participants emphasised the importance of critical awareness. Educators were especially concerned about student over-reliance and misinformation, as well as the need to embed AI literacy into teacher education:

> Quotation 16: "Students can easily become too reliant on these tools. The problem is they don't always use them critically. AI-generated content can have issues like hallucinations or misinformation, and students need to be trained to assess the information and not blindly rely on it." (T.7, South Africa)

However, the ability to access meaningful training was often constrained by time, workload, and relevance:

> Quotation 17: "Who's got time to attend those short courses? There should be a more coordinated effort." (T.13, Greece)
> Quotation 18 The webinars mostly show how AI can create typical lesson plans, but that's not what I need. (T.11, Cyprus)

Educators also identified sustained and collaborative formats as particularly effective.

> Quotation 19: Every Tuesday, we have two hours to sit in groups and discuss what's new in education. Often, AI is one of the topics. (T.8, Qatar)

And they highlighted the importance of cultural and context sensitivity:

> Quotation 20: "We had a professional development workshop about DALL E, which is generating pictures because where I'm living now, they have lots of cultural considerations, and all content should be culturally appropriate…We've done a workshop with teachers regarding how to benefit from these platforms." (T.8, Qatar)

Finally, educators acknowledged the value of peer-to-peer learning:

> Quotation 21: "Sometimes, we receive software from our institution, but the most useful support comes from our peers. They are approachable and always around to share tips. Some colleagues share new apps in group chats, and we exchange ideas about what works best." (T.5, China)

Together, these findings reveal a strong consensus among TESOL educators for professional development opportunities that are sustained, collaborative, and sensitive to their local realities. Whether through formal workshops, peer networks, or institutionally supported reflection, TESOL educators emphasised the need for training that promotes critical engagement, cultural responsiveness, and professional confidence.

In addition to exploring teachers' needs and preferences for professional development for GenAI integration, the survey also investigated how educators view it as a tool for their own professional development (see Fig. 6.3). Findings indicate that the majority of TESOL educators (76.9%) increasingly recognise the value of GenAI not only for instructional purposes but also for their own professional learning and development. This enthusiasm reflects a broader shift towards self-directed learning, where teachers engage with GenAI to explore new possibilities for practice, as well as improve their productivity. However, the 14.1% who were unsure, along with the 9% who saw no value in it, indicate the presence of uncertainty which may be linked to concerns about trust, relevance, or a lack of formal training. These patterns highlight the centrality of teacher agency in shaping how GenAI is adopted or resisted in professional practice.

This finding resonates with research on teacher agency in digital contexts. Nøhr et al. (2023) found that Danish university teachers often reported high levels of digital agency and tended to exercise this by making selective decisions about whether, when, and how to employ digital tools in their teaching. Their agency was thus shaped both by personal will and skill and by structural factors such as time, institutional support, and decision-making power. These findings underscore the need for teacher education programmes and professional development initiatives that not only build technical competence but also strengthen

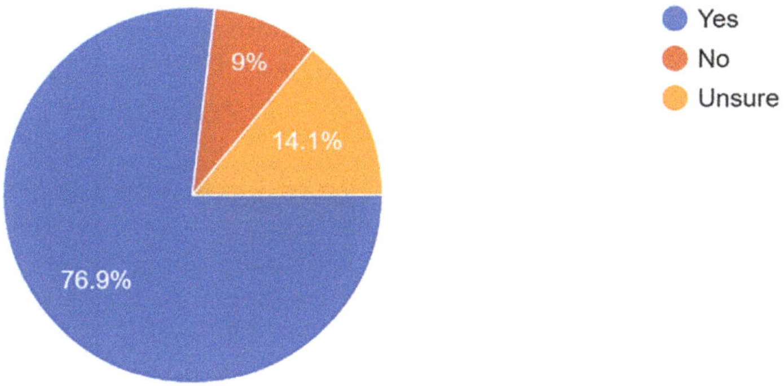

Fig. 6.3 Educators' perceptions of GenAI training as a valuable professional development tool

educators' sense of agency, supporting them in exploring how GenAI may be used as part of their own professional growth.

6.4.1 GenAI as a Professional Copilot

Interview data illustrate how TESOL educators are actively incorporating GenAI into their own professional learning through a range of self-directed practices. Many teachers described using GenAI for planning, materials development, and assessment design:

> Quotation 22: "I use ChatGPT to generate texts for reading and to create vocabulary games. I also use it for writing, especially in correcting writing tasks for my students." (T.14, Algeria)

Others framed it as a "copilot" to improve their own linguistic accuracy,

> Quotation 23: "I'm the pilot, of course, and these tools are my copilots, especially for editing in English, Spanish, and sometimes Greek." (T.9, Cyprus)
> Quotation 24: "For more complex sentences, I ask AI to help me analyse the syntax and explain why certain words are used. It's a tool I use a lot for teaching preparation." (T.4, China)

However, several limitations were also noted. Educators expressed concern about the accuracy and reliability of AI outputs. Teachers reported issues such as fabricated references or vague content:

> Quotation 25: "Yes, for instance, when creating exams, some of the questions provided by ChatGPT were vague. Also, if I ask it for references, sometimes it provides references that don't exist. When I searched for them, I couldn't find the information it provided." (T.12, Cyprus)

As such, teachers often need to filter or adapt GenAI outputs carefully and critically evaluate GenAI outputs.

6.4.2 Risks of Over-reliance

One educator highlighted the risks of over-reliance, particularly when AI-generated content is used uncritically without reflection on its appropriateness for specific teaching contexts:

> Quotation 26: "Teachers have become so over reliant that sometimes they take the content as it is. And later on, when we sit together and discuss whatever they have used, then they come to realize, oh, no. That actually doesn't fit what I want to use it for. So this is very important, over reliance. And we always tell them technology is there to help to facilitate your work, but do not use it as it is." (T.8, Qatar)

These findings suggest that while GenAI holds potential for supporting teacher learning, its effectiveness depends on critical use, professional judgement, and contextual awareness. As Nøhr et al. (2023) argue, technology becomes empowering only when teachers are positioned as active agents in shaping how, when, and why it is used.

6.4.3 Self-directed vs. Structured Learning

Educators' strong support of GenAI as a tool for their own professional development raises the question of how educators are learning to use these tools effectively, and who is responsible for supporting their learning. Across the interviews and survey responses, two distinct approaches emerged: self-directed versus institutionally supported professional development.

Many educators described their engagement with GenAI as self-initiated, often driven by personal interest or necessity. This approach enabled them to explore tools at their own pace, experiment with prompt design, and adapt outputs to their specific teaching contexts, as described by one teacher:

> Quotation 26: "I'm kind of trying to train myself, I have been using it [ChatGPT] to do simple things like improving my prompts. I phrase what I really want to request from the chatbot and see how well it adjusts." (T.13, Greece)

However, this autonomy often comes with significant costs. Teachers reported feeling isolated, overwhelmed by the pace of technological change, and uncertain about best practices. Without structured training, they were left to make ad hoc decisions about suitability of content, how to use ethically, how to integrate into their teaching:

> Quotation 27: "I don't feel prepared enough as a teacher to use it. I don't think I have the right tools or knowledge yet. We definitely need professional development on AI. If I knew how to incorporate it properly, I'd definitely use it." (T.11, Cyprus).

While most participants relied on self-directed learning, a smaller number described experiences with structured or semi-structured professional development, including long-term seminars and targeted online sessions. These opportunities allowed educators to engage with GenAI tools in more sustained and guided ways, often drawing on multiple learning modes:

> Quotation 28: "Last year, I took a 9-month seminar on technology and language education, which included AI tools like Gemini and Copilot.

> I've also attended shorter online seminars, like one offered by [university name] about AI. So, I've gathered knowledge from various sources." (T.11, Cyprus)

The interview data also reveal disparities in access to GenAI-related professional development, shaped by institutional resources and support structures. Educators working in well-resourced environments often had opportunities to engage with AI tools through organised training initiatives embedded within their institutions. As one participant noted:

> Quotation 29: "Yes, because we're a Microsoft Showcase School, we get opportunities to learn how to use AI tools like Copilot." (T.10, Cyprus)

In contrast, as one participant explained, access to professional development was not simply about availability but also affordability and workload. Attending AI-focused training often required both financial investment and additional time that teachers could not easily spare (see Quotation 6, T13, Greece).

In sum, the findings highlight that while many TESOL educators are turning to self-directed exploration of GenAI tools, this approach often leaves them isolated, uncertain, and without clear ethical or pedagogical guidance. Structured professional development opportunities, when available, provide more sustainable and equitable pathways for building competence, but access to these opportunities remains uneven across institutions and regions. To move forward, teacher education and institutional policy must prioritise inclusive, funded, and context-sensitive professional development, ensuring that GenAI training is not left to individual initiative alone but becomes a systematic and supported part of TESOL practice.

6.5 Critical Issues in GenAI Teacher Education

Beyond questions of technical competence, teacher education in TESOL must tackle the broader ethical, pedagogical, and epistemological implications of GenAI. Four critical areas stand out: the need to develop ethical and pedagogical literacies, promote culturally and linguistically responsive teaching, avoid technocentric approaches, and engage with theoretical perspectives, such as critical posthumanism. Each of these areas highlights the importance of preparing TESOL teachers to understand how GenAI is a new and integral force shaping teacher knowledge, authority, and the very nature of teaching itself.

First, one of the most urgent challenges identified by both scholars and international policy bodies is the need to develop rigorous ethical and pedagogical literacies among educators engaging with AI technologies. As noted earlier, many TESOL teachers report uncertainty about how to evaluate the reliability of AI-generated content and how to integrate these tools responsibly into their teaching. Several interviewees expressed concern about the accuracy of AI outputs, the risk of student over-reliance, and the lack of guidance for evaluating content for bias or appropriateness. These accounts highlight the need for structured opportunities to build informed and critical engagement with GenAI.

This concern is reinforced by global policy frameworks. UNESCO's Recommendation on the Ethics of Artificial Intelligence (2021) and the European Commission's Ethics Guidelines for Trustworthy AI (2019) both stress that AI systems in education must uphold human agency, transparency, fairness, and accountability. For TESOL educators, this means being prepared not only to use GenAI tools but also to critically interrogate how these systems influence language norms, assessment practices, and learner autonomy.

The academic literature echoes this emphasis. As Kohnke and Zou (2025) argue, TESOL educators must develop critical digital literacy to evaluate how GenAI tools may reproduce biases in feedback and content. Similarly, Zawacki-Richter et al. (2019) call for AI literacy that includes the capacity to question the social and pedagogical implications of automated technologies. Ethical and pedagogical literacies, therefore, must be treated as core competencies for professional practice.

A second critical issue in GenAI-related teacher education is the need to cultivate cultural and linguistic responsiveness. TESOL educators often work in multilingual, multicultural classrooms where sensitivity to language variation and identity is essential. Yet research shows how GenAI tools frequently reproduce standard British or American English while overlooking or even misrepresenting other legitimate non-standard varieties, or regional accents and idioms. Some educators in the survey also noted how AI-generated materials sometimes lacked cultural relevance, requiring them to invest time in adaptation and correction. These concerns are supported by recent research findings: Fleisig et al. (2024) found that language models, like ChatGPT, are more likely to show stereotyping, demeaning, or condescending content, indicating measurable bias against non-standard English. Such patterns risk reinforcing Anglocentric ideologies that marginalise diverse linguistic practices, which is especially concerning in TESOL where inclusivity and learner identity are central to pedagogy.

Global policy frameworks address this concern. UNESCO (2021) and the OECD (2023) both emphasise the importance of developing digital competences to promote culturally sensitive and inclusive AI integration in education. For TESOL educators, this means being trained not only to recognise and adapt biased outputs, but also to interrogate the cultural assumptions embedded in AI-generated vocabulary, examples, imagery, or values. Educators need support in adapting GenAI outputs to ensure relevance, appropriateness, and respect for learners' identities, values, and goals. As noted in some of the interviews, this also involves having the confidence and pedagogical judgement to adapt AI-generated content when it conflicts with local values or learner needs.

A third critical issue in GenAI-related teacher education is the risk of technocentrism, which is an overemphasis on tools and automation at the expense of pedagogy, context, and human judgement. As Papert (1988) observed, "Technocentrism is the fallacy of referring all questions to the technology" (p.4). This fallacy is highly relevant in contemporary discussions of AI in education, where the appeal of innovation is often seen as more important than fundamental questions about learning, equity, and purpose. For instance, several TESOL educators in this study expressed concern that institutional training often prioritised the showcasing of AI tools rather than exploring how they could be meaningfully integrated into language pedagogy. Teachers described webinars that focused on how to generate lesson plans or quizzes with GenAI but offered little guidance on how to align these outputs with instructional goals or learner needs. Others noted that training sometimes felt like a "box-ticking" exercise (T.6, Japan), reinforcing the sense that GenAI was being promoted as an end in itself, rather than a tool to support reflective practice.

This concern is well documented in the literature. For example, Selwyn (2019) argues that overly technocentric approaches reduce education to a matter of digital efficiency, sidelining questions of pedagogy, ethics, and professional judgement. Additionally, Köseoğlu et al. (2023) call for critical digital pedagogy to humanise education in a way that views learners and teachers as complex, culturally situated individuals, and challenges technocentric solutions as the remedy for educational problems.

Teacher education programmes must therefore prioritise pedagogical intent over technological novelty. As educators in this study made clear, they are not simply asking how to use GenAI; they have had several decades of adapting to technological innovations in TESOL. Rather, they are asking whether it aligns with their learners' needs, their teaching contexts, and their professional values.

Building on this, teacher education in TESOL must promote the kinds of professional environments that help educators develop informed and reflective digital literacy. As Wu and Miller (2025) demonstrate, AI literacy develops not merely through exposure to new tools, but through supportive ecosystems that encourage experimentation, dialogue, and critical engagement. Their study of two TESOL educators illustrates how contrasting institutional conditions shaped each teacher's ability to integrate GenAI meaningfully into their practice: one, with access to professional development and a strong educational background, actively sought alternatives, engaged in research, and experimented with new tools, while the other, constrained by workload, lack of training, and institutional pressures, resisted change and avoided integration. These findings suggest that TESOL teacher education programmes play an important role in creating conditions for educators to integrate GenAI in ways that are responsive to their learners, aligned with their teaching goals, and grounded in professional values.

The fourth critical issue shaping GenAI-related teacher education involves the adoption of posthuman theoretical perspectives, which challenge traditional views of teaching and technology. Critical posthumanism asks educators to reconsider how agency, knowledge, and pedagogy are co-produced through entangled relationships between people, technologies, environments, and institutional discourses (Barad, 2007; Calderwood, 2025). From this perspective, GenAI is not merely a tool but part of a dynamic "assemblage" in which agency is distributed and meaning arises through "intra-action.".

Supporting this theoretical stance, Satvati et al. (2025) conducted an empirical study involving 16 language educators in Iran. Through narrative frames and follow-up interviews, the study revealed that GenAI integration significantly influenced participants' sense of professional identity. At the classroom level, teachers reported increased confidence and professionalism when using GenAI for tasks such as resource creation. At institutional level, the degree of support offered to teachers shaped their ability to adopt GenAI meaningfully, with supportive environments strengthening their sense of professional identity and autonomy. Finally, at a macro-sociocultural level, teachers' beliefs and anxieties about job security influenced how they positioned themselves in relation to technology. Apart from one educator who saw it as an existential threat to the teaching profession, most participants believed their roles would remain but evolve in a more positive way.

This perspective moves teacher education beyond skills-based training by positioning GenAI as an active participant in teachers' pedagogical practice, influencing their instructional choices, their classroom interactions, and the construction of their professional identities. As such, TESOL teacher education can encourage teachers to examine how GenAI alters the very conditions of teaching. This includes asking questions, such as 'what assumptions about language and learning are embedded in this tool?', 'how does AI influence how they position themselves as educators?' and 'how are learners' roles and identities affected?'.

Together, these four issues—ethical and pedagogical literacies, cultural and linguistic responsiveness, the risks of technocentrism, and posthuman perspectives on teacher identity—highlight the complexity of preparing TESOL educators for GenAI integration. Effective GenAI-related teacher education must therefore foster not only technical competence but also ethical reasoning, cultural awareness, and pedagogical agency within evolving digital landscapes.

6.6 AI Policy Support for Teacher Education in TESOL

TESOL educators are currently navigating the integration of GenAI within what many perceive as a policy vacuum. Despite the rapid adoption of AI tools across educational contexts, teachers report operating with little to no structured support or official guidance. One educator noted, "There's no clear directive at my university" (T.6, Japan), while another observed, "Unfortunately, schools are not helping. So, if you're not doing it yourself … there is no upper authority telling us let's use it" (T.8, Qatar). This lack of institutional leadership risks exacerbating inconsistencies in training, assessment, and ethical use, leaving teachers to navigate complex issues, such as plagiarism detection, data privacy, and task design, without adequate support.

In the absence of clear institutional policies, it is essential to examine broader policy frameworks that may offer relevant guidance for TESOL educators. Given the European perspective of this study, this chapter draws on three key regional documents, including the European Commission's (2022) Ethical Guidelines on the Use of AI and Data in Teaching and Learning for Educators, the legally binding Artificial Intelligence Act (The European Parliament and the Council of the European Union, 2024), and the General-Purpose AI Code of Practice (European Commission, 2025, July 10), to explore how these frameworks can inform teacher education in the context of GenAI.

The European Commission's Ethical Guidelines on the Use of AI and Data in Teaching and Learning for Educators (2022) provide a foundational framework that encourage educational institutions to foster not only technical competence but also critical awareness, ethical responsibility, and pedagogical sensitivity when integrating AI tools into classrooms. The guidelines emphasise human oversight, transparency, fairness, and learner protection, aligning closely with TESOL's commitment to inclusive, learner-centred practices. These guidelines offer a set of guiding questions that are particularly instructive for TESOL teacher education, as they move beyond technical functionality to address deeper concerns around human agency and oversight, transparency, diversity, non-discrimination and fairness, societal and environmental wellness, privacy, technical robustness and safety, and accountability.

For example, questions such as "Is the teacher role clearly defined so as to ensure that there is a teacher in the loop while the AI system is being used?" and "How does the AI system affect the didactical role of the teacher?" foreground issues of professional authority and pedagogical integrity, especially relevant in TESOL where classroom interactions are socially and culturally nuanced. Other questions, like "Are procedures in place to monitor and intervene where empathy is required?" and "Does the AI system clearly signal that its social interaction is simulated?" encourage educators to reflect on the relational and affective dimensions of teaching, which are central to language learning but easily overlooked in automated systems.

Other questions such as "Is there sufficient security in place to protect against data breaches?" and "Does the AI system comply with General Data Protection Regulation" draw attention to the need for educators to be trained in data governance and accountability structures, not only as users but as active participants in AI decision-making. Equally important for TESOL is the question "Does the system adapt to learners with disabilities or special needs?" and 'Are there procedures in place to ensure that AI use will not lead to discrimination or unfair behaviour for all users?' emphasise the need to address bias, inclusivity, and accessibility in the classroom.

Integrating these questions into teacher education programmes can equip TESOL educators to adopt a critical, context-sensitive stance towards GenAI tools that not only supports technical skill development but also ethical reasoning, pedagogical reflection, and professional agency.

However, while offering a valuable foundation for AI integration in education, the guidance is also limited when applied to TESOL. It remains broad and lacks subject-specific relevance, offering little direction on how AI tools may affect teaching in multilingual contexts. In particular, it does not offer practical strategies for integrating these principles into TESOL teacher education. Crucially, it predates the use of GenAI, leaving current challenges around large language models largely unaddressed. As a result, its applicability to current challenges in TESOL is limited.

In parallel, the European Union's Artificial Intelligence Act (The European Parliament and Council of the European Union, 2024) is the world's first legal framework for AI. Adopted in 2024, the Act grades AI systems into four risk categories: unacceptable, high, limited, and minimal, with corresponding levels of regulatory obligation. Educational applications such as automated grading, learner profiling, and admissions tools are designated as high-risk, requiring strict safeguards including transparency, human oversight, data quality assurance, and user training. Under the Act, AI systems must allow for human intervention, include risk mitigation protocols, and respect fundamental rights such as privacy, fairness, and non-discrimination .

For TESOL, the AI Act has important implications. If GenAI tools are used to assess learner writing, generate feedback, or recommend instructional materials, institutions may be subject to high-risk system requirements. This includes ensuring that teachers are properly trained to evaluate and intervene in AI-generated outputs. This means that teacher education programmes must prepare educators not only to use AI tools, but to understand their regulatory context, ensuring alignment with professional, ethical, and legal responsibilities.

However, the AI Act also carries limitations similar to those in the Ethical Guidelines on the Use of AI and Data in Teaching and Learning for Educators (European Commission, 2022). While it establishes strong principles for risk governance, it does not offer subject-specific guidance for language education, nor does it address the pedagogical and cultural implications of GenAI in TESOL classrooms. The Act's focus remains on system-level compliance rather than teacher-level support, leaving institutions responsible for interpreting how best to implement safeguards for their specific context.

Most recently, the European Commission released a General-Purpose AI (GPAI) Code of Practice (European Commission, 2025, July 10), that offers practical implementation guidance for developers and deployers of high-capability AI systems, including large language models (LLMs) such as ChatGPT. While the Code is voluntary, it complements the EU AI Act (The European Parliament and Council of the European Union, 2024) and sets expectations for responsible development, transparency, copyright compliance, and safety within general-purpose models widely used in educational settings.

Although the Code is primarily directed at AI developers and platform providers, its implications for TESOL education are significant as GPT-based tools increasingly appear in TESOL classrooms. For example, TESOL educators using GPT to support academic writing must be aware of how AI-generated outputs complicate conventional understandings of plagiarism and authorship in language learning.

The European Union's recent AI policy instruments are broadly aligned with the principles outlined in UNESCO's Recommendation on the Ethics of Artificial Intelligence (2021), which is a foundational international framework endorsed by 193 Member States. UNESCO's recommendation centres on four core values: respect for human rights, promotion of inclusivity, social justice, and sustainability. These values are operationalised through ten ethical principles (e.g., human oversight, transparency, fairness, privacy) and eleven policy action areas, including a strong emphasis on inclusive, equitable, and responsible AI in education. However, while these international and regional policy frameworks establish strong ethical and legal foundations, they offer limited guidance for TESOL educators.

In response, more tailored initiatives are beginning to emerge. The AI Literacy Framework (AILit) (OECD & European Commission, 2025), currently under development, aims to offer actionable strategies for curriculum designers, teacher educators, and institutions. The framework outlines twenty-two competencies that are highly relevant to

TESOL educators and can be meaningfully adapted to teacher education. For example, the competence "Decide whether to use AI systems based on the nature of the task" can help TESOL educators evaluate which classroom activities are appropriate for GenAI integration, such as using it to generate vocabulary practice but avoiding it for feedback on student writing. Similarly, the competence "Delegate tasks to AI systems to appropriately automate or augment human workflows" encourages teachers to offload routine tasks, such as generating gap-fill exercises or sample dialogues, while saving time for higher-order responsibilities like personalised feedback and classroom dialogue.

In another example, the competence "Direct generative AI systems by providing specific instructions, appropriate context, and evaluation criteria" can be applied in TESOL by having teachers model how to craft precise prompts. For example, they might ask ChatGPT to generate a B1-level opinion essay with defined structure and word limits. Students can then critique the AI-generated output for linguistic accuracy, coherence, and cultural appropriateness, encouraging both their language development and critical AI literacy.

By mapping AILit competencies onto TESOL teaching practices, teacher educators can help current and future teachers not only use AI tools effectively but also develop a critical digital pedagogy. In this evolving landscape, educational institutions and policymakers must play an active role by embedding critical AI literacy into initial teacher education (ITE), supporting collaborative professional learning communities, and developing institutional policies that reflect international policies and frameworks relevant to the specific needs of TESOL.

6.7 A Pedagogical Framework for TESOL Teacher Education

As this chapter has shown, TESOL educators are integrating GenAI into their teaching amid significant institutional and pedagogical uncertainty. While interest and experimentation are high, both survey and interview data reveal that educators often operate without clear training, guidance, or ethical protocols. As previously discussed, teacher readiness is shaped not just by digital competence but by access to professional learning opportunities, collaborative support, and coherent policy frameworks that are relevant to the specific teaching context. In the absence of such structures, there is a pressing need for a pedagogical framework that can guide TESOL teacher education in engaging with GenAI critically and constructively. Such a framework should provide more than technical training and offer ways to support teachers in understanding the broader pedagogical, ethical, and professional implications of AI in language education.

Drawing on the findings of this chapter, as well as international policy documents, including UNESCO's Recommendation on the Ethics of Artificial Intelligence (2021), the European Commission's Ethical Guidelines for Educators (2022), and the draft AI Literacy Framework (OECD & European Commission, 2025), the following section proposes a principle-driven framework that can be used to inform both initial teacher education and in-service professional development. The framework consists of five interrelated dimensions that reflect pedagogical priorities and challenges that TESOL teachers face. These include developing pedagogical literacy skills, ethical and reflective practice, collaborative and situated learning, teacher agency, professional identity, and policy and regulatory alignment (see Fig. 6.4).

6.7.1 AI Pedagogical Literacy

First, developing AI pedagogical literacy involves a shift from general digital literacy focusing on developing skills and technical competence in utilising digital tools to AI pedagogical literacy demanding a deeper understanding of the broader ethical and pedagogical implications of AI. Teachers must not only know how to use AI, but also when and why to use it, and how its integration aligns with broader pedagogical values and learner needs. Zawacki-Richter et al. (2019) argue that informed, responsible AI use requires educators to assess the pedagogical and ethical implications of adopting automated technologies, rather than focusing solely on their technical potential.

6.7.2 Ethical and Reflective Practice

The second dimension involves ethical and reflective practice, an issue that has been raised consistently by educators in this study and in international frameworks. Teacher education must prepare teachers to engage with the ethical implications of GenAI, including issues of bias, transparency, authorship, and data privacy (European Commission, 2022; UNESCO, 2021). Building reflective capacity will help TESOL teachers decide how and when to use AI tools, model ethical use for learners, and address issues such as misinformation or plagiarism.

6.7.3 Collaborative and Situated Learning

A third dimension is the importance of professional learning communities, mentoring, and informal peer support, which educators in this study repeatedly described as essential. Rather than relying on top-down training models, this dimension focuses on the relational learning processes that are situated and context-sensitive, that allow teachers to co-construct knowledge, share practices and experiment. This is particularly important in under-resourced settings where professional development opportunities are limited.

6.7.4 Teacher Agency and Professional Identity

Fourth, the integration of GenAI into TESOL reshapes teachers' roles and sense of professional identity and agency. This dimension encourages teachers to see themselves as active agents who can mediate how the technology is used in their classrooms. Wu and Miller (2025) demonstrate that teachers who receive institutional and peer support often reframe AI as an opportunity for professional growth, while those without support may view it as a threat to their role. These contrasting experiences underscore the importance of fostering reflective digital agency so that educators feel confident in negotiating their evolving professional identities.

6.7.5 Policy and Regulatory Alignment

Finaly, TESOL educators should be able to interpret and apply relevant regulatory frameworks. Under the EU Artificial Intelligence Act (The European Parliament and Council of the European Union, 2024), the use of AI in education is classified as high-risk when it influences learner access, assessment, or performance tracking. As GenAI tools become more embedded in feedback and personalised learning, teachers need both policy awareness and pedagogical judgement to ensure compliance while upholding TESOL values such as linguistic diversity, equity, and learner autonomy.

To illustrate the framework, Fig. 6.4 presents a central circle representing context-sensitive, ethical, empowering teacher education, surrounded by five connected circles, each depicting one of the core pedagogical dimensions. This visual representation highlights that each pedagogical dimension is interconnected rather than independent. For example, AI pedagogical literacy must be informed by ethical considerations, while teacher agency is strengthened through collaborative practices and policy awareness. This framework reflects the need for an integrated, multidimensional model of teacher education in TESOL in the age of GenAI.

It is important to consider a holistic model of professional development that is context-sensitive to allow for adaptability across different settings—different types of schools, different regions in the Global South and Global North, and contexts with varying levels of infrastructure, technological access, and regulatory framework. Such differences mean that professional development cannot be one-size-fits-all. For example, teacher education programmes in contexts with strong regulatory oversight (e.g., the EU) might emphasise legal compliance and policy literacy, whereas programmes in under-resourced or rapidly changing contexts might prioritise collaborative learning and reflective practice.

The framework also responds to the asymmetries in teacher experience highlighted throughout this chapter. Some educators reported institutional support, peer dialogue, and opportunities for structured learning, while others relied solely on self-directed experimentation. The framework accommodates these differences by offering a multidimensional

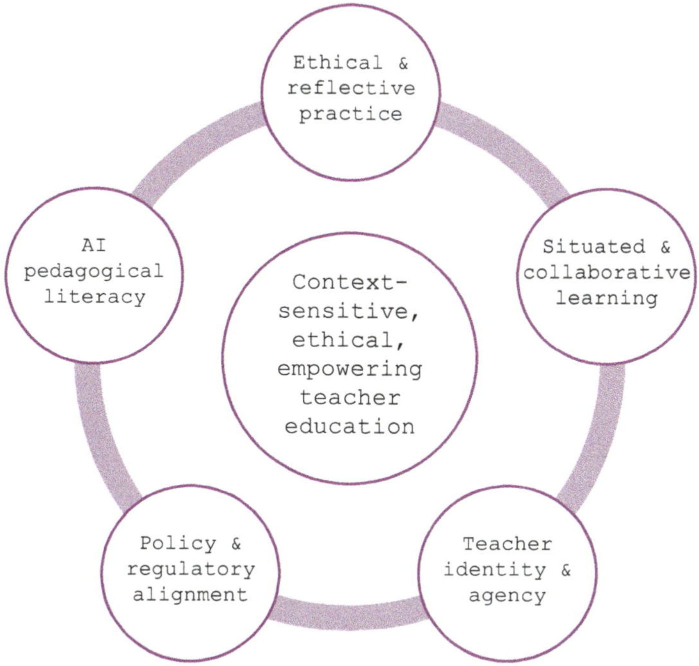

Fig. 6.4 A pedagogical framework for TESOL teacher education in the age of GenAI

model where dimensions such as AI pedagogical literacy and ethical awareness can be developed in response to local conditions and teacher needs.

Importantly, this framework is not a checklist or fixed curriculum. Rather, it offers a set of principles for curriculum developers, policy-makers, and teacher educators to design learning experiences that are ethically responsible, pedagogically sound, and aligned with the evolving role of GenAI in TESOL. It reflects the pressing need for TESOL teacher education to move beyond ad hoc experimentation and towards a more coherent, principled approach to GenAI integration that centres on pedagogical integrity, ethical responsibility, and teacher agency.

6.8 Conclusion

This chapter has examined the role of teacher education in preparing TESOL educators to engage with GenAI in informed, ethical, and pedagogically meaningful ways. Drawing on survey and interview data, it revealed widespread interest in GenAI across the TESOL profession, but also highlighted significant variability in preparedness, institutional support, and access to professional development. Teachers consistently reported a need for training that is practical, context-sensitive, and pedagogically relevant. The chapter also explored critical issues related to the use of GenAI in TESOL, such as bias, teacher agency, and the risk of technocentric approaches. By drawing on posthuman theoretical perspectives, this chapter framed GenAI not simply as a tool, but as a means to reshape pedagogical relationships, assessment standards, and professional identity.

In response to these findings, the chapter proposed a five-dimensional pedagogical framework to support GenAI integration in TESOL teacher education focusing on (1) AI pedagogical literacy, (2) ethical and reflective practice, (3) collaborative and situated learning, (4) teacher agency and professional identity, and (5) alignment with regulatory and policy frameworks. Together, these dimensions offer a structure for designing teacher education programmes that are both principled and adaptable to the diverse realities of TESOL educators working across different regions and institutional contexts.

As AI becomes increasingly embedded in educational systems, TESOL educators must position themselves both as users of technology and critical mediators of its pedagogical, ethical, and cultural implications. This dual role requires teacher education that moves away from one-off training workshops to foster sustained enquiry, reflective practice, and critical engagement.

Moving forward, several actions are essential. First, teacher educators must embed AI literacy across pre-service and continuing professional development programmes. Second, institutions must create time and space for educators to explore, experiment, and reflect collaboratively on GenAI use. Finally, policymakers must provide subject-specific guidance aligned with broader frameworks, such as the EU AI Act

(2024), UNESCO's Ethics of AI (2021), and the AI Literacy Framework (OECD & European Commission, 2025). Finally, further research is needed to investigate how GenAI affects teaching practices, learner outcomes, and the broader sociocultural dynamics of language education.

It is evident that learning to use GenAI in teaching is not enough. TESOL professionals must be empowered to use it in a way that supports inclusive, ethical, and contextually relevant language education for all learners.

References

Arefian, M. H., Esfandiari, R., & Zarei, A. A. (2025). Exploring AI-based collaborative reflective practice in light of ChatGPT: Insights from EFL preservice teachers. *Applied Linguistics Inquiry*, *3*(1), 31–43. https://doi.org/10.22077/ali.2025.9022.1108

Barad, K. (2007). Meeting the universe halfway: Quantum physics and the entanglement of matter and meaning. *Duke University Press*. https://doi.org/10.2307/j.ctv12101zq

Barnes, M., & Tour, E. (2025). Teachers' use of generative AI: A 'dirty little secret'? *Language and Education*, 1–16. https://doi.org/10.1080/09500782.2025.2485935

Bui, T. H. (2022). English teachers' integration of digital technologies in the classroom. *International Journal of Educational Research Open, 3*, Article 100204. https://doi.org/10.1016/j.ijedro.2022.100204

Calderwood, S. J. (2025). An exploration of human and platform intra-actions in a digital teaching and learning environment. *Learning, Media and Technology*, *50*(2), 263–275. https://doi.org/10.1080/17439884.2023.2285820

Chapelle, C. A. (2024). Open generative AI changes a lot, but not everything. *Modern Language Journal (John Wiley & Sons, Inc.)*, *108*(2). https://doi.org/10.1111/modl.12927

Chiu, T. K., Ahmad, Z., Ismailov, M., & Sanusi, I. T. (2024). What are artificial intelligence literacy and competency? A comprehensive framework to support them. *Computers and Education Open, 6*, Article 100171. https://doi.org/10.1016/j.caeo.2024.100171

European Commission. (2019). Ethics guidelines for trustworthy AI. High-Level Expert Group on Artificial Intelligence. https://digital-strategy.ec.europa.eu/en/library/ethics-guidelines-trustworthy-ai

European Commission. (2025, July 10). *General-purpose AI Code of Practice.* https://digital-strategy.ec.europa.eu/en/policies/contents-code-gpai

European Commission: Directorate-General for Education, Youth, Sport and Culture. (2022). *Ethical guidelines on the use of artificial intelligence (AI) and data in teaching and learning for educators.* Publications Office of the European Union. https://data.europa.eu/doi/https://doi.org/10.2766/153756.

Fleisig, E., Smith, G., Bossi, M., Rustagi, I., Yin, X., & Klein, D. (2024). Linguistic Bias in ChatGPT: Language models reinforce dialect discrimination. *Proceedings of the 2024 Conference on Empirical Methods in Natural Language Processing*, 13541–13564. https://doi.org/10.18653/v1/2024.emnlp-main.750

Holmes, W., Bialik, M., & Fadel, C. (2019). *Artificial intelligence in education: Promises and implications for teaching and learning*. Center for Curriculum Redesign. https://doi.org/10.58863/20.500.12424/4276068

Jandrić, P., & Ford, D. R. (2022). Postdigital ecopedagogies: Genealogies, contradictions, and possible futures. *Postdigital Science and Education, 4*, 692–710. https://doi.org/10.1007/s42438-020-00207-3

Kern, R. (2024). Twenty-first century technologies and language education: Charting a path forward. *Modern Language Journal (John Wiley & Sons, Inc.), 108*(2). https://doi.org/10.1111/modl.12924

Kohnke, L., & Zou, D. (2025). Artificial intelligence integration in TESOL Teacher education: Promoting a critical lens guided by TPACK and SAMR. *TESOL Quarterly*. https://doi.org/10.1002/tesq.3396

Köseoğlu, S., Veletsianos, G., & Rowell, C. (Eds.). (2023). *Critical digital pedagogy in higher education.* Athabasca University Press. https://doi.org/10.15215/aupress/9781778290015.01

Minna, V. (2024). Digital education to address global inequalities in access to technology. *Journal of the American Institute, 1*(1), 22–26.

Nøhr, L., Stenalt, M. H., & Hagood, D. (2023). University Teachers' agency in relation to technology use in teaching: A quantitative investigation. *Edutec, Revista Electrónica de Tecnología Educativa*, (86), 40–61. https://doi.org/10.21556/edutec.2023.86.2915

OECD & European Commission. (2025). *Empowering learners for the age of AI: An AI literacy framework for primary and secondary education (Review draft).* https://ailiteracyframework.org

OECD. (2023). OECD digital education outlook 2023: Towards an effective digital education ecosystem. *OECD Publishing*. https://doi.org/10.1787/c74f03de-en

Papert, S. (1988). A critique of technocentrism in thinking about the school of the future. In *Children in the information age* (pp. 3–18). Pergamon. https://doi.org/10.1016/B978-0-08-036464-3.50006-5

Satvati, N., Kamali, J., Boldaji, F. S., Khodadadi, M., & Akhondi, S. (2025). AI integration into language education and teacher identity: An ecological perspective. *Language Teaching Research Quarterly, 47*, 1–19. https://doi.org/10.32038/ltrq.2025.47.01

Selwyn, N. (2019). *Should robots replace teachers?* John Wiley & Sons.

The European Parliament and the Council of the European Union. (2024). Regulation (EU) 2024/1689 of the European Parliament and of the Council of 13 June 2024 laying down harmonised rules on artificial intelligence and amending other acts (Artificial Intelligence Act). *Official Journal of the European Union,* L 1689. https://eur-lex.europa.eu/eli/reg/2024/1689/oj/eng

UNESCO. (2021). *Recommendation on the ethics of artificial intelligence.* UNESCO. https://unesdoc.unesco.org/ark:/48223/pf0000381137

Weiner, S., Lake, R., & Rosner, J. (2024). *AI is evolving, but teacher prep is lagging: A first look at teacher preparation program responses to AI*. Center on Reinventing Public Education.

Wu, J. G., & Miller, L. (2025). Smart or sweat: The bittersweet journey of teachers' AI literacy. *International Journal of TESOL Studies*, 1–10. https://doi.org/10.58304/ijts.250124

Zawacki-Richter, O., Marín, V. I., Bond, M., & Gouverneur, F. (2019). Systematic review of research on artificial intelligence applications in higher education—Where are the educators? *International Journal of Educational Technology in Higher Education, 16*(1), 1–27. https://doi.org/10.1186/s41239-019-0171-0

7

Conclusion and Future Directions

7.1 Introduction

This book set out to explore the complex and rapidly evolving role of GenAI in TESOL, framed by diverse theoretical, pedagogical, and empirical perspectives. Amid widespread reaction, ranging from enthusiasm to apprehension, it responds to what many perceive as a crisis for second language teaching. For instance, at a conference in the summer of 2023, one presentation predicted the impending demise of the TESOL educator in the physical classroom, replaced by students independently engaging with LLMs on their mobile phones. As AI technologies accelerate into second language classrooms, often with minimal critical mediation, the idea for this book emerged from moments of anxiety and urgency. Its aim has been to pause, examine, and critically reflect on this perceived crisis.

From the outset, this book has argued that GenAI is not simply another educational tool, but a profound disruptor of the core dynamics of language education, such as pedagogy, assessment, ethics, authorship, and even the notion of what it means to "know" a language. Yet rather than positioning GenAI as an existential threat, the central premise has been to view it as an opportunity to reimagine, reframe, and transform

C. Savvidou, *AI-Powered Language Teaching*,
https://doi.org/10.1007/978-3-032-14502-4_7

second language teaching in ways that remain grounded in pedagogical values and ethical responsibility.

Drawing on theories of Social Constructivism, Critical Theory, the Technology Acceptance Model (TAM), and Posthuman Pedagogy, this book has charted the terrain from historical evolutions in CALL to the current GenAI landscape. It has drawn on the voices of TESOL educators around the world, whose practices, hopes, and anxieties have guided the analysis. While acknowledging GenAI's potential, the book has also explored the ethical, ideological, and pedagogical tensions it raises. This concluding chapter brings together those insights and offers new conceptual directions.

The writing of this book also reflected these themes. GenAI supported the process by assisting with tasks such as formatting references, refining grammar, and clarifying structure, but the critical voice, empirical analysis, and conceptual framing emerged from the author's professional expertise and pedagogical values. In this sense, the book itself illustrates a central argument advanced throughout: that GenAI can enhance creativity and scholarship without displacing human authorship, critical judgement, or ethical responsibility.

7.2 Key Insights

The following insights synthesise key themes that emerged across the book's chapters, highlighting how GenAI is reshaping TESOL practice, pedagogy, and professional identity.

7.2.1 From CALL to GenAI: A Pedagogical Evolution

The trajectory from CALL to GenAI reflects a fundamental shift in how technology is conceptualised in TESOL. Early CALL, rooted in behaviourist models, focused on drills and limited interactivity. This later evolved into Technology-Enhanced Language Learning (TELL), which promoted communicative and collaborative approaches through multimedia platforms and online tools.

GenAI represents the next phase in this progression but with a significant ontological shift. Rather than simply enhancing instruction, GenAI co-generates pedagogical content, simulates interaction, and provides adaptive, real-time feedback. As such, it embodies core principles from SLA theories: Krashen's input hypothesis (via tailored reading levels), Swain's output hypothesis (via interactive writing/chat tools), and Long's interaction hypothesis (through simulated negotiation of meaning). Crucially, GenAI blurs traditional boundaries between technology and user, as it evolves from being a passive instrument to an active pedagogical partner in the learning process.

This shift brings opportunities and challenges. As discussed in Chap. 2, educators with prior experience with online learning tools like Duolingo, Moodle, and multimedia platforms, often reported a smoother transition to GenAI. At the same time, other educators raised concerns about student overreliance, the erosion of collaboration, and the risk of replacing pedagogical judgement with algorithmic convenience. The historical progression from CALL to TELL has prepared the ground for GenAI, but its adoption requires not just technical readiness; it requires critical reflection on how the pedagogy is being reshaped. Ultimately, TESOL educators are being asked to reimagine their roles not just as adopters of GenAI tools, but as co-designers of ethical, equitable and human-centred AI-mediated learning environments.

7.2.2 Current Practices and Perceptions

As demonstrated in Chap. 3, this pedagogical evolution is more than theoretical, TESOL educators are already experimenting with GenAI in a variety of ways. Empirical data from surveys and interviews reveal a strong uptake of tools for writing support, lesson planning, conversational practice, and personalised feedback. Teachers highlight how GenAI has the potential to lower learner anxiety, enhance creativity, and support more autonomous engagement. At the same time, they expressed concerns around academic integrity, over-reliance, and uneven adoption across regions and age groups. These lived experiences confirm the theoretical shift from CALL to GenAI, while also emphasising the need for increased opportunities for pedagogical reflection, ethical guidance, and context-sensitive implementation.

7.2.3 Possibilities and Practices in the Classroom

Chapter 4 illustrated how GenAI is being integrated into the teaching of core language skills— listening, reading, speaking, writing and intercultural communication. Educators report using GenAI to generate adaptive prompts, scaffold learner output, and provide real-time feedback. In writing instruction, for example, GenAI can be aligned with sociocultural and cognitive learning theories to support different stages of the writing process from brainstorming and outlining to revision and peer review. In speaking and pronunciation, AI chatbots and speech recognition platforms offer low-anxiety environments for practice and self-monitoring. Similarly, in reading and listening instruction, GenAI is being used to generate level-appropriate materials and interactive simulations that are personalised to learners' needs and preferences. Importantly, these tools are being implemented across age groups, from gamified storytelling for young learners to academic writing feedback for university students and professional communication support for adults.

Yet, the effectiveness of GenAI in TESOL depends not on the tool itself but on the instructional design and teacher mediation. As many educators emphasised, the key is not in replacing the teacher but in freeing up teacher-time for more interactional, critical, and creative engagement in the classroom. In other words, the role of GenAI lies in augmenting, rather than replacing, teachers' practice. The goal is not just to integrate GenAI, but to do so in ways that align with learning goals and enhance student agency and autonomy.

7.2.4 Ethical and Ideological Tensions

One of the central findings of this book is that GenAI integration is never a neutral act. It raises deeply ethical and ideological questions that go beyond functionality or instructional convenience. As Chap. 5

demonstrated, these tensions are evident in several critical domains: bias, privacy, academic integrity and teacher agency.

Bias remains one of the most pressing concerns for TESOL educators. GenAI tools often reproduce dominant language ideologies, favouring Standard American or British English while marginalising World Englishes and non-Western cultural references. Research demonstrates that AI-generated feedback can marginalise plurilingual identities, perpetuate cultural stereotypes, and subtly devalue non-standard or context-specific expressions. These patterns highlight how GenAI can reinforce existing hierarchies in language education, unless they are mediated by educators who are committed to inclusive TESOL pedagogy.

Ethical concerns about surveillance and data privacy are equally urgent. TESOL teachers typically work with students' spoken and written work, which may reveal personal, cultural, or political information. Chap. 5 discussed how such sensitive student data is at risk from misuse, considering how issues of informed consent, data storage and handling lack transparency. This issue is exacerbated with institutional policies that shift ethical responsibility onto individual educators rather than shared governance frameworks.

The concern around academic integrity, particularly in writing assessment, was expressed repeatedly. The ease with which GenAI generates fluent text challenges long-held notions of authorship, originality, and assessment in TESOL. Educators described a tension between wanting to support learners' use of GenAI yet, unintentionally, enabling plagiarism or overreliance. As AI detection tools remain unreliable, TESOL educators are being challenged to question whether the traditional essay can still serve as a reliable measure language competence, critical thinking and authentic student authorship.

Teacher autonomy and agency also emerged as a recurring theme. While GenAI offers efficiency, there is concern that it may replace professional pedagogical judgement and reduce teachers to the role of curating content. There is also a concern AI-generated lesson plans impose implicit epistemologies of what "good" language teaching looks like. As Chap. 5 argued, tools often embody unspoken values about correctness, fluency, and appropriateness, which may conflict with non-Western pedagogies or inclusive language practices. As such, the challenge is not whether GenAI should be used, but how it can be integrated in ways that prioritise transparency, fairness, and inclusion.

7.3 New Contributions

While much of this book is largely descriptive and analytical, it also gestures towards new theoretical and practical contributions that can help transform the future of TESOL in the GenAI era. These contributions are framed around four key areas: teacher identity, critical AI literacy, GenAI as a pedagogical actor, and the disruption of knowledge. Together, they suggest new ways of reimagining what it means to teach and learn English through intra-action with GenAI.

7.3.1 Reimagining TESOL Teacher Identity

A new TESOL landscape demands a reimagined conception of teacher identity. Rather than being framed as passive recipients of AI tools, TESOL educators can take on an active identity as critical mediators, human-AI co-designers, and ethical caretakers of AI pedagogy. The roles of teachers have always extended beyond just delivering the curriculum and now this is even more important as they are required to interrogate how GenAI tools frame knowledge, decide when and how to integrate GenAI tools into their teaching, and advocate for tools that reflect inclusive linguistic values.

As Chap. 6 makes clear, this reimagining can only happen through significant tailored teacher education, directed to both pre-service and in-service teachers. Survey and interview data reveal that over 90% of educators have received little or no formal training on GenAI, leaving them to rely on informal experimentation or peer networks. While many educators expressed enthusiasm for GenAI's potential in lesson planning, feedback generation, and learner engagement, they also reported uncertainty about its ethical use, bias, and alignment with pedagogical goals. These gaps in teacher preparedness highlight the urgency of developing structured, context-sensitive professional development that integrates critical AI literacy.

Importantly, Chap. 6 also demonstrated that TESOL educators particularly value collaborative and sustained models of professional learning, such as professional learning communities, peer mentoring and workshops, that allow space for experimentation, reflection, and co-construction of practice. This reimagining of teacher identity in TESOL highlights teacher agency in a context where many teachers fear displacement by AI, and it reinforces the idea that teaching cannot be reduced to content generation and facilitation of AI tools. Ultimately, TESOL teaching depends on the relational and ideological practices that support teacher identity and agency, dimensions that no technology can fully replace.

7.3.2 Towards Critical AI Literacy in TESOL

Digital literacy alone is no longer sufficient. TESOL educators require a critical AI literacy that is ethical, context-specific and pedagogically grounded. This involves not only understanding how GenAI tools operate but also interrogating the values, biases, and assumptions embedded within them. Such literacy enables teachers to identify when AI-generated content aligns with learning goals and when it risks undermining them.

A TESOL-specific model of critical AI literacy should therefore prepare teachers to make these judgements while also equipping learners to reflect on what GenAI produces, how it produces it, and whose interests are served in the process. As highlighted in Chap. 6, many teachers feel underprepared in these areas and explicitly call for targeted professional development that blends hands-on training with critical pedagogy.

7.3.3 GenAI as a Pedagogical Actor, Not Just a Tool

GenAI is not merely a neutral tool to be used within language teaching. It increasingly functions as a pedagogical actor that shapes teaching-learning interactions, influences the types of language learners produce, and even affects the criteria by which their work is evaluated. In other words, it participates in the co-construction of meaning alongside teachers and students.

From a posthuman perspective, GenAI's role extends beyond that of a teaching aid: it actively generates, filters, and models language, thereby shaping how learning unfolds. For example, when GenAI suggests "improved" sentences, it promotes notions of correctness, fluency, and appropriateness that may or may not align with local pedagogical goals or values. While norms of linguistic "correctness" have always existed, they are now much more evident.

This shift calls for intentional instructional design that treats GenAI as a participant to be managed and critically engaged with, rather than a neutral assistant. When approached this way, teachers retain their central role as mediators, ensuring that GenAI's involvement enhances rather than distorts the social, cultural, and human dimensions of language education.

7.3.4 Disrupting Knowledge

Finally, GenAI challenges TESOL's epistemological assumptions, or what it means to "know" English when machines can simulate fluency? Questions such as "how do we assess originality when AI can generate plausible essays?" and "what is the value of memorization or grammar drills when AI can supply answers on demand?" challenge educators to rethink how we define learning, assessment, and competence in TESOL. These questions compel the profession to reconsider what kinds of knowledge are valued and how they are demonstrated in GenAI teaching environments. This disruption is not just a threat; it also opens space for reimagining assessment, prioritising creativity, collaboration, and critical reflection over the reproduction of knowledge.

7.3.5 Research and Policy Agenda

To guide the future of GenAI in TESOL, research and policy development must work together to ensure that innovation is guided by ethical governance. Chap. 6 highlighted the absence of coherent institutional policies for GenAI in many educational contexts, leaving educators to tackle issues of ethics, privacy, and assessment on their own. Aligning TESOL practice with emerging AI governance frameworks such as the UNESCO guidelines (UNESCO, 2021), the OECD principles (OECD, 2019/2024), the EU Artificial Intelligence Act (The European Parliament and the Council of the European Union, 2024), and the General Data Protection Regulation (European Union, 2016) provides an important starting point. However, these efforts remain preliminary, and regulatory development needs to move faster to keep pace with technological advances, which are currently outpacing governance. While some TESOL institutions are already responding to these shifts, much more needs to be done to support educators to engage with GenAI responsibly and ethically.

7.3.6 Research Priorities

Future research on GenAI in TESOL must address both its immediate applications and its long-term consequences. Longitudinal studies are needed to track how sustained engagement with GenAI affects language development, learner autonomy, and teacher roles over time. Comparative, cross-cultural research will help identify how diverse linguistic, educational, and cultural contexts shape both adoption patterns and pedagogical impact. There is also a pressing need for educator-driven tool design, in which teachers collaborate directly with developers to create AI resources that reflect local pedagogical priorities rather than generic, one-size-fits-all solutions. Equally important is the integration of critical AI literacy into teacher education, ensuring that technical competence is accompanied with ethical and sociolinguistic awareness. Finally, equity-focused studies on access and outcomes are essential for identifying and addressing the risks that GenAI may even exacerbate existing educational inequalities.

7.3.7 Policy Priorities

This research can then be used to inform policy and create robust ethical and pedagogical frameworks for the integration of GenAI in TESOL. Institutions need clear ethical-use guidelines that align with both emerging national and international AI regulations and TESOL's broader social mission of promoting equity, inclusivity and learner empowerment. Learner voices must also be included in shaping these policies, particularly in decisions that affect assessment, privacy, and classroom practice. Policies should also advocate for plurilingual AI development, ensuring that GenAI supports multiple Englishes and the multilingual realities of TESOL classrooms. Assessment models will need to be revisited in light of AI's capacity to generate human-like output, shifting the focus towards evaluating process, critical engagement, and originality. Finally, institutions should establish ongoing review procedures to keep policies aligned with evolving legislation, pedagogical values, and technological development.

7.4 Final Reflections

This book began with a sense of curiosity and urgency about the impact of GenAI on the future of TESOL. It has argued that GenAI is neither a passing trend nor a force that will necessarily disempower educators and learners. Its influence depends on the values and decisions that educators bring to its use. The challenge is not whether to use GenAI, but how to use it in ways that sustain TESOL's core commitments to pedagogy, ethics, equity, and teacher agency. Only when teachers are equipped with the skills, awareness and confidence to direct GenAI towards these ends can it truly empower language education.

As Paulo Freire reminds us, education functions "as a practice of freedom, as opposed to a practice of domination" (Freire, 1970, p. 81).

Guided by this vision, the task is not to fear for the future of TESOL but to embrace it critically and creatively. Keeping Freire's words in mind, we can use GenAI to expand access, empower learners, and equip teachers to transform the future of language education.

References

European Union. (2016). *Regulation (EU) 2016/679 of the European Parliament and of the Council of 27 April 2016 on the protection of natural persons with regard to the processing of personal data and on the free movement of such data, and repealing Directive 95/46/EC (General Data Protection Regulation). Official Journal of the European Union, L119,* 1–88. https://eur-lex.europa.eu/eli/reg/2016/679/oj

Freire, P. (1970). Pedagogy of the oppressed (M.B. Ramos, Trans.). Continuum, *2007*.

OECD. (2019/2024). *Recommendation of the Council on Artificial Intelligence* (OECD/LEGAL/0449). OECD. https://legalinstruments.oecd.org/en/instruments/OECD-LEGAL-0449

The European Parliament and the Council of the European Union. (2024). Regulation (EU) 2024/1689 of the European Parliament and of the Council of 13 June 2024 laying down harmonised rules on artificial intelligence and amending other acts (Artificial Intelligence Act). Official Journal of the European Union, L 1689. https://eur-lex.europa.eu/eli/reg/2024/1689/oj/eng

UNESCO. (2021). *Recommendation on the ethics of artificial intelligence.* UNESCO. https://unesdoc.unesco.org/ark:/48223/pf0000381137

Index

C. Savvidou, *AI-Powered Language Teaching*,
https://doi.org/10.1007/978-3-032-14502-4

GPSR Compliance
The European Union's (EU) General Product Safety Regulation (GPSR) is a set of rules that requires consumer products to be safe and our obligations to ensure this.

If you have any concerns about our products, you can contact us on

ProductSafety@springernature.com

In case Publisher is established outside the EU, the EU authorized representative is:

Springer Nature Customer Service Center GmbH
Europaplatz 3
69115 Heidelberg, Germany

www.ingramcontent.com/pod-product-compliance
Ingram Content Group UK Ltd.
Pitfield, Milton Keynes, MK11 3LW, UK
UKHW020753220926
475829UK00004BA/91
* 9 7 8 3 0 3 2 1 4 5 0 1 7 *